THE SOCIAL WORLD
OF BIBLICAL ANTIQUITY
SERIES

General Editor
James W. Flanagan

MONOTHEISM
AND THE
PROPHETIC
MINORITY

An Essay in Biblical History and Sociology

BERNHARD LANG

The Almond Press · 1983

THE SOCIAL WORLD OF BIBLICAL ANTIQUITY SERIES

General Editor:
James W. Flanagan (Missoula, MT)

The Social World of Biblical Antiquity, 1

Monotheism and the Prophetic Minority:
An Essay in Biblical History and Sociology
by Bernhard Lang

British Library Cataloguing in Publication Data:

Lang, Bernhard
    Monotheism and the prophetic minority.
    - (The Social world of biblical antiquity,
    ISSN 0265-1408; 1)
    1. Bible. OT. - Prophecies
    I. Title   II. Series
    221.1'5   BS1198

ISBN 0-907459-30-7
ISBN 0-907459-31-5 Pbk

Published by
The Almond Press
P.O. Box 208
Sheffield S10 5DW
England

Printed in Great Britain by
Dotesios (Printers) Ltd
Bradford-on-Avon, Wiltshire
1983

CONTENTS

DEDICATED TO
THE LONDON SCHOOL OF ECONOMICS
AND POLITICAL SCIENCE
DEPARTMENT OF SOCIAL ANTHROPOLOGY

ACKNOWLEDGEMENTS

Earlier, and with one exception German versions of the papers included in this volume appeared in periodicals or books. They have been revised and updated (hence of interest for the German reader as well) and are used with the original publishers' permissions. Here is a list of the original versions:

(1)   The Yahweh-Alone-Movement and the Making of Jewish Monotheism, adapted from Lang 1981b, 47-83 (Kösel-Verlag, Munich).

(2)   What is a Prophet?, adapted from Lang 1980, 11-30 (Patmos-Verlag, Düsseldorf); the appendix from Lang 1981c (Wewel-Verlag, Munich).

(3)   The Making of Prophets in Israel, adapted from Lang 1980, 31-58 (Patmos-Verlag, Düsseldorf).

(4)   The Social Organization of Peasant Poverty in Biblical Israel, revised from the Journal for the Study of the Old Testament 24(1982).

(5)   The Making of Messianism, adapted from Lang 1980, 69-79 (Patmos-Verlag, Düsseldorf).

(6)   From Prophet to Scribe: Charismatic Authority in Early Judaism (unpublished).

Revising and partly re-writing the material would have been impossible without a Fulbright travel grant which enabled me to stay at Temple University, Philadelphia, PA., during the fall semester of 1982.

As the translations are my own I gratefully acknowledge the help received from Susan G. Blackall, Marilyn Fraser, Nancy Hall, Colleen McDannell and Rosamunde Jones. Most of the final version was typed by Marie Jester.

I would like also to explain the dedication of this volume to the London School of Economics, Department of Social Anthropology. After initial contact with Fritz Kramer of Berlin and John Rogerson of Sheffield who whetted my appetite for social anthropology, I was able to spend eight months at the LSE. I would like to thank the staff members of this distinguished department for their warm reception and manifold inspiration, especially my teachers and friends: Maurice Bloch, Chris J. Fuller, Alfred Gell, Joanna O. Kaplan, Jean S. La Fontaine, Ioan M. Lewis, David McKnight, Jonathan Parry, Michael J. Sallnow and James Woodburn.

Most authors thank their friends for moral support. I, however, feel that I ought also to acknowledge their immoral support of providing me with exciting excuses for leaving my study.

- Bernhard Lang
May, 1983

PREFACE

I will do my best to give as probable an explanation as any other - or rather, more probable.

- Plato, Timaeus 48d

NE of my predecessors at the Johannes Gutenberg University of Mainz, Johann Lorenz Isenbiehl, was imprisoned from December 1777 until December 1779 because of his allegedly heretical view of biblical prophecy in general and Isaiah 7.14 in particular, a passage he did not take to be messianic in the traditional sense of the word. He simply dropped the passage from the list of messianic prooftexts and suggested a different reading. After having recanted his heresy, he was released one Christmas Day - aptly enough on the day celebrating the fulfillment of that prophecy by Isaiah. According to Isenbiehl biblical prophets were more deeply involved in contemporary society than concerned with some vague and distant future. Now, two centuries later, there is hardly any ecclesiastical supervision of historical research in the Bible, and critical issues are left to scholarly debate.

In a new age of scholarship Isenbiehl's problem is no longer on the agenda (though there has been some discussion whether a certain Hebrew word of Isaiah 7.14 should be rendered as 'virgin' or 'young woman' in an official German translation of the Bible). However, it seems to be difficult to find two specialists in the field whose views of prophecy as a powerful institution in ancient Israelite society are identical. By focussing on biblical texts rather than on the society in which they originated, most textbooks avoid the issue altogether and are therefore of little help. This situation is equally unsatisfactory for both scholars and students who have to find their way through an almost impenetrable jungle of periodical literature with its characteristic thicket of assumptions that are often as wild as they are widespread. The present publication is my personal path through this jungle which is, of course, much more untidy than may be apparent from the unavoidable notes, learned references and bibliographical details.

The essays which make up this book must speak for themselves, but it may be helpful to indicate some general conclusions which I have arrived at and approaches I recommend. Firstly, there is the ongoing debate about literary criticism a term which, in this field, has nothing to do with literary evaluation but is concerned with secondary passages or words in our biblical sources. There can be no doubt about the non-authenticity of some prophetic texts. Recent scholarship, however, seems to have exaggerated the possibility of establishing the secondary nature of texts to such a degree that one starts doubting both methods and achievements. Generally speaking, I have not found many valuable insights in studies which seem to rely on an almost infallible approach of divide et impera. The preoccupation with minutiae is so complete that the larger issues often seem to be obscured. Nobody would argue that the many volumes of hermetic textual analysis so characteristic of our discipline cannot contribute anything; but is it not obvious that the specialist argument can work quite effectively to block the larger, the more interesting and, perhaps, the more intellectually serious perspective?

Secondly, there is the question of the prophets' 'intention' or, more precisely, their involvement in day-to-day politics. The issue, dealt with at some length in my book on Ezekiel (Kein Aufstand in Jerusalem: Die Politik des Propheten Ezechiel, 1978), is taken up in the review of literature appended to the second essay of this volume. I had the opportunity to study the problem at the Collège de France in Paris in 1975/76 under Professor André Caquot who has contributed a valuable essay on the political objectives of Hosea. There is now a much wider recognition of prophetic politics than before when I first studied the problem. However, prophetic politics still seems to be a neglected factor in biblical studies.

The third point to be emphasized is the state of uncertainty, if not crisis in biblical scholarship. Many of its leading theories are in eclipse. Assumptions which have been upheld for many decades are suddenly questioned, e.g. the theory of four pentateuchal sources or certain views of patriarchal religion which can no longer be taken for granted. The established version of Israel's religious history seems to be largely questionable, but a new one not yet emerged. I

Preface

have worked on the problem myself and with my students, and I have received much inspiration from Morton Smith's 'Palestinian Parties and Politics that Shaped the Old Testament' a book which has not yet received the attention it deserves. It may be worth mentioning that Smith's work can be seen in continuity with that of some earlier writers, and that his view of ancient Israelite polytheism was anticipated by the American scholar, Louis Wallis. The cooperation with Morton Smith, Hermann Vorländer and the Iranian scholar, Mary Boyce (School of Oriental and African Studies, London) was extremely stimulating and has helped me to come back to a radical version of De Wette's and Wellhausen's distinction between Israel and Judaism, and to see the truth of the saying that Israel went into exile a nation and returned a church - indeed a monotheistic one.

Put briefly and somewhat simplified, my view entails a four-stage-development of biblical religion: (a) The first period of Israelite religion (or, Hebrew paganism, ca. 1250-586 B.C.) is as polytheistic as any other West Semitic cult but includes (b) a group which demands and promotes the exclusive worship of Israel's state god, Yahweh. The religion of the Yahweh-aloneists, the first clear evidence for which is found in the Book of Hosea (ca. 750), can be called Proto-Judaism. (c) The Babylonian exile of the sixth century sees the formation of (Early) Judaism which continues and further develops the case of the Yahweh-alone movement. (d) During the first half of the second century B.C., a new feature of Jewish belief emerges: the expectation of a new, universal and eternal kingdom of (the Jewish) God. Beginning with the Book of Daniel one can speak of an 'eternal-kingdom movement' which soon develops into the Eschatological Judaism of Pharisees, apocalypticians, Christians, Essenes, etc. Morton Smith's attempt to carefully distinguish between different groups, 'movements' and 'parties' within Israel was extended to first century A.D. Judaism by one of his students, Jacob Neusner, in a particularly fruitful way: Both Yahweh-aloneists and Pharisees were a minority among eighth century B.C. prophets and the sages active before 70 A.D., respectively.

Last but not least, mention must be made of <u>social anthropology and the scientific study of religion</u> which have an ever-growing impact on biblical studies and, indeed, will give it a new dimension if not a new direction. Several essays of this volume refer to studies by social scientists and adopt their approach, their results, or both. However, one section is almost exclusively based on comparative evidence and anthropological theory: the article on 'The Social Organization of Peasant Poverty'. I feel that the use of a concept developed in the 1950's and 1960's, that of 'peasant society' (a social system in which peasant communites are controlled by urban centers) was overdue. Given the wide interest in prophetic social criticism one wonders why this has not been done earlier. For some of the other essays I found particularly helpful and illuminating the old-fashioned functionalist theory and the work of Hjalmar Sundén, the Swedish psychologist of religion. Max Weber's work, too, has been a constant source of inspiration. Perhaps one can say that the present influx of anthropological, sociological - and to a certain extent: literary - methods, together with the above mentioned 'crisis' in the established historical-critical tradition, constitute 'the state of Old Testament studies'. This 'state' is not static, but a state of change, and what may at first appear uncomfortable to the beginning student may very soon reveal its exciting and even revolutionary nature. The obstacle can become a challenge.

Chapter One

THE YAHWEH-ALONE MOVEMENT AND THE MAKING OF JEWISH MONOTHEISM

There is no God but Yahweh and Israel is his prophet.
                        - Julius Wellhausen (1921, 152)

The introduction of monotheism into the consciousness of mankind is the greatest single achievement of the ancient Hebrews.   - Raphael Patai (1977, 349)

N terms of the biblical evidence it seems almost natural that 'heathen' polytheism should be the illegitimate offspring of a much older monotheism. According to such a view, polytheism derives from the still pure beliefs held by the immediate descendants of Noah, hero of the flood. Time and again, the idea of a primitive and primordial monotheism (the German 'Urmonotheismus') is even recognized by critically and empirically orientated scholars. For instance, the English philosopher Herbert of Cherbury (1582-1648) took the veneration of one single god to be the essence of religion in the classical world, its polytheistic character being nothing but its facade. Actual polytheism, however, is an invention of 'priestcraft': by pretence and deceit, priests have dissuaded their peoples from a thoroughly monotheistic 'Urreligion'. It is not difficult to see what the father of English deism is aiming at: he is looking for a reassuring empirical and historical basis for his belief in the deistic god and, overwhelmed by discovering this god in ancient sources, he feels happier than the Greek thinker, Archimedes /1/.

The first to relate the idea of a primordial monotheism to both ancient and contemporary religions is the French Jesuit, Jean-François Lafitau (1681-1740), a former missionary in Canada and one of the founders of modern comparative religion. Starting from the fact that classical religion, as well as that of the Chinese, the Indians, Peruvians, Amerindians and many other peoples, includes a Supreme Being, he goes on to conclude that this reflects a primordial monotheism, mediated to man by an original revelation. Polytheism, on the other hand, is taken to be some degenerate form of the belief in angels which must ultimately derive from the same supernatural source /2/.

The great Enlightenment critic, Voltaire, is still of the same opinion. "I dare to believe", he writes in his 'Dictionnaire Philosophique' of 1764, "that in the beginning, people knew of one god only and that later on a plurality of gods was assumed due to human frailty" /3/. In the twentieth century, this theory of decadence was revived by Father Wilhelm Schmidt SVD (1868-1954) in his many-volumed 'Ursprung der Gottesidee' on the basis of anthropological research. Nowadays, critics differentiate Schmidt's evidence from the dogmatic framework in which it was presented and conclude, that the idea of a High God is almost universal. This concept, however, is not to be confused with monotheism proper /4/.

How Old is Yahweh-Alone Worship?
Review of Some Theories /5/

The student of the Old Testament whose documents recall the beginnings of recorded human history is easily led to endorse the theory of a primordial monotheism. How will he react when being assured that one can only think in terms of an evolution which makes monotheistic belief a later form of religion? Since 1757, when David Hume published his famous 'Natural History of Religions', this view has been gradually gaining ground and is now generally accepted. Hence, the beginnings of Israelite monotheism, or, to be more cautious, the beginnings of monolatric religion, are sought in the history and, especially, the early history of the biblical people. Various authors place the nomadic religion of the patriarchs, the religion of Moses, that of some tribal league, or the prophets at the first stage of the developing belief in one god. The view which one adopts does not only depend on actual historical evidence (which is meager), but also on the requirements of one's church doctrine or personal bias, as we see in the cases of Father Schmidt, Father Lafitau, and Herbert of Cherbury quoted above.

The same is true for Abraham Kuenen (1828-1891) who is remembered as one of the founders of modern Old Testament criticism. His theory of the prophetic origins of Jewish

14

monotheism is aptly summed up in the concept of 'ethical monotheism', an expression Kuenen seems to have introduced himself and which has enjoyed wide circulation:

> What did the Israelitish prophets accomplish? What was the result of their work, and what value are we to assign to it? Ethical monotheism is their creation. They have themselves ascended to the belief in one only, holy, and righteous God, who realises his will, or moral good, in the world, and they have, by preaching and writing, made that belief the inalienable property of our race /6/.

In Kuenen's work, as later in that of Max Weber, Israel's prophets figure among the first to promote the ethos which became normative for Western society. The emphasis on progress ("they have themselves ascended"), the implied concepts of evolutionary perfection, and of morality as the center of religion are typical ideas of the late nineteenth century. The liberal Dutch theologian's book on prophecy was published in the same decade as Charles Darwin's 'Descent of Man' (1871)!

To most contemporary scholars, Kuenen's view of monotheism seems out of date, as it clearly over-estimates prophetic creativity. Recently, however, the same view was eloquently advocated by Nikiprowetzky. This author returns to the concept of 'ethical monotheism' and recognises the prophets as the actual creators and promotors of a monotheistic belief which is one of the "moral and intellectual bases of modern society" /7/. "Born of national pride and self-confidence, it grew and gained strength along with it", Kuenen writes on monotheism /8/. In Nikiprowetzky, we read:

> As intolerant and fanatic champions of Yahweh, the prophets started the religious war in reaction to the Philistine expansionism that led to the conquest of the highlands. The preaching of the prophets represented, on a religious level, calls to battle against the Philistines and to form an Israelite state. Monolatry became symbolic of an imperative duty to Yahweh and to the Hebrew nation /9/.

Prophetic nationalism, then, is the cradle of monotheism - at least in the view of the authors quoted. Would Durkheim have taken this as confirming his theory that the divine is a symbolic abstraction or representation of society, and hence, in the final analysis, society itself?

Monotheism and the Prophetic Minority

Although Kuenen's late dating of the birth of Yahwistic monolatry may be historically accurate, his work is now passé. Scholars prefer to look at earlier periods of Israel's history for the origins of monotheism, without, of course, immunity from ideology or bias. This is particularly true of writers of 'dialectical theology', advocates of a sternly dialectical exegesis, the classical representative of which is Gerhard von Rad (1901-1971). He opens his 'Theology of the Old Testament' with an interesting, yet somehow inadequate outline of the history of Yahwism. In the middle of a well-documented report that gives evidence to the long and undisputed co-existence of Yahweh with a host of other gods in Israelite religion, one is surprised to encounter the following dogmatic statement:

Right from its beginning (...) Yahwism's claim to exclusivity did not tolerate peaceful co-existence with other cults. One cannot conceive of a worship of Yahweh which did not respect the First Commandment /10/.

Such a statement would be quite fitting for a Karl Barth, but can it be accepted as a historian's judgement? Its source seems to be the Deuteronomist's work, which was aptly called the implicit or 'secret' center of von Rad's Theology /11/. Was he aware of the limitations and doubtful historical accuracy of the Deuteronomist's perspective? Von Rad's view may be explained, and perhaps excused, by saying that our problem, the origin of Jewish monotheism, was not his. He was concerned with the distinctive traditions of Israel.

From this strictly inner-biblical, phenomenologically orientated approach, which has always been stressing rather than actually demonstrating the distinctiveness of Israel in all respects, monotheism was no subject to be discussed at any length; for monotheism is only meaningful as the opposite of polytheism which is not particularly prominent in Israel's national traditions /12/.

One may add that, during the Third Reich, this simple view of Israel's uncompromising worship of Yahweh alone contributed to the status of the Old Testament as the unquestionable property of the Confessional Church /13/. But should such indisputable merit silence scholarly argument?
While von Rad allows for an Israelite origin of the exclusive worship of Yahweh, which he relates to a sacred tribal league prior to the monarchy, Victor Maag /14/ goes far back into the desert to look for origins. He refers to a

documentary film by the famous Sven Hedin which deals with the Bachtiars of Iran. When the usual pastures of these herding people are insufficient or unavailable, they migrate for long distances, often venturing into unfamiliar territory. They base their hope in finding rich pasture-ground on a divine promise mediated by an inspired leader. Maag identifies this with the religion of the patriarchs Abraham, Isaac and Jacob, and even with that of Moses, as an exclusively workshipped god of the wilderness guiding his people. This interesting and extremely witty view of Maag has often been criticized and refuted, even by Maag's own students /15/.

Ulf Oldenburg looks even further back in desert society than Maag /16/. Coming out of the desert earlier than 3000 B.C., the Canaanites have a purely monotheistic religion whose god is called El. Their belief, however, does not remain in its original form as other peoples enter their society along with their gods. When, from the late Third Millennium onwards, the Near East is flooded by the Amorites who come out of the Arabian peninsula, El is supplanted by the Amorite pantheon, the best known representative of which is Baal, a young character full of vitality. The Israelites are the only ones to resist foreign influence and continue their exclusive worship of El, whom they call Yahweh, the intolerant god of monotheism. Thus, the Israelites appear to be the true Canaanites, the genuine Semites who stubbornly conserve and defend their inherited religious identity. The reader of Oldenburg's book is strongly reminded of Ernest Renan's (1823-1892) famous phrases that "The desert is monotheistic" [now transformed into: Canaan is monotheistic] and "The Semites never had a mythology". Further, "The intolerance of the Semitic race is the logical consequence of their monotheism" /17/. Perhaps echoing Renan, Lawrence of Arabia, who had a first-hand knowledge of the desert, wrote in the same vein that the Arab's "desert was made a spiritual ice-house, in which was preserved intact but unimproved for all ages a vision of the unity of God" and further, that "this faith of the desert was impossible in the towns" /18/. However, such views have long rested in the graveyard of out-dated theories, and R. de Vaux's comment on Oldenburg's book is to the point: "There are accurate observations, but unfortunately they are marred by views no longer used in the history of religions (Urmonotheism, the pure religion of the desert, etc.) and by an entirely uncritical reading of biblical texts" /19/.

17

A different approach is taken by N. K. Gottwald in his
bulky study on 'The Tribes of Yahweh' the subtitle of which
reveals the author's perspective: 'A Sociology of the Religion
of Liberated Israel'. According to Gottwald, mono-Yahwism
is the out-growth of an innovative social revolution taking
place in pre-state Israel. Whereas polytheism is a feature of
the traditional, hierarchically stratified city-states of
Canaan, mono-Yahwism is Israel's own property and is related
to the conscious creation of a classless commonwealth:

One way of viewing the relationship of religion and
society in old Israel is to recognize in Yahwism an
experimental, conceptual-institutional alternative to
repressive human authorities. In Israel the element of
experimental calculation is reflected in the people's free
choice of the covenant relationship with the deity. Thus,
while in explicitly cultic terms the demands of Yahwism
were strict and excessive compared to the demands of
official Canaanite religion, the actual empirical
situation was that the 'tolerant' Canaanite cult justified
the centralized political rape of human and natural
resources and energies by a small elite, whereas the
'strict' Israelite cult justified the development and
enjoyment of human and natural resources and energies
by the entire populace. Yahweh, in appearing to demand
much more than Canaanite gods, actually gave back to
his worshippers the benefits of productive human life
which a small Canaanite minority had arrogated to itself
under the symbolic approval of hierarchic polytheism /20/.
[In brief:] Yahweh forbids other gods in Israel as Israel
forbids other systems of communal organization within
its intertribal order /21/.

I am afraid that this eloquently conjured 'monotheistic
experiment' is a modern idealization of Israel's origins, the
romantic idea of an ancient peasant revolt, wishful thinking
rather than a plausible reconstruction of historical events!
In his book on 'Palestinian Parties and Politics that Shaped
the Old Testament', Morton Smith engages in a truly critical
reading of the Bible. Coming from von Rad's outline you have
to slowly adapt your eyes to a new perspective. According to
Smith, the notorious worship of many gods by the Hebrew
people is not a lapse, or defection, from an earlier and
metaphysically higher faith revealed at Sinai, but merely
exemplifies the polytheism of all ancient and primitive
nations. Israel's religious history is not characterized by the

fight for restoring the original, monolatric orthodoxy, but rather by the fluctuating fate of a minority Yahweh-alone movement, whose own presentation of the story in the Books of Kings should not mislead the modern scholar as it is the biased view of the victorious party.

We cannot confidently reconstruct the origin of monolatry. The factors that may have contributed to its formation include, (a) rivalry between the priests and prophets of Yahweh and those of other gods, (b) opposition of conservative nomads against Canaanite cult and culture, and (c) the wish to keep the ritual and cultural life of the immigrating overlords separate from that of their native subjects. Rivalry in cultic matters can be illustrated by the destruction of the Yahweh temple in Elephantine by the Egyptian priests of Khnum (5th century B.C.), and by the return to the 'gods of the fathers' implied by a passage in Herodotus on the Caunians in ancient Greece. Actual influence of the monolatric idea is not attested before the 9th century B.C. when it is advocated by the prophets, Elijah and Elisha, in the northern kingdom, and by the reforms of kings Asa and Jehoshaphat in the south. The exact aims of the monolatric movement are as difficult to grasp as the origins of its ideology. In the southern kingdom, temple prostitution and icons are abolished, and in the north there is a fierce battle, not between the adherants of Baal and Yahweh, but between an official polylatric cult patronized by King Ahab and a group supporting Yahwistic monolatry. Ahab's spouse, Jezebel, persecutes the members of the monolatric movement, while King Jehu appears to support them, most probably for political rather than religious reasons.

For a long time to come there are no records on the monolatric movement; perhaps they saw their foremost objectives fulfilled. It is documented again when Hosea appears on the scene in eighth century Israel, when King Manasseh persecutes the Yahweh-aloneists, and when, in the late seventh century, the reform of King Josiah inaugurates a true growth period for monolatry.

Despite the brevity of his presentation, Smith tries to include many well-argued details. He notes that unlike Hosea, Amos does not seem to be an advocate of monolatry but the monolatric movement takes up his interest in social matters, and that political pressure in favour of polylatric worship applied by the Assyrian overlords, often assumed by modern scholarship, is unlikely /22/. The cultic monopoly of

Jerusalem, realized under King Josiah, may be taken to be a new objective of the movement, dating from the days of Hezekiah or Manasseh. The Josianic reform seems to be supported by various groups which have dissimilar interests. The priests of the Jerusalem temple favour the idea of making it the center of worship, merchants are interested in the lucrative business connected with pilgrimages, and the king in political centralism, while nomadic and ascetic circles want the suppression of fertility rituals and to re-invigorate the legendary figure of Moses /23/, etc.

Although one may have reservations about some of the details, it seems clear that this fresh view is the most probable and empirically sound interpretation of available facts.

The following pages try to reexamine the sources and, adopting Smith's approach and some of his conclusions, give an outline of the history of the exclusive worship of Yahweh. We have to start with the oldest form of Israelite religion, i.e. polytheism.

The Background: Israelite Polytheism

During the four and a half centuries of Israelite monarchy (ca. 1020-586 B.C.), the dominant religion is polytheistic and undifferentiated from that of its neighbours. The religions of the Ammonites, Moabites, Edomites, Tyrians, etc., are local variants of the common Syro-Palestinian pattern which is not transcended by their individual traits and distinctive features. The original religion of Israel belongs to this group of West-Semitic cults. Every individual Israelite clan, from the king down to serfs and slaves, honours its own tutelary god or spirit who is taken to be responsible for the family's health and well-being. It respects the local god whose name is used in oath-taking and who is thought to punish the wicked members of the residential community be it village or town. It worships Yahweh, the god of country and nation, whose special domains are kingship, war, and peace. Finally, there are 'departmental gods' whose fields of competence may be weather, rain, female fertility, and the like. It may be that the Baalim, so often mentioned in the Bible, are but the gods of cities and provinces of Israel, whereas Yahweh is the great Baal, or lord, of all the kingdom. In any case, Yahweh, the 'god of hosts', is surrounded by a host of gods.

Female prestige depends on male children, since only they can provide old-age pension. Hannah does not take comfort in her husband's tender assurance that, to him, she is worth more than ten sons; she prays to the clan god, worshipped on the occasion of a yearly feast, for a son (1 Sam 1). Other women direct their prayers to the 'Queen of Heaven', apparently their special patronness, who is honoured by burning incense, by libations and by offering of a particular kind of cake /24/.

From the vast repertoire of religious ideas, institutions and practices, let me single out just a few, especially those that were suppressed or transformed later, and analyze them briefly.

(1) The National God

Yahweh's position as Israel's national god is undisputed even in polytheism. All the neighbouring peoples have one single national god each - the Moabites worship their Kemosh, the Ammonites Milcom, the Assyrians Ashur, and the Egyptians Amun-Re. Just as Israel is the people of Yahweh, so Moab is the "people of Kemosh" - and the Moabites the sons and daughters of the same divinity /25/. Generally speaking, aliens are "the people of a foreign god" (Dan 11.39). The idea of a national god is well expressed in Micah:

All peoples may walk, each in the name of his god, but we will walk in the name of Yahweh our god for ever and ever /26/.

As god of the country where he resides, Yahweh's sphere of responsibility and influence may be conceived of as either very limited or relatively extensive. Aramean enemies take him to be a 'god of the hills', i.e. of the Palestinian hill country, whereas Amos thinks in terms of the Davidic-Solomonic empire and even includes some adjacent areas /27/. A much more modest idea can be seen in a Hebrew inscription found some years ago and now on exhibition in the Israel Museum in Jerusalem. Around 700 B.C. a Judaean has the following sentence engraved on the wall of his tomb chamber: "Yahweh is the god of all the country, the hills of Judah belong to the god of Jerusalem" - possibly the refrain of some psalm or national song /28/.

The close correlation between god, land and people implies 'other countries, other gods', and to go abroad means 'to serve other gods' (1 Sam 26.19-20). "How could we sing Yahweh's song in a foreign land?" (Ps 137.4) the exiled psalmist asks melancholically. On the other hand, national gods may be worshipped even abroad, and foreign gods enjoy the right of

21

hospitality in the Yahweh temple of Jerusalem, where their statues and altars are installed. Further, the Moabite Kemosh and the Ammonite Milcom have their own separate shrines on the hill immediately east of Jerusalem (1 Kgs 11.7). In these sanctuaries there are icons of these gods which are tended and maintained by a special, and possibly foreign, clergy.

The images of gods may be taken abroad or even deported in war (Jer 49.3). But how to worship Yahweh, the aniconic god, in another country? The Aramaean commander, Naaman, finds a solution which does honour even to a military leader's ingenuity. He takes a load of soil on two mules and thus is able to worship the owner of this soil, Yahweh, even in Damascus (2 Kgs 5.17). Naaman's promise to worship Yahweh exclusively, and his apology for his involvement with the cult of Rimmon may be the product of the imagination of a biased narrator, rather than the usual logic of polytheism. Israelite polytheists are people "who bow down before Yahweh, yet at the same time swear by Milcom" /29/. Even after his rise to world dominion, the Yahweh of the fifth century does not loose the nature of a god whose sphere of influence is geographically defined, "Yahweh's greatness reaches beyond the borders of Israel" (Mal 1.5). If it is to be properly understood, this statement must be read in terms of its implication that there was a time when Yahweh's power did not extend beyond the borders of the country.

(2) The Creator God

A national god such as Yahweh need not be conceived of as the creator of the universe. For most of ancient Israel, as well as for its immediate neighbours, man and world were created by a mighty god called El or Elohim. Accordingly, one text speaks of "El, the Most High, creator of heaven and earth" /30/. Some passages give clear evidence to a later and quite conscious identification of Elohim and Yahweh, see above all the well known creation narrative: "Then Elohim, (i.e.) Yahweh, formed a man from the dust of the ground" (Gen 2.7). The added name of Yahweh betrays how the earlier concept of Elohim was supplanted by the belief in Yahweh alone. The same process of identification and assimilation can be seen in Am 9.6:

He builds his stair up to the heavens and arches his ceiling over the earth, he summons the waters of the sea and pours them over the land. Yahweh is his name.

The concluding exclamation, "Yahweh is his name" is

repeated several times in secondary passages /31/ in Amos, and is the creed of a later period which sees a struggle to supplant Elohim by Yahweh and exclusively worships the latter. "Yahweh is his name" means to say that Yahweh is the creator god, not Canaanite El! Belief in El, however, is not directly opposed, but El or Elohim are simply identified with Yahweh, so that both merge into one, single deity. (The emergency of the 'aloneist' creed will be discussed later in this chapter.)

(3) Iconolatry

Another feature of Israel's oldest religion is an array of idols, or cult images representing gods or goddess in human shape, or symbolizing some divine power, perhaps some secondary aspect of a deity, in animal or vegetable form. It seems that Yahweh himself is never represented in iconic form /32/, but that a bronze serpent, a golden calf-bull and a sacred tree /33/ can symbolize his power to heal and to dispense fertility in various domains, serving as the focal points for sacrificial activities - see, e.g., the altar which Aaron erects in front of the Golden Calf (Ex 32.5). The idols themselves are so powerful that just by looking at them one can receive divine blessing, soaking it in, as it were, with one's eyes. Fortunately, later tradition did not altogether suppress what may be called the 'sacrament of seeing'. "When a snake had bitten a man", one passage reads, "he can look at the bronze serpent and recover" (Num 21.9). At least one psalm echoes what it means to the worshipper to 'see', i.e., to meet, his god in iconic representation: "I seek thee early with a heart that thirsts for thee (...) So longing I come before thee in the sanctuary to look upon thy power and glory" /34/. Some features of the famous golden calf incident at Mount Sinai, in particular the priest's formal presentation of the image to the people, suggest the existence of an elaborate ritual of consecration and induction, which in the Book of Daniel is reported for Babylonia /35/.

(4) Divine Kingship

This expression does not just entail that kingship is a divine institution, but that the monarch himself is a divine figure and can legitimately be called a 'god' or a 'god's son' /36/. The precise meaning of these terms in the framework of Hebrew mythology escapes us as the idea could survive later censorship only in poetry open to a metaphoric or 'sterilized' re-reading. How can it be that the king is the son of Yahweh, a god without a consort? Or are we looking for too much consistency in the realm of myth, and of ideology presented in the form of myth? (Some possible interpretations are suggested in this volume's section on the Making of Messianism.)

(5) Human Sacrifice

One of the institutions of the polytheistic cult, later considered heresy, is human sacrifice. It is not a regular feature of worship, but is thought to be powerful in the event of a national disaster. When the king of Moab was encircled in one of his towns by the Israelite military, leaving him no possibility of escape, "he took his eldest son, who would have succeeded him, and offered him as a whole-offering upon the city wall" (2 Kgs 3.27). Incidentally, the Israelite military, afraid of some supernatural action on behalf of their enemy, immediately returned to its own country. Micah 6.7 leaves no doubt that the Israelites themselves occasionally resort to the same practice of human sacrifice. The Phoenician large-scale sacrifices, where two hundred or more children have to satisfy some god's insatiable appetite, seem to be the product of the unrestrained imagination of such story-tellers as Diodor and Flaubert /37/, who are writing with an eye toward a readership which expects sensations.

(6) Temple Prostitution

Many sanctuaries have their own temple brothel which includes both female and male prostitutes. Contrary to widespread assertion, there is no evidence for a religious or magical meaning of copulation, such as the ecstatic experience of the divine in orgasm or the promotion of fertility. According to biblical texts, the brothel is one of the temple's sources of income, perhaps an important one /38/. The temple women of Jerusalem, and elsewhere, may be obedient servants of some goddess of love who has her icon in the temple. Their actual business, however, is as profane as that of the prostitute who may seek a female innkeeper's protection or keep an inn herself. The temple brothel probably provides shelter and income for a woman who, for whatever reasons, can no longer count on the help and solidarity of her clan. The temple brothel serves humanitarian ends, at least from the temple management's point of view.

(7) Ancestor Worship

The cult of the dead /39/ seems to play an important role, but as it is rejected by a later phase of Israelite religion, it is hardly recognizable in the sources. According to the older view, the ancestors are not the weak and feeble beings of later dogma, but rather powerful ghosts or 'gods' (the latter designation being used by 1 Sam 28.13) who are able to influence their descendants. Extra-biblical data suggest that the injunction to honour one's father and mother refers not only to the care for the aged parents but also to some form of cult of the dead. Ancestor worship is the basis of the idea of a family tomb and of the wish to live close to it. Writing in the sixth century B.C., the prophet and priest, Ezekiel, is shocked by the fact that the, seemingly unclean, family tomb of the Davidic dynasty is within the 'city of David', probably even within the royal palace itself /40/, and, in any case, quite close to the temple. Although this situation fills the priest with horror, it is actually encouraged by an earlier tradition, which confines the idea of ritual impurity to a short period of mourning and burial.

This polytheistic and 'pagan' religion did not remain static. Some of its transformations may be seen as steps towards monolatry, whereas others lack such direction. Of the Judaean king, Asa (912-871), we are told: "He even deprived his own grandmother Maacah of her rank as queen mother because she had an obscene object (?) made for the worship of the holy tree /41/. Asa cut it down and burnt it in the gorge of the Kidron" (1 Kgs 15.13). The passage reveals an intimate connection of politics and religion: "It seems likely that the king removed a particular cult object, perhaps the image of a mother goddess of special concern to the queen mother, from the temple, in order to express, even by this, the end of the gebirah's political influence" /42/. However, this reading is far from certain. The reason the biblical writer gives for Maacah's deposition sounds "so typically Deuteromonistic that doubts about the historical accuracy can hardly be suppressed" /43/. Maybe the biblical author, known for his interest in religious reforms, has modelled the ex-queen mother on the prototype of other idolatrous women associated with the royal court. In this case, he would have indulged not only in arbitrarily supplementing the sources available to him, but also in falsely attributing the cultic ideal of a later age.

An episode involving Nadab and Abihu is less obscure, even though, in its brevity, it is not entirely clear. These two

25

priests once "presented before Yahweh illicit fire which he had not commanded" and were, so the story tells, killed by the sacrificial fire (Lev 10.1-5). This anecdote seems to reflect an argument about some sort of incense offering which was rejected or tabooed by a certain group of priests, for whatever reasons. Undoubtedly, the story of the two disobedient priests' fate was told to all apprentices at the temple in order to inculcate the strictest obedience and to eliminate a former feature of the cult. For us, this conflict about the incense offering indicates that there were issues unrelated to monolatric worship. Even the cult is not free from human rivalry - just as any other realm of society.

The Fight against Baal in the Ninth Century (Phase 1)

We have several highly interesting politico-religious reports for the northern kingdom in the ninth century:

(1) In the period of King Ahab (874-853) the Yahweh prophet, Elijah, has a large number of Baal prophets murdered, after the king's consort, Jezebel, had killed those of Yahweh (1 Kgs 18; 19,1).

(2) King Jehoram (852-841) removes a stone monument of the god Baal from the temple of Yahweh in the capital of Samaria (2 Kgs 3,2).

(3) Following a coup d'état, the usurper king, Jehu (841-813), has a temple of Baal destroyed and orders the killing of the priests and prophets of this divinity (2 Kgs 9-10).

With the exception of the brief report about King Jehoram, we are dealing here with texts which are to be classified as prophetic legend or history recast in terms of later religious concerns. Their immediate evaluation as historical sources is therefore impossible. Because the narrator projects his particular preoccupation, the exclusivity of the workship of Yahweh, on to the events of the ninth century, we can no longer determine the true extent of the conflict between Yahweh and Baal, and between their respective supporters. Whether the murder of prophets and priests really took place we do not know, though it is certainly possible. The key to the events lies in the figure of Jezebel. A daughter of the Sidonian king, Ethbaal, she is a fervent worshipper of the god of her Phoenician home town /44/. King Ahab demonstrates his pro-Phoenician policy through the marriage to Jezebel and through promoting her to chief wife. This invigorates trade and strengthens Ahab against the Assyrian Empire, which is rising threateningly on the horizon, and results in the increased worship of Baal.

King Ahab himself endows an altar for the foreign god, perhaps even a shrine, if 1 Kgs 16.32 is not an exaggeration. This is nothing unusual; in the middle of the ninth century, Bar-Hadad, king of Damascus, erects a stela for the Tyrian Melcart and calls the foreign god "his lord (baal)" /45/.

What can be the meaning of the alternative, 'Yahweh or Baal', stressed in the biblical reports, in the context of polytheistic religion? The following considerations may be offered:

(1) Perhaps the newly introduced cult, with its center on or at the Carmel mount /46/, is very popular and leads to a financial loss for Yahweh's priesthood. We can see that these priests are ill-disposed towards Baal and his, certainly, foreign priests /47/, and that the rivalry can escalate into open conflict.

(2) Following a suggestion by Astour /48/, one must reckon with an opposition to the Phoenician traders, whose financial center is the temple of Baal. This supposition is by no means irrelevant. In antiquity, temples are institutions for religious cults, and also fulfil many a task of the modern bank. "So great was your sin in your wicked trading that you desecrated your sanctuaries" (Ez 28.18) says Ezekiel to the king of Tyre, a sentence which makes little sense unless the temple functions as a trading bank. Even though we have no immediate evidence for the rejection of foreign traders in this period, it is not totally unthinkable. Foreign traders' branches require royal protection just for this reason (1 Kgs 20.34).

(3) The political re-orientation under King Jehu, away from Phoenicia and towards Assyria, is certainly no spontaneous decision. Clearly, an anti-Phoenician circle with sees its future in an alliance with Assyria had existed for a long time. Such circles have as little respect for the Baal cult as they have for Sidon and Tyre, and are easily won over to a 'Yahweh instead of Baal' slogan, if it is not created within their own ranks. One does not worship the god of the enemy. In a parallel illustration, the Shilluk of southern Sudan are forbidden to worship the tribal god of the Dinka, their neighbouring enemies. The ethnographer, Hofmayr, can even document a violation: In an extremely dry year, a desperate Shilluk who set up a secret shrine to the powerful god, Dengit, is discovered and fined one ox /49/.

(4) In addition to the financial and political rivalries, there may be some which can be regarded as directly religious confrontations. Perhaps the adherants of Baal really

27

try to make the Phoenician god into the national god of the northern kingdom, leaving only an inferior place for the traditional god of the country. Or does this particular historical situation result in two gods of the country, sharing more or less equal status, i.e., Yahweh and Baal? Even the flexible logic of polytheism cannot accommodate two national gods at a time, and the result is not a fight between Yahweh and the Phoenician Baal, but "between Yahweh and what one might call the duo-theistic posture of the kings" /50/. Just the thought of such a situation offends Yahweh's prophets and injures their national feeling. Whatever may be the historical truth about the bloody fights under Ahab and Jezebel, Ahab's second /51/ successor, Jehoram, bears, perhaps consciously, a name containing Yahweh's, and removes a stone monument consecrated to Baal from the temple of Yahweh in the capital city.

The events of the Jehu revolution are harder to judge. The records assume prophetic incitement and, accordingly, that Jehu allows full rein to religious, and not just power-political interests. However, it seems to me that the greatest caution is advisable on this point.

The participation of prophetic circles in the plotting of the coup d'état looks more like royal propaganda than historical fact. A prophetic oracle of the type, "This is the word of Yahweh, the god of Israel: I anoint you king over Israel, over the people of Yahweh" (2 Kgs 9.6) can only strengthen a powerful chief and will not miss its mark with the people. But what about Jehu's pitiless action against the god Baal and his priests? It is a priori probable that the new king replaces the priests devoted to his predecessors Ahab, Ahaziah and Jehoram, with new ones, in order to eliminate a possible or even probable opposition. We know from his merciless extermination of the families of his predecessors that Jehu does not shrink from murder in such cases (2 Kgs 10.1-14). Even if the destruction of a Baal temple corresponds more to a wish of a Deuteronomistic writer than to historical fact, one must nevertheless reckon with measures against the cult of the Phoenician god. For Jehu does not continue the pro-Phoenician policy of his predecessors, but takes sides with the enemies of the Phoenicians, i.e. the Assyrians /52/. A contemporary Assyrian stela shows King Jehu kissing the dust at the feet of the Assyrian king, Shalmaneser /53/. The logical implication of Jehu's policy is that opponents of the pro-Assyrian course are to be found among the friends of the Phoenician temple and have to be eliminated.

Chapter One - The Making of Monotheism

In the events of the generation of 874-840 later adherents of the Yahweh-alone movement see key concerns of theirs realized or, at least, enhanced. In the ninth century, however, the struggle between Yahweh and Baal is still contained within the framework of polytheism, and has its closest counterpart in the rivalry between Ashur and Marduk, the major gods of Assyria and Babylonia, respectively. Every time Babylon is incorporated into the Assyrian Empire, the cult of the Babylonian Marduk loses prestige and is consciously reduced at least twice. Tukulti-Ninurta I (1244-1208 B.C.) conquers Babylon and takes the statue of Marduk to Assyria. Sennacherib (704-681) destroys the temple of Marduk in the enemy's capital and carries the statue of Marduk back to his homeland with him. It is his grandson, Ashurbanipal (669-627), who brings it back to Babylon. According to W. von Soden /54/, Sennacherib has prop-agandistic cult theatre performed which shows Marduk in the pitiful role of the accused before the court of the gods. All of these are measures for the defamation of the Babylonian national god and to the greater glory of Ashur.

Such acts originate from a narrow-minded national pride and it is the known characteristic of most peoples to brand everything strange as barbaric and reject it, especially when it appears right on their doorstep. That is the end of the tolerance otherwise practised or declared. Even Roman history provides an illuminating example for this. When many people turn to foreign (and hence, allegedly, superior) cults during a devastating epidemic, they are denounced as mentally ill, or superstitious, or they are defamed as the victims of profit-hungry swindlers, and, finally, these cults are formally forbidden. The conservative Romans of 428 B.C. defend themselves successfully against the importation of foreign cults with the slogan, 'Only Roman Gods'.

And not only were men's bodies smitten by the plague, but a horde of superstitions, mostly foreign, took possession of their minds, as the class of men who find their profit in superstition-ridden souls introduced strange rites into their homes, pretending to be seers; until the public shame finally reached the leading citizens, as they beheld in every street and chapel outlandish and unfamiliar sacrifices being offered up to appease Heaven's anger. The aediles were then comm-issioned to see to it that none but Roman gods should be worshipped, nor in any but the ancestral way /55/.

Monotheism and the Prophetic Minority

Because neither an Ashur-alone movement nor an 'Only Roman Gods' party did arise from this rivalry, caution must be exercised in the interpretation of the corresponding events in Israel. The violence and radicalism of certain episodes in the religious battle should not mislead us. The opponents of the Phoenician Baal are not monotheists, nor do they worship Yahweh exclusively to the detriment of all other gods. One can realize only later that the beginnings of the Yahweh-alone fanaticism lie here, and it is this which will finally drive out polytheism.

The Prophet Hosea (Phase 2)

In the period between the coup d'état of Jehu (841) and the appearance of the prophet Hosea (around 750) a religious movement comes into being in the northern kingdom which, following Morton Smith's suggestion, can be called the 'Yahweh-alone party' /56/. Our knowledge of this group is very limited and essentially rests on the Book of Hosea, whose value as a source is not above suspicion. The Book of Hosea must be regarded as the oldest, classical document of the movement and its influence can be proved without difficulty even two hundred years later. As the movement further develops its teachings and objectives, these are partly incorporated into the book. At any rate, critical research takes this factor into account, though it is, admittedly, very hard to prove for individual passages. In our context, however, it is less important to reconstruct the original wordings of Hosea's oracles, than to read the book as a reliable witness to the intentions of the Yahweh-alone movement. In this way, we can placate the critical consciousness by pointing out that the typical teachings of the seventh and sixth centuries, limiting the sacrificial cult to Jerusalem and actual monotheism, are not to be found in that book. It can be valid as a thoroughly genuine document of the eighth century.

A second important source is the book of the Prophet Amos /57/ who lives in the same generation as Hosea. It is a source in a totally negative sense, because Amos reveals nothing of a polemic against false gods. Amos is indeed a prophet of Yahweh but the Yahweh-alone idea does not find expression in his written legacy. Not every worshipper of Yahweh is simultaneously a supporter of the Yahweh-alone movement, which one should not imagine to be too influential. If we evaluate the Book of Hosea we see that the programme of the movement at that time includes criticism of gods other than Yahweh and criticism of temple prostitution. We will now take up these points.

(1) The Israelites should worship Yahweh and neglect all other gods on principle

In the words of Hosea's god this reads:

But I have been Yahweh, your god, since your days in Egypt. You shall know no god but me! There is no saviour beside me! (Hos 13.4)

What sounds like a play on the words of the decalogue to the ears of a later Jew or Christian well-versed in the Scriptures is, in fact, the basis of the Ten Commandments, which appear much later and allude to the words of Hosea. The worship of Yahweh alone is the cause of a small group only. The official trend of the religion of the Temple remains, of course, polytheistic:

They must needs sacrifice to the Baalim and burn offerings before carved images. (Hos 11.2)
They resort to other gods and love the raisin-cakes offered to their idols. (Hos 3.1)

Raisin-cakes, therefore, are not part of the Yahweh cult. In short, "Ephraim, keeping company with idols" (Hos 4.17). More than once it can be perceived clearly that this conception is an extension and escalation of the fight against Baal. 'The other gods' are simply called the "Baalim":

I will punish her (i.e. Israel) for the holy days when she burnt sacrifices to the Baalim (Hos 2.13)

says one oracle, and another one:

and I shall wipe from her lips the very name of the Baalim; never again shall their names be heard. (Hos 2.17)

Now opposition is not only to the Phoenician Baal alone, but also to all his local manifestations. Wherever a Baal, whether it is the Phoenician or any other, is worshipped, the Yahweh-alone movement rejects his cult. Apparently, the opposition is now extended to deities who do not belong to the Baal type, for example the god of the plague, the god of death, etc., and of course the female deities as well. The Baalim are mentioned emphatically, but this is probably less due to the wide distribution of Baal shrines than to the memory of the 'original conflict' between supporters of Yahweh and those of the Phoenician Baal. Now all the gods are denounced as 'Baalim', as supposed rivals of Yahweh.

(2)   Prostitution should be banned from the temple area

Hosea, husband of a temple woman (Hos 1.2-3), is a harsh opponent of the temple brothels:

At Israel's sanctuary I have seen a horrible thing: there Ephraim played the wanton, and Israel defiled herself. (Hos 6.10)

Apparently, prostitution in the temple can barely be differentiated from the same trade carried on at the edges of simpler venues for worship, such as the village threshing floors. The reproach here is:

You have loved a harlot's fee on every threshing-floor heaped with corn. (Hos 9.1)

It is hard to decide what the prophet in chap. 4.13-14 is referring to. Is he talking about the orgiastic cults at holy shrines, in which every male participating in the service of worship is paired with a woman at its end? In this sense, W. Rudolph paraphrases the prophet's reproach:

The men who indulge in these practices must notice that they offer a bad example to the female members of their own families, who are also present at the cult festivals. If anything happened to them a hue and cry would be raised (the woman is not allowed to do what the man lays claim to as his obvious right). But Yahweh says that he cannot count it ill if the young girls and wives, befuddled by wine, take the heads of their own families as a model and give in to their impulses /58/.

But the prophet may be referring to a fertility rite which the women undergo before marriage. In the shrine, they have sexual intercourse for the first time with any stranger present or with a priest /59/. Whatever the intent may be, Hosea, and with him the Yahweh-aloneists, condemns all sexual practices which occur in connection with Israelite temples and worship. He is a 'Puritan'.

The reader of Hosea may note that I have not dealt with the rejection of images and of idols, which plays a role in the prophet's book. I consider the polemic against icons to be post-Hoseanic additions /60/. As Yahweh is never presented in iconic form /61/, the condemnation of other gods must simultaneously be the rejection of images. The Golden Calf symbolizing Yahweh's power and potency, set up as a statue in the Temple of Bethel, is clearly mentioned without polemic in Hos 10.5-6. If Hosea considers the fabrication of idols of silver and gold a sin (8.4), then he is thinking of the statues of Baal, and not of this calf-shaped icon. That is the opinion of the editor who added 8.5-6 and 13.2. Hosea does not take exception to the Golden Calf of Bethel. Only the temple brothel disturbs him. In the secondary polemic against the Calf we can grasp a teaching of the Yahweh-aloneists which only appears after Hosea's days, but perhaps before the end of the eighth century. It is interpolated by the editors of the book for the sake of completion and elucidation.

At this point it is necessary to look back at the development of the worship of Yahweh alone. By now it should be clear that no straightforward path leads from the confrontations of the ninth century to the developed Yahweh-alone theology of Hosea. If we lack sources to reconstruct this path, we can at least reconstruct some of the forces which must have been at work. We can refer to the 'temporary monolatry' known in the Ancient Near East and first analyzed by the Dutch Assyriologist, A. van Selms /62/. In certain situations, larger groups of Mesopotamians, Persians, and apparently Israelites, too, practised the exclusive worship of one divinity. Such a cult suggests neither the rejection nor the absence of other (i.e. non-worshipped) gods. Instead, in a period of crisis, worship is directed towards a single divinity from whom, after this extraordinary attention, help is expected. The temporal bounds of such worship shows that this sort of monolatry remains within the framework of polytheism. As sources, van Selms quotes two texts from the Babylonian Atrahasis-Epic where, on one occasion, Namtara, and on another, Adad, temporarily receive monolatric worship, in order to bring an end to plague or draught, respectively. A passage from the first tablet of the Atrahasis Epic is particularly impressive:

> Command that heralds proclaim
> and make a loud noise in the land,
> "Do not reverence your gods,
> do not pray to your goddesses,
> but seek the door of Namtara,
> and bring a baked loaf in front of it.
> The offering of sesame-meal may be pleasing to him,
> then he will be put to shame by the gift
>   and will lift his hand."

Such an effort cannot prove unsuccessful:

The offering of sesame-meal was pleasing to him,
he was put to shame by the gift
    and lifted his hand.
Plague left them,
the gods returned to their (men's) offering /63/.

The same practice was current among the Arabs to whom
Mohammed preached his message. To the prophet's dismay
people discontinued the exclusive worship of Allah as soon as
they saw their prayers answered:

When distress touches a man he calls his Lord, turning
repentant to Him. Then when He confers on him a favour
from Himself, that man forgets what he had called upon
Him for before, and makes peers for God (i.e., returns to
polytheism) to lead people astray from His way! (Surah
39.11)

Further examples for such concentration of the cult are
the thirty-day monolatric worship which the Persian king
demands for himself, according to Dan 6.8, and the exclusive
worship mentioned in 1 Sam 7.2-14 during a war against the
Philistines, if the latter text is not already stamped by the
later views of the Yahweh-alone movement. Dan 11.37-38
may be read as a clear statement of temporary monolatry by
order of some king who considers himself to be the prophet of
the god who is to be worshipped exclusively:

He will ignore his ancestral gods, and the god beloved of
women; to no god will he pay heed but will exalt himself
above them all. Instead he will honour the god of the
citadel, a god unknown to his ancestors, with gold and
silver, gems and costly gifts.

Finally, Jer 44.18 may give evidence to the fact that all
cults except Yahweh's were discontinued during the siege of
Jerusalem in 587/586 B.C.:

From the time we left off burning sacrifices to the
Queen of Heaven and pouring drink-offerings to her, we
have been in great want, and in the end we have fallen
victims to sword and famine

protest the people whom Jeremiah tries to convince of the
Yahweh-alone idea.
If we suppose that 'temporary monolatry' is known in Israel
and practised from time to time, then we can, at least
provisionally, consider it the prototype of the Yahweh-alone
idea. Israel, afflicted by continual inner social crises and

34

military-imperialistic threats from the outside, is a milieu in which the idea can arise of adopting, not just a temporary, but a permanent monolatry of the state god. Consequently, Yahweh-alone worship can be understood as a crisis cult which is continued beyond the actual crisis situation. Or, rather, the crisis situation is perceived as permanent. Moreover, Yahweh's capacity to become an opponent of Baal, and of any other god or goddess, must be found in his being, which is developed and explained in myth. Eastern mythology usually does not report about an individual and isolated god but about god-figures who are joined to one another in multifarious ways. The customary link is that of marriage, family and kinship. The gods appear, like men, not as single or isolated 'individuals', but are social beings who meet in a network of kin-like relationships. To give just one example, the Egyptian Isis is the wife of Osiris and the mother of Horus. Apart from genealogical organization, mythology also presents the nation of the gods, with king, council and allocations of rank, especially among the Sumerians. The idea of a heavenly court is also known from the Old Testament. Just think of the prologue to the Book of Job or Ps 82, where Israel's god sits in judgement in the circle of the gods (or, following the Hebrew wording, stands up in order to pronounce judgement). But, as Yahweh lacks every link to a family of gods, so the idea of a gods' state is rather incidental. Yahweh appears as a lone figure who is outside the usual bonds. Later, in the Koran, it is written: "He begets not nor is he begotten" (Surah 112.3). From a polytheistic point of view, this signifies that in the normal cases a god has a father and son and thus is in the web of kinship and pantheon. The childless god is the exception /64/. To have kinship relationships implies a certain diminution of power. In kinship-based societies the leader's kinsmen want to share in his power and privileges or, alternatively, tend to encroach upon his autocracy. The really powerful leader, therefore, does not surround himself with kinsmen, but with followers and dependents such as slaves. The proverb, "A prophet is not without honour, except in his own country, and in his own house", suggests that he is not respected by his family who wants him to be like the other kinsmen. Sons, moreover, involve a father in endless generational conflicts that ultimately aim at replacing him.

Yahweh, as the 'Lord of Sinai' (Ps 68.9), has little to do with the well-organized world of the gods of Canaan. He is as much a foreigner as are his immigrant worshippers in the land, who are, or consider themselves to be, foreigners. The outsider in the world of the gods is the god of the outsiders.

Because the Israelite tribes are not, or only in part, related to the Canaanites, their god cannot be genealogically linked to the latters' gods. The lack of a kinship relationship means, consequently, possible enmity. Clearly, it is this special position of Yahweh which makes possible his enmity with Baal and the other gods. One result of this elective affinity is not seen until later, i.e. the exclusivity of the relationship between Yahweh and Israel. Whoever worships a 'normal' god-figure comes into contact with the clan and nation of gods. Just as a person cannot be isolated from the net of genealogical associations, so it is for a god and goddess. What, then, if a god has no kinship? Here may lie an important cause of the Yahweh-alone idea and thereby, ultimately, a root of monotheism. The lonely Yahweh becomes the only god.

The Hezekian Reform (Phase 3)

While the Book of Hosea gives clear evidence for the existence and concerns of the Yahweh-alone movement in the northern kingdom, we know virtually nothing about the situation in the southern kingdom of Judah. Prophets Isaiah and Micah appear in the time of kings Jotham, Ahaz and Hezekiah (ca. 739-699), but the traces of the Yahweh-alone idea which we find in their books seem to be later additions /65/. In his poem on the birth or ascension to the throne of Hezekiah, Isaiah describes the king, according to polytheistic courtly style, as god-like (Isa 9.5). Isaiah is no Yahweh-aloneist.

Yet, the influence of the Yahweh-alone movement, or, more exactly, the influence of one of its demands, can be assumed from the cult reform of King Hezekiah (728-699). In the cult reform, according to the existing text, Hezekiah fulfils all the objectives of the movement: abolition of the high places, smashing the images of the false gods, cleansing the Jerusalem Temple of heathen features. But it has long been recognised that here the later period incorporated its conceptions of an orthodox cult reform.

In reality, Hezekiah's reform consists of the relatively modest measure of removing a certain serpent-shaped cult symbol from the temple. He "broke up the bronze serpent that Moses had made; for up to that time the Israelites had been burning sacrifices to it; they called it Nehushtan ('bronze image')" (2 Kgs 18.4). This serpent is not an image of

Yahweh, nor is it a divinity in its own right, but it is probably meant to symbolize Yahweh's healing and rejuvenating powers which find expression in the well-known legend of its healing effect during the Moasaic journey through the wilderness (Num 21.6-9). The Yahweh-alone movement seems to have extended to such symbols a much older taboo which originally only prohibited the iconic representation of Yahweh himself. Now the movement demands the abolition of all images somehow related to Yahweh and perhaps understood by the people as representations of the national god himself. We can probably link the rise of the polemic against the images of the Golden Calf with the age of Hezekiah, those statues which King Jeroboam I of the northern kingdom (931-910) had endowed, in reality or supposedly, to the shrines of Dan and Bethel (1 Kgs 12.28-30). In the Deuteronomist we find a continuous hostility towards these statues. He goes so far as to connect the political fall of the northern kingdom (722) with them by giving them first place in a list of all the ritual abominations which called forth Yahweh's wrath (2 Kgs 17.16). This sort of polemic is certainly from a later phase of the Yahweh-alone movement, but the basic idea, opposition to cultic symbols of Yahweh, must have been alive in the age of Hezekiah. Scholarship dates the story of the Golden Calf which Aaron had made, and around which the people danced while Moses met his god in the solitude of Mount Sinai, to the same period. The story receives its polemical propagandistic point of criticism from the fact that Moses does not sanction the action of Aaron and the people (which must have been the common attitude of the priests), but angrily grasps hold of the Calf, burns it and grinds it to powder (Ex 32).

Perhaps one can explain the facts as follows: after the fall of the northern kingdom in 722 B.C., the supporters of the Yahweh-alone idea come into the southern kingdom, - so that the movement already in existence there receives a political stimulus. The movement links the traumatic fall of the northern kingdom to the fact that their objectives, as advocated by Hosea, for instance, were not followed. Additions and clarifications in the Book of Hosea and a special version of the story of Aaron's image of the Golden Calf impart greater weight to the argument.

The objectives and arguments of the movement do not lack effect on King Hezekiah, who must tremble for the survival of his own kingdom. The crisis brought about by the Assyrian policy of expansion - in 722 Samaria is destroyed, and in 701

Sennacherib's troops are in front of Jerusalem - offers the movement its first chance to realize one of its goals in the southern kingdom. Apparently, Hezekiah's reform marks "the beginnings of a prophet-inspired cult praxis in Judah" /66/.

The Josianic Reform (Phase 4)

We have no further sources on the influence of the Yahweh-alone movement until the time of King Josiah (641-609) and the subsequent decades of the Judaean state. However limited our documentation may be, it is more detailed than for the whole of the preceding period. This is not due to a chance transmission, but is connected with the success the movement experiences.

During the first two years of Josiah's reign the prophet Zephaniah appears. In the collection of his words there is an oracle which shows him to be an adherent of the Yahweh-alone movement:

> I will stretch my hand over Judah
> and all who live in Jerusalem;
> I will wipe out Baal from this place
>   to the last remnant /67/,
> and the very name of the heathen priests,
> those who bow down upon the house-tops
> to worship the host of heaven
> and who bow down before Yahweh,
> yet at the same time swear by Milcom,
> those who have turned their back on Yahweh,
> who have not sought Yahweh or consulted him. (Zeph 1.4-6)

The editor of the book of Zephaniah, himself clearly an adherent of the movement, places the oracle at the beginning. In this the special hatred for the priests of Baal is conspicuous, and is obviously an established tradition in the movement.

Although we are not informed about Zephaniah's actual influence he must be among the forerunners of the events of 622 B.C. /68/. Even before this year there are supporters of the Yahweh-alone movement among the priests of the Jerusalem Temple and at court, but it is in this year that the king himself is won over to the movement and immediately puts a comprehensive and drastic programme into practice. The report given in 2 Kgs 22-23 may in some respects be exaggerated and idealized, yet it is clear to see that the movement has succeeded in the coup d'état of a reform. Hilkiah, high priest of the Temple, presents the still youthful king, twenty-six years old at that time, with a book which has supposedly come to light during restoration work on the Temple. According to 2 Kgs 22.11 the king accepts the regulations of the book in a spontaneous act of devotion - he rents his garments. It has become customary in recent historical writing, it is true, to reckon with a genuine find; on the other hand, scholars such as J. Wellhausen and Morton Smith may be right to suppose a forgery: when the book is read out aloud to King Josiah the ink is barely dry. Ashurbanipal, who had just died in 627 B.C., ordered all the archives to be searched for old texts in order to incorporate them into his library in the Assyrian capital, Niniveh. One is wont to point to this in order to credit the age with an interest in ancient writings, so that the finding of Hilkiah gains credibility /69/. This fashionable antiquarianism may have been welcome to Hilkiah and his friends, however, in order to secure attention for their 'find'. If one considers the fanaticism and unwillingness to compromise of the Yahweh-alone preaching of some prophets, as well as the blindness to history with which Israel's past is judged in the movement, then the 'find' is by no means out of place. Yahweh-aloneists stop at nothing to achieve their objectives. Religious zeal shrinks at no method.

Because the report of the reform agrees with the substantial provisions of the law of Deuteronomy, one usually identifies Hilkiah's book with the nucleus of Deut 12-26. The most important measures of the reform are:

(a) Centralization of the cult

The legitimate cult of Yahweh is only to be carried out at the Temple of Jerusalem. The provincial shrines will be closed.

(b) Purification of the cult

Both unity and purity of the cult are demanded. All features are removed from the Temple of Jerusalem which offend the eye of the Yahweh-aloneists. The king orders: "remove from the house of Yahweh all the objects made for Baal and the sacred tree and all the host of heaven" (2 Kgs 23.4). As to be expected, the dethronement of Baal is mentioned first.

In second place comes the 'sacred tree' (Hebrew: asherah) which represents Yahweh's power of blessing made visible in vegetable form; there is no goddess called Asherah as is presumed by modern translation /70/. The banning of the

39

images is extended to this symbol because it is plainly popular and adorned with all sorts of ornaments, especially with the pieces of fine cloth mentioned in verse 7. Perhaps these were sold to visitors to the temple, who decorated the cult symbol with the items bought so that the tree shifted into the role of a god's icon to which one made sacrifice. That the temple brothels also fall victim to the cleansing goes without saying.

(c)   The new order declared national law

With this measure the Yahweh-aloneists reach their actual goal, viz. the permanent control of the entire worship in Judah. We do not know how far the reform can actually carry through its programme in fact. There is certainly no mass-conversion to mono-Yahwism, but the latter becomes an officially established fact.

When Josiah falls in the battle against the Assyrian army in 909 B.C., the reform is not continued and the movement loses control of national worship. As we know from Ez 8, the images of the gods return to the temple. The prophet Ezekiel, active in a Babylonian colony of Jewish exiles from about 593 B.C. onwards, lashes out at this; he comes from a family of priests and from his youth belongs to the Yahweh-aloneists. He now supports the movement far from his homeland. His invective against idolatry pervades his whole book, provoking Wellhausen's judgement that he is "more a judge at the court of the inquisition than a prophet" /71/. He wants to have only adherents of the Yahweh-alone idea among his clients. He gives oracles only to them, others receive a tirade of insults which he extends into an attack on Israel's religious policy in the whole of its history /72/. Simultaneously, Jeremiah is active in Jerusalem (from 609 B.C. /73/). He too is an uncompromising exponent of Yahweh-alone theology. Like Ezekiel, he comes from a priestly family who has shared in Josiah's reform. After the destruction of Jerusalem (586) he is driven to Egypt where we meet him, once again, quarrelling with the opposition party. The latter stands firm on its point of view:

> We will burn sacrifices to the Queen of Heaven and pour drink-offerings to her as we used to do, we and our fathers, our kings and our princes, in the cities of Judah and in the streets of Jerusalem. (Jer 44.17)

The eloquent rhetoric of Jeremiah that follows cannot hide the fact that the Yahweh-alone idea is innovative, rather than traditional polytheism. The Jews and Aramaeans of the military colony of Elephantine even have a temple dedicated to this Queen of Heaven. In any case, a letter addressed to an inhabitant of the island in the Nile was found with "greetings to the Temple of Bethel and to the Temple of the Queen of Heaven" /74/.

The Breakthrough to Monotheism (Phase 5)

In 586 B.C., when Jerusalem is reduced to ruins, the hour of the Yahweh-aloneists has come. Polytheistic Israel is dead, and out of its ashes arises Judaism, being firmly based on the teachings of the aloneist movement. The decline of the state and the Babylonian exile are represented as results of polytheistic heresy and as punishments of the god who is to be worshipped exclusively. The bulky history of the Deuteronomist /75/ starts with the exhortations of Moses, who, time and again, impresses Yahweh-alone worship upon his audience and promulgates or repeats all the laws which are now edited in their final form /76/. The work proceeds with the history of Israel, which is a story of how a people "turned wantonly to worship other gods and bowed down before them; all too soon they abandoned the path of obedience to Yahweh's commands which their forefathers had followed. They did not obey Yahweh" (Jdg 2.17). During the course of seven centuries there were not many events to be reported that find the Deuteronomistic historian's approval. Both monarchies, north and south, are dealt with in impressive parallelism. The northern kingdom dies of its idols first, but it is followed by the south. We read about Josiah, "He did what was right in the eyes of Yahweh; he followed closely in the footsteps of his forefather David, swerving neither right nor left" (2 Kgs 22.2), but his successors revert to polytheism, so that the comment on Jehoahaz, Jehoiakim, Jehoiachin and Zedekiah, the four kings of the last twenty-five years of Judah, is the same as pronounced on many kings before: "He did what was wrong in the eyes of Yahweh, as his forefathers had done" /77/, and, "Jerusalem and Judah so angered Yahweh that in the end he banished them from his sight" (2 Kgs 24.20). Accordingly, the course of history follows rules that are clear and straightforward; no one can help but hear Yahweh's footfall through the history of his people. The immense work which comprises several long scrolls is a detailed sermon of repentance, urging obedience to the law of Moses and, in particular, to its central tenet: the exclusive worship of Yahweh. Actual

41

historiography, on the other hand, is less important. For many details the reader is referred to the 'Chronicle of Solomon' or the 'Chronicle of the Kings of Israel' /78/ and similar books, writings which were, unfortunately, not transmitted to posterity.

The most important literary sources for the Yahweh-alone movement dating from the exile are, apart from the Deuteronomistic History, the books of Ezekiel and Deutero-Isaiah. The Yahweh-alone idea contributes to the foundation of Judaism through four major issues which stand out in this literature: education, the sabbath, control of orthodoxy, and national restoration. Let me briefly comment on each of them.

(a) Education

Deuteronomy shows a remarkable interest in education and is, at times, quite emphatic in this. Every Jew is to be taught the basic elements of religion from early childhood, so that "a wise and understanding people" (Deut 4.6) will be the consequence. Learning and teaching become the essential religious duty, and parents are their children's instructors. The Decalogue which I date to this period is a brief statement both of law and creed, reduced to a form that is easily memorized. It is prefaced by the formula, "I am Yahweh your God who brought you out of Egypt, out of the land of slavery. You shall have no other gods to set against me" (Deut 5.6-7), clearly reminiscent of Hosea, one of the earlier and classical authors of the aloneist movement. Though an original creation of a Deuteronomistic writer /79/ the rest of the Decalogue, too, echoes Hosea (Hos 4.2; 13.4). It is true that the Ten Commandments may provide the commoner with sufficient religious knowledge, but for the expected king of a restored Israel this text is inadequate. He is supposed to

> make a copy of this law in a book (...) He shall keep it by him and read from it all his life, so that he may learn to fear Yahweh his God and keep all the words of this law and observe these statutes (Deut 17.18-19).

Although it is presumed that the king would be able to read, this is not expected from the commoner, so it is important to teach him his duties on ritual occasions. According to Deut 31.9-13, this education is to occur every seventh year, during the feast of Tabernacles. Since there is no thanksgiving in the fallow year, then, everybody is expected to "listen and learn (by heart)". Later, this rather modest program of religious instruction once in seven years (!) develops into more regular teaching on every seventh day, on sabbath in the synagogue.

(b) The Sabbath

I take the sabbath to be an institutionalization of the Yahweh-alone idea. This weekly day of rest is not an ancient, religiously tabooed day, but a conscious creation of the sixth century /80/. In using the sabbath to moor monolatry in popular custom, it cannot be introduced in a vacuum, but has to be connected with some already existing practice. The founding fathers of the sabbath start from two institutions which are undoubtedly very popular. The first is the seventh day of rest which ancient Israelite law grants to the agricultural labourer at ploughing time and harvest, i.e. at the period of hardest work /81/. The second is the day each month when the moon is full, which, since time immemorial, is called the sabbath. It is not just a day without work, but a day set aside for ritual observances /82/. It is clear that in pre-exilic times, ritual obligations were not only due to Yahweh but also to other gods; in Hosea, the sabbath is one of those holy days called 'days of the Baalim' /83/. The fathers of the exilic sabbath make every possible effort to rededicate this day to the exclusive worship of Yahweh. The Decalogue is quite explicit on this point; "the seventh day is a sabbath of Yahweh your God" /84/. 'Sabbath of Yahweh' is a cliché common to literature of the sixth and fifth centuries /85/ which seems to reflect the élite's insistence on the connection between Yahweh and the sabbath; the sabbath is for Yahweh, and for him alone. Thus, the sabbath is subordinate to the first commandment, "you shall have no other gods to set against me", and exists to promote its observance. One may even say that in the 'sabbath of Yahweh' the first commandment is given a tangible, practical, and, as it were, sacramental form. Early Judaism outside Palestine which is suddenly forced to lead a life poor in ritual creates the sabbath as a substitute for the distant temple and uses the emerging synagogue as the people's meeting place on sabbath. A secularist's use, or rather misuse, of the sabbath as a day for leisure, and not for religious ritual, would no doubt have horrified the Yahweh-aloneists.

(c) Control of Orthodoxy

By introducing a series of statues, the founding fathers

of Judaism try to safeguard the new community's loyalty /86/. They leave no doubt about their intolerance. Prophecy calling for following other gods is punishable by death (Deut 13.2-6). If such an invitation is pronounced by one's brother, son, daughter, wife or friend, then "you shall have no pity on him, you shall not spare him nor shield him" (Deut 13.9). In this way, a system of control is established which even interferes with, and works within, the family. The religious community is considered to be more important than kinship solidarity - a revolution in a kinship-based society, but characteristic of new religious movements such as early Christianity, Islam and some well-known contemporary cults /87/. In particular, marriage arrangements are subject to public control. Traditional endogamy (marriage within the closer kin group, Gen 24.3-4) is developed to take on a new meaning. Mixed marriage with non-Jews is not only discouraged but formally forbidden, as it endangers the community's stock of members /88/.

(d) National Restoration

One of the main objectives of the Yahweh-aloneists is the future restoration of the Jewish state, with its only cultic center to be the temple of Jerusalem. For this purpose the legal code of Deuteronomy is substantially revised; the new texts inserted provide the most vital regulations for the new Jewish commonwealth and is official religion. Ezekiel's book, too, includes a detailed draft of a national constitution dating from 573 /89/, the outlines of which most probably go back to the prophet himself. While Deuteronomy and Ezekiel are concerned rather with constitutional theory and planning, Deutero-Isaiah (546-539) is the prophet of a return to Palestine. According to one of his oracles, Israel "has fulfilled her term of bondage" (Isa 40.2). As for the head of the new commonwealth, there is no uniform idea in our three authors. Deuteronomy thinks in royal terms, Ezekiel pictures a rather simple cult warden and mayor. By transferring the name of messiah, an ancient ritual title of the Israelite king, to the Persian monarch, Cyrus, as the liberator from the yoke of Babylon, Deutero-Isaiah /90/ seems to imagine the new commonwealth as a purely religious community under Persian political control. In spite of such differences there is a common objective to all of these practical and theoretical activities - to firmly establish monolatric Judaism and to provide for it in perpetuity.

Some of the texts which doubtlessly belong to the

Yahweh-alone tradition are interested in completing the monolatric belief by introducing a totally new principle: the denial of the existence of other gods, i.e. monotheism. The formula of Deut 6.4, which was to become the classical creed of Judaism, is still monolatric and expresses the traditional programme of the Yahweh-aloneists: "Yahweh is our God, Yahweh alone" /91/. But there is another and quite new dimension in its variants:

Yahweh is God, there is no other. Deut 4.35
Yahweh is God in heaven above and on earth below; there is no other. Deut 4.39
Yahweh is God, he and no other. 1 Kgs 8.60
... so that all kingdoms of the earth may know that thou, O Yahweh, alone art God. 2 Kgs 19.19

Such expressions are not only to be found in Deuteronomy and the Deuteronomist's work, but also in Deutero-Isaiah:

There is no god but me; there is no god other than I, victorious and able to save. Isa 45.21
... for I am God, there is no other. Isa 45.22
Before me there was no god fashioned nor ever shall be after me. Isa 43.10

Deutero-Isaiah imagines how the Egyptian subjects of the then world-ruling Israelites bow down in supplication and humbly confess: "Surely God is among you and there is no other, no other god" (Isa 45.14). This conviction is underlined by repeated polemic against idolatry. One ironical text reads: "Those who squander their bags of gold and weigh out their silver with a balance, hire a goldsmith to fashion them into a god; then they worship it and fall prostrate before it." For the Yahweh-alone movement there can be no doubt about what the prophet adds: "Let a man cry to it as he will, it never answers him; it cannot deliver him from his troubles" /92/.

This is monotheism, but it never disregards the national conviction that Yahweh is and will remain the god of Israel; the only god is Israel's god. Time and again this national dimension is brought to the attention of the later Jew in the liturgical "Hear o Israel: Adonai is god, Adonai alone" /93/. Therefore, a Talmudic saying is quite appropriate: "Whoever rejects the worship of other gods is called a Jew" /94/, and not simply a monotheist. There is no God but Yahweh and Israel is his prophet! /95/

No doubt there is a polytheistic variety of Judaism which survives the exile and can be studied from the 5th century documents of the Jewish colony at Elephantine in Egypt. However, the restored temple of Jerusalem, consecrated in 515 B.C., remains from the outset under the rule of a Yahweh-alone priesthood. The monolatrists or, as we may call them now, the montheists, are no longer a minority but rather assume the leading role and set the fashion. The political and religious élite of post-exilic Judaism is firmly rooted in the monotheistic faith. Jerusalem remains the only legitimate place for sacrificial ritual, and the exclusive worship of Yahweh becomes a general feature of Judaism in so far as it adopts the temple and the emerging synagogues as its centres.

Monotheism is born, but how to account for this major event in Jewish and, perhaps, universal religion? First of all let me state that our source material is too fragmentary to allow for a comprehensive and satisfactory answer. In fact, there are hardly any sources at all, so that one could reasonably give up any attempt to elucidate the advent of monotheism. When I try to consider some suggestions and develop some possibilities, this proviso has to be kept in mind.

The first theory to be considered is that of Norbert Lohfink /96/. He challenges the usual clear-cut dichotomy of polytheism and monotheism and argues that there has always been a latent monotheism or montheistic undercurrent within the ancient Egyptian and Near Eastern religions. Paganism, too, sensed the fundamental unity of the divine. The urban or national deity often worshipped exclusively and taken to be the ultimate cause of all life is the focus of the divine in its entirety. The local god is god 'tout court'.

There can be no doubt that the Sumerians actually believed in the many gods, and in every single city another god took the role of the urban deity just described. But in the final analysis they experienced the one and universal deity whose hidden presence they felt in their particular god. In their god they had the whole /97/.

This latent monotheism had only to be grasped and made explicit theoretically, as well as to be verified in ritual practice. This final step was taken in Israel and in other places, and mainly so in the sixth century B.C. Lohfink points out

that monotheism proper emerged in Israel not before new theoretical insights into the divine were discovered in other parts of the ancient world. Zoroaster in Persia

46

Chapter One - The Making of Monotheism

and the pre-Socratic philosophers of Greece are Deutero- Isaiah's contemporaries /98/.

Hence, the religion of Israel does not have an individual and isolated development but participates in the general development of the other religions of antiquity, just as Israel's culture does in other respects, too. However, by virtue of its firm commitment to Yahweh-alone worship, Israel was in a position to take the final step towards monotheism.

Recently, Hermann Vorländer /99/ proposed a theory which is far more detailed than Lohfink's. In fact, Vorländer takes Lohfink's acticle as his basis, but takes us beyond a general account of Israel's affinity with its neighbours. His key figures are Zoroaster and Deutero-Isaiah. Apparently, Zoroaster's monotheistic worship of Ahura Mazda dates from the second millennium, but it became more and more influential during the reign of the Achaemenid kings of the sixth and fifth centuries. In his inscriptions Darius I (522-468 B.C.) mentions no god but Ahura Mazda whom he seems to acknowledge as the only god and creator. Around the middle of the sixth century the teaching of Zoroaster spread to the Jews exiled in Babylonia and served as a catalytic agent in the restatement of their theology, an observation which was anticipated by the Enlightenment philosopher, Lessing, in the eighteenth century. Influenced by Zoroastrian teachings, Deutero-Isaiah proclaimed his monotheistic kerygma which is, even verbally, echoed in the Deuteronomic secondary texts quoted earlier.

This suggestion comes as no surprise, as there are other well established or very cogently argued connections between Deutero-Isaiah and Persian sources. As early as 1898, Rudolf Kittel /100/ was able to notice some parallels between the cylinder inscription of Cyrus and several passages of Deutero-Isaiah. They are now understood as not merely reflecting the 'Babylonian court style' (this was Kittel's original suggestion), but rather as a clear echo of Persian imperial propaganda. To the Judaeans, the agents of Cyrus must have represented their king as chosen by Yahweh to punish Babylon and restore Israel. Deutero-Isaiah accepted this view and supported it with his own prophetic authority. The fact that Deutero-Isaiah got his political programme from propaganda for Cyrus makes it plausible to look for other Persian connections in his book. Morton Smith /101/ has made, I think, a good case for tracing Deutero-Isaiah's theology of creation back to the same source on which Yasna

47

44 is based, one of the oldest Zoroastrian texts.

Vorländer's view is well argued and his presentation is the most satisfactory one available. In pointing out the likelihood of a powerful Persian influence, he has opened up neglected, if not new and promising, perspectives for research /102/. It may be too wide a perspective to be dealt with in the present context. However, we can take up Deutero-Isaiah's monotheism and theology of creation, both of which appear to be a fitting response to the problems raised by the exile. In the sixth century, Jewish theology has to face two serious problems:

(1) Is Yahweh, whom Jewish theology professes to be its only god, less powerful than the gods acknowledged by other nations? To answer this question in the positive means to renounce Jewish identity. Uprooted from a comfortable, home-grown Israel-centered theology, Jewish thought has to clarify the relationship between Yahweh and the other gods once and for all.

(2) The second problem is closely related to the first and concerns the mythic dimension, without which it is impossible to make any statements about the divine. How to speak about Yahweh meaningfully after much of the older tradition on his special concern for kingship, nation and land has suffered a loss of prestige?

The solution to these problems is that Yahweh is the only god, and that the only god is the creator and ruler of the whole world. In this period, the least useful item of Israel's theological repertoire is the royal tradition. Even Ezekiel makes little use of it. When speaking of Israel's future leader he does not use the royal title at all, but presents him as the mayor of Jerusalem. Largely ignoring the royal and Jerusalem traditions, exilic theology refers to unexhausted subjects such as the Mosaic period, the patriarchal times and creation. Among these traditions, the theme of creation enjoys special privileges as the creator god, by his very nature, is concerned not with Israel alone but with the entire world, thus meeting the challenge of exile.

Let me add that I do not want merely to repeat what Wellhausen said almost a century ago. Impressed by the fact that Gen 1 and Deutero-Isaiah date from about the same period, he concluded that the belief in Yahweh as creator and ruler of the universe did not antedate the exile. I do not share this view. It seems to me that there are at least two original oracles pronounced by Jeremiah which clearly express belief in Yahweh as creator and lord of the world, viz. Jer 27.5-6 and 32.27. The former text reads as follows:

> It is I who by my great power and my outstretched arm have made the earth, with the men and the animals that are on the earth, and I give it to whomever seems right to me. Now I have given all these lands into the hand of Nebuchadnezzar, the king of Babylon, my servant, and I have given him also the beasts of the field to serve him.

Interestingly enough, the situation is not altogether different from Deutero-Isaiah. Both he and Jeremiah support a foreign overlord whom they try to integrate into the religious system of their people, and for both of them creation theology provides the basis for doing so. I am well aware of the fact that the history of Israel's doctrine of creation is far from clear; there is the problem of the cosmological hymns in the book of Amos and there are secondary texts in Jeremiah of an almost Deutero-Isaianic flavour such as chap. 10.1-10. In any case, it seems almost certain that Jeremiah paved the way for Deutero-Isaiah's theology of creation. If we are justified in looking for a foreign influence on Deutero-Isaiah, we are still more justified to look for inner-Israelite precedents.

To refer to Jeremiah, however, is not to say that his belief in Yahweh's creative activity is an autonomous and original feature of Israelite religion. Isaiah, for example, did not link his god's control of history to his status of cosmic creator, and it seems reasonable to assume that Jeremiah was the first explicitly to claim that Yahweh had power over all the kingdoms of the earth by virtue of being the cosmic creator. In a lecture delivered at the School of Oriental and African Studies in 1975, and now published as 'The Encounter with the Divine in Mesopotamia and Israel' /103/, Professor Saggs has suggested that Jeremiah was taking over for Yahweh claims he found already made for Marduk of Babylon. Indeed, one can demonstrate that the very language of Jer 27.5-6 reflects conventional Babylonian, rather than Israelite, phraseology /104/. But let us return to Deutero-Isaiah and the birth of monotheism!

In Deuteronomy we can see both the novelty of Deutero-Isaiah's monotheism and the way in which it became part and parcel of the Jewish mind. Monotheism was neither incorporated into the legal collection of chaps. 12-26, nor into the so-called historical creed of chap. 26, nor even into the Decalogue. All of these texts are still based on the older conception of the Yahweh-alone idea. No more than a handful of scattered references in Deut 4 and the Deuteronomistic History attest the advance or final victory of an idea which was to become the central, and possibly only, dogma of Judaism.

The Assimilation of Polytheistic Survivals

How does monalatric, if not monotheistic, Judaism cope with its polytheistic past? In the Deuteronomistic History the official polytheism of the nation is unsparingly stigmatized. Perhaps the 'reform kings', Hezekiah and Josiah, were transfigured into national heroes, but otherwise we see no inclination to gloss over faults of any member of the royal dynasty. The Deuteronomist's denunciations are even surpassed by Ezekiel, whose chap. 20 finds nothing positive or even edifying in Israel's past.

In the world's whole literature there is hardly a document which represents the history of the author's own people in such a negative and uncompromising manner. Israel is a human community which stubbornly refuses its own salvation from the very start, never fulfills the meaningful and judicious precepts of its god and behaves worse than any other nation of the world /105/.

Given this attitude towards the past, it is clear that the canon of sacred literature which emerged gradually after the exile does not contain anything of the polytheistic literature which must have existed. It is completely lost. However, defamation of the fathers and the outlawing of their literature are not the only methods for dealing with the past. In addition to these relatively unsophisticated methods there are more subtle ones: assimilating, adopting and re-interpreting traditions which may conserve polytheistic elements within a monotheistic context.

The divine name of Shaddai provides an example for this. Just as the Babylonian called his protecting spirit 'shedu', which is a kind of guardian angel whom he considers to be a minor but very accessible deity, so the Israelite polytheist achnowledged his Shaddai. Yahweh-aloneists identified Shaddai with Yahweh, who thus acquired the new role of the individual's protecting spirit to supplement his status as the national deity. However, this identification did not imply that the name and notion of Shaddai were forgotten and no longer used. In the Book of Job, a monotheistic document dating from the fifth century /106/, Yahweh, in his role as personal god, is called Shaddai. Klaus Koch who studied this curious phenomenon concludes his analysis as follows:

> The deity, not polymorphous but manifold, approaches man in various extensions, refractions or modes, however one may call this concept. The poet's monotheism is not monolithic. Shaddai is one of these specific refractions, one aspect of God which relates to the human individual, comes close to his body to make him either happy or to wound him deeply. The Shaddai of the Job dialogue is not the Almighty One as some of the modern translations have it, but rather the divine neighbour, somehow to be compared to the personal guardian angel of later centuries /107/.

As Shaddai, Yahweh is particularly responsible for the human individual and the well-being of his family. Just compare how happy Job was,

> while Shaddai was still there at my side, and my servants stood round me, while my path flowed with milk, and the rocks streamed oil (Job 29.5-6).

The name of Shaddai conserved its own message for a long time after the abolition of its originally polytheistic meaning. This can be seen from a Jewish custom based on Deut 6.9 which is still alive and practiced today. This commandment tells us of the Deuteronomistic creed formulae to "write them up on the doorposts of your houses and on your gates". The commandment is fulfilled by writing Deut 6.4 and some parallel texts on a slip of parchment, the reverse of which is inscribed with 'Shaddai'. The rolled-up parchment is enclosed in a little case, and through a small opening one can read the name of Shaddai. This amulet, called 'mezuzah', is attached to the doorpost to ensure the blessing of God or, to use the older and more original name, of Shaddai. A rendering of this name would be 'my god', which is, in fact, occasionally used by the Septuagint /108/.

Beautiful polytheistic texts about an Israelite goddess can be found in Proverbs, chaps. 1-9, a self-contained little book which I date to the pre-exilic period /109/. The goddess is called 'Hokhmah', in English 'wisdom' or 'shrewdness', and was later taken to be a simple poetic personification of school wisdom or of God's own wisdom. But to take Prov 8.22-30 as referring to the wisdom of the only God is contrary to sound textual analysis, as was observed by the Hispano-Arabic

Muslim polemicist Ibn Hazm in the eleventh century /110/. And he is right, for wisdom is the goddess of school and instruction or, more precisely, the patroness of scribal education and training. She is a relative of the Sumerian school goddess, Nisaba, bearer of the beautiful title 'Mistress of Science' /111/. At least according to their teachers, the students are expected to entertain an especially intimate and personal relationship with the school goddess. Prov 8.17 alludes to the relationship of love when the goddess says, "Those who love me I love". Even more explicit is Prov 7.4, where the student is invited to declare his love to her. He is to say, "You are my sister", what is in plain English something like, "You are my darling (or sweetheart)". (For the Hebrew, 'sister' was a pet name for girl friend or wife.) A further example of erotic language is Prov 4.5-9, where the sequence of 'acquiring' and 'embracing' is unambiguous. The student is not to have just an affair with this goddess, but a permanent marital relationship.

Mythologically, Wisdom's father is Yahweh, but no mother is mentioned, and Prov 8.22-31 does not provide any information on this point. I do not recommend postulating a mother, as the history of religions knows of several gods without mothers, see, e.g., Athena, whose father is Zeus but who has no mother. In mythical parlance this is represented by saying that Athena sprang from Zeus's forehead, and Pindar adds to this information, given by Hesiod, that Hephaestus struck open the head with an ax. Similarly, the Egyptian god Thoth, himself inventor of the hieroglyphs and therefore related to writing and school, sprang from the head of Set, in this case because Set involuntarily had swallowed the semen of Horus. Such a paradoxical phenomenon is labelled 'male pregnancy' and 'male birth', an idea not entirely foreign to Gen 2.21-22, where Eve is taken from within Adam's body. Concerning Wisdom, the relevant idea may perhaps be taken from Sir 24.3 which is, however, a much later text. According to this source, Wisdom came forth from the mouth of God. We can never be quite sure of the details of Israel's lost polytheistic mythology. However, let me indulge in a little speculation and propose that the original father of Hokhmah may not have been Yahweh at all, but rather El, the actual Semitic creator god /112/.

Apart from passages dealing with Lady Wisdom, there is at least one further hint at the original polytheistic nature of Prov 1-9. It is in the final paragraph and reads: "The first step to wisdom is the fear of Yahweh and knowledge of the Holy One(s) is understanding" /113/.

The 'Holy Ones' are either taken to be angels (thus the Septuagint), or, if one prefers the translation 'the Holy One' in the singular, Yahweh himself. Without doubt, the couplet is open to both interpretations, which can be justified with reference to the parallelism in biblical poetry. For this reason, the sentence could be transmitted in monotheistic Judaism. But originally, the 'Holy Ones' are the gods of polytheistic Israel, among whom Lady Wisdom belongs.

Perhaps the school goddess was a rather pale figure of which the students were not very fond, in spite of her erotic attraction. It was all too evident that the school masters were putting their own exhortations into her mouth, see Prov 1.20-33. Hence, she cannot be dangerous to Yahweh-alone or to monotheistic doctrine and, reduced to a mere figure of poetic speech, she leads a miserable life in the text-book of post-exilic apprentice scribes. However, there is the possibility that her original nature was remembered in polytheistic, i.e. non-converted, Jewish circles. In 1906/08, German archaelogists, while working on the Nile island of Elephantine, discovered a bundle of papyrus leaves which eventually turned out to be an Aramaic version of the well-known Assyrian Ahiqar story. The leaves date from the fifth century B.C. and were read by members of the polytheistic Jewish military colony. One passage, first reconstructed by A. Ungnad from two papyrus pages, refers to a goddess who bears exactly the same name as Israel's patroness of wisdom /114/. Like the Ahiqar story as a whole, the home of this goddess must be seventh century Mesopotamia. Unfortunately, the Ahiqar passage on wisdom is too short and fragmentary to allow for further conclusions. Israel's school goddess may have had innumerable parallels in Near Eastern mythology, but considering her an imported element cannot be argued on the basis of the Ahiqar passage.

A polytheistic reading of the poems on Lady Wisdom may help us to understand their original meaning, but misses the intention of the editors who are committed monotheists. In the process of demythologizing, a vital figure in religion degenerates into a mere poetic being of ornamental value. For the monotheist reader, Wisdom loses much of her original reality and vitality; what remains is a shadowy figure with some poetic charm. The orthodox reader has to be satisfied with this. A nostalgic memory of the pagan gods is possible and permissible, not for a Jew, but for a Friedrich Schiller:

Keine Gottheit zeigt sich meinem Blick,
Ach, von jenem lebenswarmem Bilde
Blieb der Schatten nur zurück /115/.

What Schiller says of Greek mythology applies as well for polytheistic survivals in Judaism: "My eyes see no deities. Alas, what remains of the picture warm with life is nothing but a shadow."

Concluding Remarks

Having now concluded our survey, we can look back and sum up. It is particularly surprising that so many factors have contributed to the formation and eventual establishment of Jewish monotheism. Let us try to single out the most important and decisive ones. Yahwistic monolatry, which was to become monotheism, develops from three premises in a particular historical situation. (1) The first premise is a common feature of ancient West Semitic religion, namely the prominence of one single deity as the national god. (2) The second premise is the particular character of the god whom Israel worships as her national deity: Yahweh's lack of kinship connections with other gods sets him apart from them. (3) The third and perhaps even more effective premise is the temporary monolatry of one single god chosen out of a pantheon of many because of some special competence, and exclusively worshipped in order to receive his help or appease his anger in a time of crisis. (4) From the eighth century B.C. onwards, these two features of Semitic religion find their particular expression in Israelite religious thought and, later on, dominate Judaism.

The most general answer to the question of why this was the case must refer to power politics. Beginning in the ninth century, the two petty kingdoms, Israel and Judah, come into the orbit of the Near Eastern superpowers. Both states become dependent on, and indeed tributary to, Assyria. In 722 B.C. the Assyrian overlord abolishes the vassal kingdom of Israel by reducing it to a mere district administrated by a governor. Likewise, in 586 B.C., the Babylonian military decides to discontinue the existence of the rebellious vassal Judah. During this apparently unending period of crisis, a small but growing group which we call the Yahweh-alone movement clings to the state deity and demands its exclusive worship. While Judah, as a political entity, is shattered by a superpower, the idea of the only god is born. Monotheism, then, is the answer to political emergency, in which no solution is to be expected from diplomatic manoeuvering or foreign military help. There is but one saviour: the only God. The story of his emergence is part of a larger story, that of a petty nation's political destruction.

Chapter One - The Making of Monotheism

It should be clear that monotheism as a doctrine cannot be the solution to problems faced by ancient Israel. There is a dimension of doctrine in monotheistic thought, it is true; but unlike later scholastic speculation, Yahweh-aloneists and Jewish monotheists are not primarily concerned with dogma and doctrine. Theirs is a theology of hope, the expression of which is embodied in Hosea's and Deutero-Isaiah's precise statement that there is no god other than Yahweh, victorious and able to save /116/. In theological jargon one could say that soteriological monotheism is older than monotheistic dogma, or that hope precedes belief.

Jewish monotheism does not appear abruptly or at one stroke, but has a history in which, as we have seen, various forces operate. Let us try to define the structure of this historical process more accurately with reference to the concepts of evolution or revolution which have often been used in this context. Does monotheism grow up slowly and steadily by mastering difficulties and antagonisms, constantly moving towards its final form, so that the concept of evolution would apply? "The rise of biblical monotheism, as an exceptional cult amidst the ancient pagan world, is analogous to the rise of the human brain in the process of biological evolution", asserts Louis Wallis /117/. Or is it an individual's conscious creation which transcends the limits of its culture, time and environment, in the sense of Gressmann's words about Zoroaster, Moses and Mohammed: "Monotheism, on the other hand, has always been the achievement of great personalities" /118/. According to another author, Pettazoni, such creativity can never be unconscious and evolutionary, but is quite conscious and revolutionary in nature: "Monotheism is not the result of evolution, but of revolution. The rise of a monotheistic religion has always been connected with a religious revolution" /119/.

Taken in its strictly dogmatic form which suggests religious virtuosi to be the true 'founders' of monotheism, Pettazoni's concept of revolution does not apply to Israel. On the other hand, the history of the Yahweh-alone movement does not seem to be due to some hidden, unconscious mechanism of evolution which guarantees the victory of Yahwistic monolatry in order to further elevate it onto the level of monotheism. There is, I feel, no equivalent of Darwin's 'natural selection' and 'survival of the fittest' in the history of religions. Further, there is neither an intrinsic and 'natural' inclination of the Semitic mind towards it, nor a geography or ecology of monotheism which could, by itself, initiate the process or create its premises. No serious scholar will today consider a view which attributes any major cultural feature to the influence of the mere physical environment as anything but an unfounded assumption.

The Yahweh-alone idea, it is true, makes its appearance suddenly, but there must always have been people who were concerned about the influence of this new form of belief, who fought against the worship of other gods, and helped the monotheistic cause to gain recognition and, finally, victory. Moreover, the survival of an idea whose superiority and persuasive power is far from self-evident is always at stake. There may be competing theories of fishing in which rival coteries of experts develop vested interests. The question can be decided with relative ease by seeing which theory is most conducive to catching more fish. But how about competing notions of female beauty and other aesthetic issues? A fortiori, no obvious criterion exists for deciding between a non-polytheistic (i.e. monolatric or monotheistic) and a polytheistic religion. Thus, theologians and religious leaders are likely to substitute abstract argumentation for pragmatic testing - see the rival claims that Jerusalem's defeat in 586 B.C. was due to an abominable monolatric experiment or to the equally abominable neglect of the exclusive worship of one single deity (Jer 44). By its very nature such argumentation does not carry the inherent conviction of pragmatic validity; what is intellectually satisfactory and convincing to one may not be to another.

Even though many of the protagonists and leaders of the minority Yahweh-alone movement remain anonymous, we may call them the 'founders' of proto-Jewish monolatry and Jewish monotheism, thereby slightly stretching a concept used by historians of religion. However fragmentary our knowledge of the development of Israel's religion is, we may describe it as a chain of revolutions which follow one another in rapid succession /120/, leading from the fight against the Phoenician Baal in the ninth century, via the Yahweh-alone idea in the eighth, through the prevalence of the monolatric system in the late seventh, to the final establishment of monotheism in the sixth century B.C.

Perhaps further research will help us to improve our still inadequate knowledge of this most exciting chapter of religious history.

Appendix to Chapter One

HOW EXCLUSIVE WAS THE WORSHIP OF YAHWEH IN TRIBAL ISRAEL?

In this appendix we will argue that Yahweh was the main, though not only, god worshipped in pre-state Israel. He was the head of a pantheon in which there was room for lesser deities invoked on minor occasions. Some pre-Islamic tribes of northern Yemen were, like Israel, defined as religious confederacies and shared its cultic pattern.

What was the religion like that Israel practised in its early and pre-state period? In the foregoing essay we did not deal with this issue since biblical sources do not provide enough reliable information. In fact, Old Testament research has not produced a satisfactory account of Israel's early history and social structure - not to mention a reconstruction of its most ancient religion. Beginnings are always shrouded in darkness. However, there are certain approaches that can serve as a basis for discussion.

According to A. Lemaire (1981b: 5-15; 1982) the following development led to what was to become Israel. In the 14th and 13th centuries B.C., Egypt looses its traditional and long-established control over Syria and Palestine. Palestinian society slowly disintegrates, possibly due to the Aramaean movement. Two new formations emerge in the political vacuum: the Bene-Jacob and Bene-Israel. The Bene-Jacob, Aramaeans in Transjordan, cross the Jordon river and settle north and north-east of Shechem. The Bene-Israel leave Egypt under Ramesses II (ca. 1279-1213, according to Hornung's chronology), live for some time in the Negev, and eventually penetrate into central Palestine, settling south of the Bene-Jacob. When, towards the end of the 13th century, the two groups conclude an alliance, Israel is born. The confederacy is soon joined by other tribes - Naphtali, Zebulun, and Benjamin. Two hundred years later in the time of David, Judah and Simeon join. Lemaire emphasizes the religious nature of the alliance arguing that Yahweh is its tutelary, and assuming this deity's exclusive worship by all its members. He even dates an early form of the decalogue to this period. The first commandment tells the league's members, "You shall have no other gods besides me". Suppressing the deity traditionally worshipped by the Bene-Jacob (Josh 24.23; Gen 35.2) and promoting the religious leadership of the Bene-Israel, the original contract establishes the monolatric principle as the foundation of religion. Yahweh is the federal god, and the confederates are nis people.

Lemaire's reconstruction of the political side of Israel's formation is well-argued and plausible, but his account of the religious aspect is open to criticism. It seems too much influenced by the dogmatic view of later 'aloneist' orthodoxy. There can be of course no doubt about the religious implications of the alliance, for who else but Yahweh could have been the federal deity? The exclusive nature of Yahweh worship and the assumed early date of the decalogue seem questionable. In his capacity of federal deity, Yahweh must have been worshipped exclusively; there is no other federal god besides him. The tribes and clans that made up the confederacy may, however, have continued the cult of former gods and goddesses. Each of these lesser deities had a domain quite different from that of the federal god, and never claimed his title. In polytheistic mythology, gods may be rivals; in polytheistic ritual, each receives his share.

Admittedly, this account is as hypothetical as Lemaire's. Any reconstruction depends on one's confidence in the reliability of the relevant biblical traditions. In such cases the informed historian has only one tool to render his views plausible, the method of checking analogies. Given reliable information about society A, and that society's sufficient resemblance to society B, it can be argued that knowledge about A can be hypothetically used in reconstructing certain features of B. Shared economic and social systems, for instance, may provide a sufficient basis for assuming similar religions. More commonly, fragmentary evidence from religion B can be elucidated on the basis of more detailed information about religion A. This method which never produces more than tentative results, or 'informed guesses', has always been used by students of the earliest history of the Hebrews.

A possible analogy to early Israel is provided by pre-islamic tribes of northern Yemen, whose religion and social structure have recently been studied by C. Robin (1982: 24-26). Like early Israel these groups formed alliances which they defined in religious and cultic terms. Each tribe or tribal league had a central sanctuary dedicated to its tutelary god, the worship of whom was exclusive without being hostile to the cult of lesser deities. Let us have a closer look at these matters.

According to evidence from 3rd to 1st century B.C. inscriptions, the ancient Yemenite tribes refer to themselves as owners of a particular territory or descendants of a common ancestor. However, the decisive definition of the tribes is neither based on genealogy nor ownership of land, but couched in religious terms. Each tribe or, in the case of larger alliances, each tribal league worships a common pantheon. Accordingly, tribes that are politically dependent are required, even forced, to acknowledge the gods of the leading group - without having to abandon their traditional gods. Their original pantheon suffers a loss of prestige, but is not suppressed and replaced. All members of a tribe or tribal league worship one main god at a central shrine. The tutelary of the Sumʿay tribe of highland Yemen is Taʿlab; his temple is called Turʿa and is located on mount Riyâm. The Maʿîn tribe of lowland Yemen worships its god ʿAthtar dhû-Qabḍ in a sanctuary called Riṣâf which is in the town of Qarnâw. The entire country is dotted with such temples that serve as cultic centers of certain groups. By offering sacrifice in an appointed shrine people express their tribal affiliation and solidarity. In some cases, religious rhetoric links individuals to a tribal deity rather than a tribe - see the expressions "children of [the god] Almaqah" for the Sabaeans, and "children of [the god] ʿAmm" for the Qatabānians.

In addition to the central shrines there are many minor cultic institutions, dedicated to the worship of lesser deities. Frequented by people living in their immediate neighbourhood, they enjoy only local importance. Interestingly enough, the tribe's tutelary is usually included in the pantheon worshipped there. Other gods neither challenge the tutelary's pre-eminence in the pantheon, nor weaken his role of providing his tribe with identity and cohesion.

Some tribes of the Yemen eventually worshipped their tutelary in an exclusive way (Robin 1982: 26). However, neither in Israel nor elsewhere can such monolatry be regarded as an original religious notion. Monolatry and monotheism presuppose polytheism. This is the lesson we can learn from studying the tribes of pre-islamic Yemen.

Chapter Two

WHAT IS A PROPHET?

RE Israel's prophets - from Amos and Isaiah in the eighth century B.C. to Ezekiel and Deutero-Isaiah in the sixth - to be rated among the great thinkers of the Ancient World, alongside Pythagoras and Plato? Or would it be more fitting, taking account of their fearless utterances against the mighty of their times, to place them among the champions of justice and social conscience along with the enlightened thinkers and founders of democracy? Are they religious virtuosi who fought against Israel's primitive sacrificial religion in order to bring their people to a new level of awareness? Or are they Utopian visionaries who tried in vain to fight against political pressures with the weapons of morality and religion?

However much truth may be contained in such generalizations, critical research remains uncertain which appellation fits their case best. There is, however, general agreement that the picture of the prophets which earlier generations had is insufficient in some respects and is even misleading in others.

Ecclesiastical tradition has long contented itself with the view that the prophets are - like John the Baptist - divinely inspired preachers of repentance and heralds of the coming of the Messiah. It is, of course, correct to hear in the angry words the Baptist addressed to the "vipers' brood" of the seemingly pious the clear echo of the Old Testament prophets, but when examining the question of messianic prophecy - as with all forecasts for the future - the orthodox conception reflected in the coining of such words as 'weather prophet' cannot be upheld. If we want to understand Israel's prophets we must, as far as is possible, disregard all previously supposed knowledge and to work our way through a series of biblical texts in order to become acquainted with the fundamental characteristics of monarchic Israelite society.

Chapter Two - What is a Prophet?

I. Prophecy as a Factor in Politics

Micaiah ben Imlah: Meeting a Prophet

Ramoth-Gilead is quite a large fortified town in the northern part of Transjordan. Under King Solomon a district capital, it falls shortly after his reign into the hands of the Arameans of Damascus who are trying to expand westwards. King Ahab of Israel who does not want to suffer defeat gathers together his own forces and those of the neighbouring land of Judah in order to reconquer Ramoth. Before the campaign King Ahab asks the prophets for their opinion: "Shall I attack Ramoth-Gilead or shall I refrain?" From the numerous prophets - the text speaks of some four hundred! - he receives the unanimous answer: "Attack, Yahweh will deliver it into your hands."

Since in the Ancient World a consultation with ritual specialists, responsible for oracles, is nothing unusual and is part of the normal customs of war, there is no point in telling the story. Not until the appearance of a prophet with an exceptional oracle do the proceedings become interesting. For Micaiah, son of Imlah, says:

I saw all Israel scattered on the mountains like sheep without a shepherd; and I heard Yahweh say, "They have no master, let them go home in peace."

Signalling defeat, this is a negative reply for the commander. From the crowd of prophets one called Zedekiah steps forward and begins to argue with Micaiah, to curse him and strike him in the face. In order to avoid a confrontation and so as to jeopardize his expedition, King Ahab has the troublemaker, Micaiah, locked up in prison on a diet of bread and water. In the mêlée of the battle Ahab is fatally wounded by an Aramean arrow whilst disguised as a common soldier. He dies on the battlefield in the evening. Having lost its royal commander the army scatters without having achieved its mission. The point of the episode, which occurs in the year 853 B.C. and is recorded in 1 Kgs 22, is that the prophet, Micaiah, son of Imlah, was right.

The agreement of prophetic pronouncement and political event should not, however, lead us to the conclusion that the prophets were simply making predictions about the future. The prophets know, or believe they know, how their god will

61

react to a human project, whether he will give it his blessing or whether he will turn his face. Only when god's blessing is certain will the prophet advise action; should divine goodwill be lacking, the person who acts is himself guilty of the misfortune into which he falls. In this way Micaiah seeks to warn King Ahab and make him abstain from military action. What at first sight appears to be a good or bad premonition of the future, reveals itself upon closer examination to be a political stance by which the prophet is seeking to influence the course of events.

We are no longer able to check whether the report corresponds to historical fact or whether it was a propaganda legend circulated by prophets of the opposition. The unpretentious tone of the narration does, however, point to a real incident whose details - such as the number of prophets loyal to the king and the wording of the oracles - are the work of an author writing a story which will entertain and edify the reader. However that may be, one thing is certain: we are dealing with a true-to-life picture of prophetic activity. We learn something of war as a trigger for prophecy: before the battle the commander wants to know the decision of the national god; this information is not common knowledge, it is available only to specialists. Whereas the Babylonian or Roman commanders turn to priests or readers of omens, in Israel only prophets are consulted, a group of ritual experts different from the sacrificial priests.

The somewhat exaggerated figure of four hundred tells us that at the time of the monarchy Israel was, as it were, crowded with prophets. Most prophets are loyal to the king and are paid for their services, if not regularly at least occasionally. But there are some who intentionally isolate themselves and do not flatter the authorities or others who may consult them. To this group belongs, alongside Micaiah, son of Imlah, his contemporary Elijah, a figure who is shrouded in legend and is difficult to grasp as a historical character. He too is an opponent of the tyrannical Ahab. When an honourable Israelite called Naboth refuses to sell his vineyard to the despot, Ahab organizes a trial with bribed witnesses which costs Naboth his life. Obviously without being asked to, Elijah appears with a devastating pronouncement from god which he hurls into King Ahab's face.

Around the middle of the 9th century, if not earlier, prophetic outsiders in the mould of an Elijah or a Micaiah become a factor in politics. True, it remains uncertain whether the dynasty of Ahab is overturned by prophetic policy or - rather more likely - by the skilled use of alleged prophetic oracles in 841 B.C., but one thing is certain: the decisive religious influence, which in other societies is executed by soothsayers, priests or popes, is in Israel in the hands of the prophets.

Even in the Persian period, when political events are largely guided by dependent governors, prophetic agitation must be reckoned with. Governor Nehemiah, who belongs to the house of David, was accused of monarchic, and hence anti-Persian activities, in particular of bribing prophets to proclaim him King of Judah (Neh 6.7). And when one considers the role of Nathan at the anointment of King Solomon then it seems that the political influence of the prophets between 970 and 450 B.C. (half a millenium!) had not changed at all. What has changed, however, is the group on the receiving end of prophetic communication. Disregarding the legends of the Elijah-Elisha cycle, one discovers that in the time before Amos no oracle is addressed to or directed at anyone outside the royal court. This changes in the middle of the 8th century B.C. in the generation of Amos, Isaiah and Micah. From then on the message of the prophet is valid not only for the royal court but also for all of the people, in particular for the influential and leading classes. Without a doubt this change is connected with the political mobilization of the public in the Assyrian Empire /121/.

Whilst the earlier Assyrian rulers had only contracted vassal treaties with the ruling houses, the later rulers also include the populace of their subject lands. In mass gatherings often held at regular intervals the vassal population is confronted with its duties as well as intimidated by well-publicized penalties for defection. It is not surprising, then, that an Assyrian messenger should appeal directly to the populace in an attempt to arouse support against Judah's rebellious king (2 Kgs 18). When Israel and Judah enter the boundaries of the Assyrian Empire and become obliged to pay tribute, the political mobilization of the leading sector of the population is inevitable. To this group belong the prophets since Amos whom we call 'classical' because of their written legacy.

The Prophet's Function in Society

It is because the prophets are politically active and hence wield political power that we must obtain a general idea of how Israel's society is structured and who else in it can become politically active, with or against the prophets/122/.

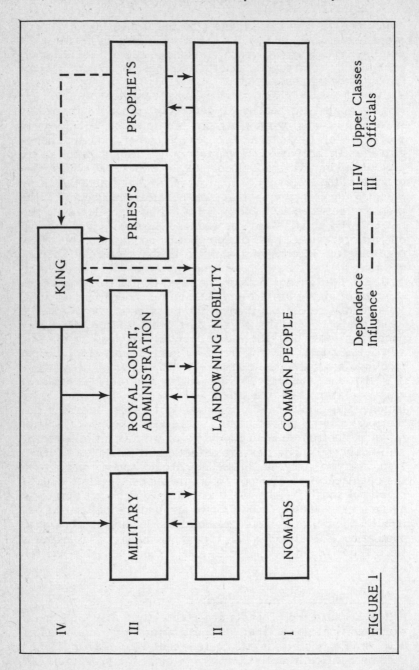

FIGURE 1

Chapter Two - What is a Prophet?

Figure 1, opposite, represents a model of the social hierarchy.

The figure shows four levels, each of which indicates a different potential for power. On the lowest level are the common people, including smallholders, cattle breeders and craftsmen, in addition to the slaves and probably the Rechabites, a group of nomads mentioned in Jer 35. Nothing is known about the political rights of this social stratum. On the other hand, we do know about the great influence of the land-owning nobility, who - meeting regularly in a form of diet - could exert considerable influence on the king. The king, it is true, comes from the dynasty regarded as legitimate, but when the ruler changes, the nobility often intervenes and chooses a successor to the throne from among the sons of the dead king or from other members of the royal lineage. When Jeroboam, who does not belong to the house of David, is named Solomon's successor at the diet of Shechem, the northern tribes break off from the kingdom of Judah to become the kingdom of Israel (1 Kgs 12). According to 2 Kgs 23.20, Josiah, one of the last kings on David's throne, owes his position to the nobility.

On the third layer to the left, the wielders of political power are indicated; they are closely linked and answerable to the king: the military and the royal court. The kings maintain a standing army to support their rule, but the army can also be dangerous. Thus in a military coup d'état Captain Jehu becomes king of the northern kingdom and founds his own dynasty. Also belonging to the royal court (in addition to the Queen Mother whose role is not entirely clear to us) are the ministers and the administrators of the crownlands, the king's most important source of income.

Alongside the military and the royal court is the priesthood of Jerusalem which serves at the royal court Temple and far surpasses the priests of the provincial temples in influence. (In the northern kingdom are the important temples of Samaria and Bethel.) The priests are probably not subject to the king's command in the same immediate sense which applies to court and army.

Next to the priests are the prophets, a very differentiated group. There are prophets who belong to the court (such as Nathan, 1 Kgs 1), prophets who are attached to the priesthood, and prophets who are free from such ties and who find a greater scope for political influence in their independence.

Given the fact that Max Weber took an interest in the social location of prophets, this author's famous distinction between legal, traditional and charismatic, i.e. prophetic, authority may help us to understand the nature of the forces and institutions which operate in Israelite society. Pre-modern societies lack the legal type of authority which, with its impersonal rules and its self-recruiting bureaucracy, represents the modern and distinctively Western development. Thus we are left with traditional and charismatic authority the dynamic interplay of which is characteristic for ancient society. In biblical Israel, the two basic forms of traditional authority co-exist, the geron-tocracy of the elders or upper classes, and the king's Sultanism. Both derive their legitimacy from tradition, i.e. they are taken for granted. According to Weber,

> A system of imperative co-ordination will be called 'traditional' if legitimacy is claimed for it and believed in on the basis of the sanctity of the order and the attendant powers of control as they have been handed down from the past, 'have always existed'. The person or persons exercising authority are designated according to traditionally transmitted rules. The object of obedience is the personal authority of the individual which he enjoys by virtue of his traditional status. The organized group exercising authority is, in the simplest case, primarily based on relations of personal loyalty, cultivated through a common process of education. The person exercising authority is not a 'superior', but a personal 'chief' /123/.

In gerontocracy, there is not one single leader but a ruling élite of elders or patriarchs who have no administrative staff at their disposal. The distinctive feature of this situation is

> that this authority, though its exercise is a private prerogative of the person or persons involved, is in fact pre-eminently an authority on behalf of the group as a whole. It must, therefore, be exercised in the interests of the members and is thus not freely appropriated by the incumbent. In order that this shall be maintained, it is crucial that (...) there is a complete absence of an administrative staff over which the individual in authority has personal control. He is hence still to a large extent dependent on the willingness of the group members to respect his authority, since he has no machinery to enforce it. Those subject to authority are hence still members of the group and not 'subjects'. But their membership exists by tradition and not by virtue of

66

legislation or a deliberate act of adherance. Obedience is owed to the person of the chief, not to any established rule. But it is owed to the chief only by virtue of his traditional status. He is thus strictly bound by tradition /124/.

With the development of a purely personal administrative staff, especially a military force under the exclusive control of a chief or king, traditional authority becomes what Weber calls Sultanism.

The 'members' are now treated as 'subjects'. An authority of the chief which was previously treated principally as exercised on behalf of the members, now becomes his personal authority, which he appropriates in the same way as he would any ordinary object of possession. He is also entitled to exploit it, in principle, like any economic advantage - to sell it, to pledge it as security, or to divide it by inheritance. The primary external support of patrimonial authority is a staff of slaves, coloni, or conscripted subjects, or, in order to enlist its members' self-interest in opposition to the subjects as far as possible, of mercenary bodyguards and armies. By the use of these instruments of force the chief tends to broaden the range of his arbitrary power which is free of traditional restrictions and to put himself in a position to grant grace and favours at the expense of the traditional limitations typical of patriarchal and gerontocratic structures /125/.

Our third force is charisma which Weber defines as "a certain quality of an individual personality by virtue of which he is set apart from ordinary man and treated as endowed with supernatural, superhuman, or at least specifically exceptional powers or qualities" /126/. Unlike its 'traditional' equivalent, charismatic authority derives exclusively from the prophet's personality and the recognition he obtains for his oracles. His authority is not given with a particular social or professional status but has to be achieved individually. This has led some authors to place prophetic authority in diametrical opposition to traditional and established authority and to speak of them as the born 'revolutionaries' or 'protestants', respectively, as figures who almost naturally transcend the restrictions imposed by law and order. Today, critics prefer the more modest and more realistic view that prophetic charisma is not free from certain traditional constraints. To transcend them requires the power and ingenuity of great personalities and hence truly independent prophecy is less frequent than the prophetic vocation as such. One of the factors conditioning and, perhaps, constraining the prophets' activity is their social background.

In fact, all the prophets belong to the landowning nobility and so to the social stratum from which highly placed state officials are recruited. Jeremiah and Ezekiel come from the priests' milieu. We know of Jeremiah that he lives in Jerusalem but owns lands of considerable size in his place of birth, Anathoth, which in a time of crisis he is able to extend by making further purchases /127/. Amos is a cattlebreeder and plantation owner from the little town of Tekoa. Elisha seems to own a house in Samaria (2 Kgs 6.32). The prophetess Huldah lives in Jerusalem as the wife of a senior temple administrator (2 Kgs 22.14). Thus, the only groups exercising influence on the king are the land-owning upper classes and those prophets belonging to them. This is why there are only two arrows pointing to the king on the figure. One arrow points from the nobility directly to the king, the other goes from the same group via the prophets to the monarch.

The king, however, is not the only addressee of the prophets; they seek more often to exert their influence on the upper classes. Not to be overlooked are finally the continual confrontations of the prophets among themselves, as we meet in the case of Micaiah ben Imlah. Thus prophecy is an institution which belongs to the landowning upper classes and which constantly plays its part in the mastery of political problems. If one looks at the position of prophecy in the social structure it appears as a channel whereby the nobility can advance its right of a say in public affairs. Structurally, prophecy serves as one of its means of political expression in public.

There is indeed one biblical text well qualified to illustrate our view of the Israelite prophet's social location and function. Ezekiel compares the role or office of prophet with that of an urban military commissioner ("watchman") whom the local nobility elects from its own circle (Ez 33.1-9). This man is appointed to signal an enemy's approach so that the citizens can take their weapons, leave their unprotected country houses and retreat to the walled city. From a sociological point of view the comparison is quite appropriate: The prophet belongs to the nobility and can be seen as its commissioner. He is not elected in any formal procedure, of course, but he does have to establish his own and his oracles' reputation. In his case, public approval is not bestowed on the occasion of an election, but is an ongoing social process. Our biblical passage is fully aware of this difference between the military commissioner and the prophet: whereas the prophet's task (and, implicitly, his social origin) equals that of the watchman, he is, unlike the latter, not appointed by men but by his god. The military watchman's office is of a democratic, the prophet's role of a charismatic nature.

Defining the prophet's place in the field of political influence in society protects us from the misunderstanding to which Israel's "speakers of Yahweh" are frequently subjected. They are often conceived of as creative outsiders who do not appear inside the normal structures of communication and who enjoy at a charismatic distance the freedom to express new, alternative and opposing ideas. A typical example of such a figure is John the Baptist, who appears in the desert "on the other side of Jordan", who keeps away from the noise of the towns, who lives like other loners/128/ as an ascetic, and who parades in his rough skins the typical features of deviant neglect in order to demonstrate his independence from all accepted norms. However rightly the anthropologist, Mary Douglas /129/, characterizes the Baptist and his untrimmed external appearance, it would be wrong to generalize this characterization and extend it to Israel's prophets. Even if there were a few strange fellows among them such as the bachelor Jeremiah, most of them are 'normal' and relatively inconspicuous members of their society. Their role did not demand of them anything which would degrade them to an existence on the edge of society.

There is another corollary of our attempt at defining the social location of Israelite prophecy. A respectable (even though now somewhat dated) anthropological theory, functionalism, reminds us of the fact that social institutions exist only as long as they contribute to a society's ability to cope with reality and, ultimately, to survive. There are, by definition, no non-functional or purely ornamental institutions which outlive and faintly echo former political, social or religious structures. The fate of prophecy, then, must be seen in the broader context of the fate of Jewish nobility. In the Babylonian exile of the sixth century B.C., prophecy continues to flourish along with the Jewish aristocracy's hope for the restoration and re-establishement of an independent state. Deutero-Isaiah, who takes the Persian king to be Israel's messiah, has a broader perspective but he remains a political figure. The fifth century, on the other hand, sees a rapid decline of the aristocracy's actual influence as well as the virtual eclipse of prophecy. In a time without any real political power in the hands of Jewish nobility there is no place for prophecy in the traditional sense. Only during days of heated political movements and expectations does one hear of prophets - e.g. when Haggai and Zechariah expect the Jewish leader, Zerubbabel, to become king, or when Nehemiah is alleged to hire prophets to proclaim him candidate for the same position/130/. None of those expectations is realized. When the aristocracy is denied political influence prophecy loses its function and becomes silent.

Our most important source of information about Israel's prophets are the books named after them, whose contents - although at first sight confusing and puzzling - document their actual activity and are therefore open to historical evaluation. The books are confusing and puzzling because they contain hardly any narrative text and are almost exclusively collections of prophecies, so that we often have to search laboriously and at times unsuccessfully for the historical circumstances surrounding the individual oracles. It is therefore all the more important to read and critically evaluate the stories of the prophets which occur in the Books of Kings and occasionally in the prophetic books themselves (see, e.g. Am 7 and Jer 36-45).

The following presentation of the prophetic 'office' or 'role' takes as its starting point an account in which we meet the prophet Isaiah in the atmosphere of political turmoil in a year of war (701 B.C.).

II. Prophetic Role and Repertoire

The Basic Role:
The Prophet as the Messenger of Yahweh

One of the most exciting chapters in Jerusalem's political history are the events of 701 B.C. In this year the Assyrian military overruns the petty state of Judah, occupies all the towns, but comes to a halt in front of Jerusalem. King Hezekiah of Judah engages in feverish diplomacy. He sends messengers to the Assyrians' military camp in order to buy off both himself and Jerusalem, and he succeeds. Yet the Assyrian military is clearly only temporarily satisfied with the tributes offered by Jerusalem. Diplomats from the Assyrian king appear in Jerusalem and try to negotiate with Hezekiah's ministers, but without success. In the end the

Assyrians withdraw without troubling Jerusalem. The reason for this, one might suppose, was the outbreak of plague in the enemy camp. In the biblical account of these events (2 Kgs 18) the continual mention of messengers, envoys, ministers and diplomats is striking, whereas both the enemy kings, the Assyrian Sennacherib and the Judaean Hezekiah, remain in the background. They never negotiate in person but make use of their delegates. Even in the Assyrian court annals Hezekiah's "personal messenger" is described as the "bearer of tributes" /131/. Hezekiah sends his messengers not only to negotiate with the enemy. They must also consult the prophet Isaiah, or more precisely consult his god, Yahweh.

Comparing the prophets with diplomats and political envoys may at first sight appear playful and fortuitous. In reality, the very report of these events in the year 701 B.C. shows that Israel's prophets can only be understood in their role as envoys. The correspondence of the two messenger roles - the prophetic and the diplomatic - is equally baffling. Let us compare the wording of the messages and statements delivered:

> [Messenger of Assyrian king to people of Jerusalem:]
> These are the words of the king of Assyria: "Make peace with me. Come out to me."

> [Messenger of Hezekiah to Isaiah:]
> These are the words of Hezekiah: "This day is a day of trouble for us, a day of reproof and contempt."

> [Isaiah to King Hezekiah:]
> These are the words of Yahweh: "Do not be alarmed at what you heard when the lackeys of the king of Assyria blasphemed me. I will put a spirit in him and he shall hear a rumour and withdraw to his own country; and there I will make him fall by the sword." (2 Kgs 18.31; 19.3.6ff)

Isaiah makes use of the same phrase, "These are the words of ...", as the diplomats; Isaiah is the messenger of, envoy of and speaker for his god. That is why he does not talk about his god but in the words of his god: the prophet bears, corresponding to the style of the diplomats, not his own message but that of his lord; this is kept in the first person which is typical of prophetic literature. Equally characteristic is the use of the messenger formula: "Hear the message of Yahweh"; cf. "Hear the message of the Great King, the King of Assyria" in the speech of the diplomats (2 Kgs 18.28), and above all the phrase: "This is the word of

Yahweh" which is to be found on almost every page of the prophetic books.

The connection between the political and the prophetic messenger role is also evident in a small - but for the understanding of prophecy not to be underrated - number of passages in the accounts of prophetic calling. From Isaiah, Jeremiah and Ezekiel - about whom we have substantial literary sources, more than for the other prophets - we possess reports about the experience of a first encounter with Yahweh, in which they receive their prophetic calling. In Isaiah's report the appointment as messenger is particularly clear:

> Then I heard Yahweh saying, "Whom shall I send? Who will go for me?" And I answered, "Here am I; send me." He said, "Go and tell this people: ..." (Isa 6.8-9)

Similarly, Yahweh says to Jeremiah:

> For you shall go to whatever people I send you and say whatever I tell you to say. (Jer 1.7)

According to all three reports the prophet is made into the envoy of Yahweh and, as emerges from Ezekiel's report, is authorized to use the phrase, "These are the words of Yahweh" (Ez 2.3ff). In one oracle Yahweh speaks of the prophets as his messengers (Isa 44.26). Once again it comes to light that: The prophetic role is a messenger role, the prophet speaks for Yahweh to the people - he is speaker of a higher power which keeps itself in the background and communicates with others only through messengers.

The reverse role of the prophet is to appear before Yahweh as intercessionary speaker for mankind, but this needs only a passing mention for the prophet's task as intercessionary is referred to only in Jeremiah (Jer 7.16; 27.18). In this role the prophet mediates on behalf of a person or for his people to, say, save the life of a sick man or to avert divine wrath. But while we have a large number of oracles, no intercessionary prayers have been handed down to us in the books of the prophets. It is not as if the prophets seldom exercised this role of messenger of the people to Yahweh, but the prophets and their friends saw no reason to record these prayers; their interest was restricted to god's word alone and not to the ordinary words of men.

Before the prophet can impart the message of Yahweh, he must receive it. How does this happen? How does Yahweh assign his envoys their tasks? One might imagine that the prophet discovers the will of god by mechanical means, such as by casting lots which answer every question posed with "yes" or "no", respectively. In actual fact the casting of lots did exist in Israel but its use was restricted to priests. In contrast to them the prophets are 'intuitive' diviners who do not observe omens (in the clouds or the flight of birds), nor do they cast lots.

His task of messenger and the permanent presence of god, which only he can feel, determines the prophets' inner life to such a degree that he hears and perceives Yahweh's voice without having recourse to mechanical procedures, i.e., 'intuitively'. Only occasionally is mention made of an external preparation for the reception of the revelation, for instance when Elisha calls a harp player and enters a state of trance through the music, or when Daniel fasts /132/. On the other hand, according to Jer 37.3; 42,2.20, prayer, we can suppose, is the regular preparation for receiving an oracle. Only after a prayer does the prophet hear Yahweh's answer. The process of revelation is portrayed as listening (audition) and more rarely as seeing (vision). The audition formula usually runs: "The word of Yahweh came to Jeremiah" (Jer 33.1) - wording which is so characteristic that it is found in the New Testament again with John the Baptist (Lk 3.2), although prophecy in its traditional form had long vanished. In vision, not only does god's voice penetrate the consciousness of the prophet, he is also put into a state of wakeful dreaming in which he sees, speaks with, is moved by his god or by god's servants; he touches, smells, tastes and therefore feels himself to be directly transposed into god's world. The brief formulae used to introduce the vision report are: "That was what Yahweh showed me," or "Suddenly the hand of the Lord Yahweh came upon me and I saw ..." (Am 7.1; Ez 8.1ff). The dream of revelation must have played a certain role as well; but in the books of the prophets one can only very loosely describe the night visions of the prophet Zechariah as dreams (Zech 1.8; 4.1). Jeremiah even informs his audience that he does not think of dreams very highly: dreams are chaff, the prophetic word is grain (Jer 23.28). Following audition, dream and vision, the fourth mode of receiving the message is symbolic perception. We can best explain this with the experience of reality described by certain modern writers. Hesse writes:

Seltsam im Nebel zu wandern!
Leben ist einsam sein.
Kein Baum sieht den andern.
Jeder ist allein.

[Strange to wander in the mist, Living is being alone. No tree sees the other. Everyone is alone.]

The trees isolated in the mist are by association of ideas formed into the image of the isolation of the individual. In the same way as the mist separates the wood into individual trees, so life makes people into lonely people. Such an association of ideas is found in the symbolic perception of Amos, who sees a basket of ripe fruit and then hears the voice of Yahweh saying: "The time is ripe for my people Israel" (Am 8.2).

The connection of thought between the name of a flowering tree and a message from Yahweh is similar in Jeremiah: an almond tree in early bloom - Hebrew 'shaked' - occasions the word of Yahweh: "I am early on the watch (Hebrew 'shocked') to carry out my purpose" (Jer 1.12).

The role of the prophet is not, however, fully described by the term messenger, called by Yahweh to receive communications from him for transmission. Also forming part of the prophetic role is an extensive repertoire which includes typical divine messages, a store of knowledge, and methods of communication. It is the combination of all these elements which constitutes the activity of prophet. We shall now consider this comprehensive repertoire which is more or less shared by all of the prophets.

The Message:
Yahweh sends misfortune and (perhaps) good fortune

Because Yahweh is the god of Israel he guides the fate of his people. The people themselves set the standard, in that they show fear of god and love to their neighbours and as a reward receive a happy carefree life; or in that they break faith and commit crime and so arouse the punishment of god. However, as we have seen Yahweh is no hidden god who retreats behind the mechanism of reward and punishment; he makes "prophets from your sons" (Am 2.11) and so makes them his envoys and speakers. In the figures of the prophets Yahweh supports a permanent legation among his people which, it is true, does not have to transmit daily the comments of their lord about all things but only about important affairs, especially those affecting the fate of the state and the people:

For Yahweh does nothing without giving to his servants the prophets knowledge of his plans. (Am 3.7)

Chapter Two - What is a Prophet?

Amos who is active in the northern kingdom of Israel, in the middle of the 8th century, sees oppression, inhumanity and crime everywhere. Yahweh has already sent famine, drought, water shortage, mildew, locusts, plague and defeat in war as a warning (4.6-10) but the people do not see in them signs of divine wrath and do not therefore take them as a cause to change their ways. Therefore, Amos is sent to reproach Israel for her atrocious deeds and to announce the punishment incurred. What the god of Amos denounces above all is the exploitation of the small farmers by the great landowning upper class. There is talk of corn dealer's profiteering in times of shortage, of untruth and bribery in the judicial system (8.5), high rent (5.10-11), the enslavement of debtors, and garments seized in pledge (2.6-7). It is impossible for Yahweh to tolerate a state of affairs in which the lesser members of society are forced by the rich to bear the costs of their luxurious and euphoric celebrations in his temples. Hence, even though they are meant to be a form of worship of god and a feast of thanksgiving, the prophet must say: "I hate, I spurn your pilgrim feasts; I will not delight in your sacred ceremonies" (5.21). The punishment Amos announces is military defeat. Without Assyria's name being spoken it must be in the prophet's mind. Assyria, the greatest power in the Near East at that time, is on the point of preparing to push the frontiers of empire further forward. Amos speaks of military decimation and deportation (4.3; 5.27).

Of course, Amos also knows about the salvation which Yahweh can send his people: "Hate evil and love good; enthrone justice in the courts; it may be that Yahweh, the God of Hosts, will be gracious to the survivors of Joseph." (5.15)

That probably implies: at least one part of the criminal upper class can avoid misfortune by a fundamental change of attitude and action. On the other hand, Amos seems to assume that the constantly betrayed lower class is not or at least not seriously affected by the coming national disaster. Whether Amos speaks of a restoration of the state after the catastrophe, or even of the renewal of the Davidic empire, is a matter of scholarly dispute; Am 9.11-15 could be a textual addition dating from a later period. (The present author considers the oracle to be genuine. The message of salvation is part of the prophetic repertoire at the disposal of Amos.)

The Book of Amos gives us little information about the public to which the prophet addresses his oracles. He often speaks to the whole of Israel (e.g., 4.4-13), sometimes only to the upper class, e.g. rich women who are - to us ungallantly - described as "cows of Bashan" (4.1-3). On one occasion he directs his words to an individual, the chief priest of the Temple of Bethel: "Now these are the words of Yahweh: Your wife shall become a city strumpet and your sons and daughters shall fall by the sword. Your land shall be divided up with a measuring-line, and you yourself shall die in a heathen country" (7.17). Thus the prophet retaliates for being reported to the royal court and for being forbidden further speech.

The audience of Amos (which, of course, cannot include "the whole of Israel") lives in Bethel and other Israelite towns. Speaking to Israelites, however, does not make them the exclusive subject of prophetic discourse. Amos not only speaks about the people of his god, but also about the neighbouring peoples: the Aramaeans of Damascus, the Philistines of Gaza, Ashdod, Ashkelon and Ekron; Tyre, Edom, Ammon, Moab. Because Amos is active in the northern kingdom of Israel we may also count his words about the southern kingdom of Judah (2.4-5) as belonging to the oracles concerning foreign nations. Israel's sister kingdom arouses Yahweh's blazing anger because she and the other neighbours all have a long catalogue of sins, so that the punishment announced is well- deserved.

Whilst Amos is chastising internal political crimes in Israel and Judah, he blames alien peoples for war atrocities and diplomatic crimes such as the breach of treaty (1.9), the slitting open of pregnant women (1.13), and the desecration of a royal tomb (2.1). Without a doubt the oracle concerning foreign nations grew out of the war prophecy which proclaims the enemy's downfall. In Amos, it is true, there is nothing more of this origin to be discovered. Rather, Amos seems to comprehend his god as the owner of Palestine as well as its neighbouring territories, and so is entitled also to act outside of his people.

When later prophets speak about the Egyptians, Assyrians, Babylonians and Persians they must be understood as words about enemy, exploiting or even friendly sovereigns who have some relationship with Yahweh's people. At the same time it is not hard for the later prophets, especially Deutero-Isaiah, to see in the god of Israel one who mocks the gods of other peoples and says of himself: "I am Yahweh, there is no other" (Isa 45.18).

Finally a table of the most important types of oracles:

Chapter Two - What is a Prophet?

Oracles of Judgement	about Israel	Am 2.4-5
	about a group	Am 4.1-3
	about an individual	Am 7.17
	about a foreign nation	Am 2.1-3
Oracles of Salvation	for Israel	Am 9.11-15
	for a group*	Jer 24
	for an individual	Jer 39.15-18
	for a foreign nation*	Ez 29.13-16

[*occurs very infrequently]

The table shows that we can refer to Amos in only one case for an example of an oracle of salvation. With him the judgement oracle prevails, whence one is justified in labelling him as a prophet of misfortune and doom. Such an expression need not, however, lead us astray into over-looking that glimmer of hope, "it may be" (5.15), and the perhaps authentic word which concludes the book of Amos.

National Story, Prophetic Tradition and Historical Knowledge as Elements of the Message

Israel's Exodus from Egypt is mentioned by Amos, Hosea and Micah (Am 2.10; Hos 2.17; Micah 7.15). Amos and Isaiah know the history of Sodom and Gomorrah (Am 4.11; Isa 1.9). Even Zephaniah - more than one hundred years after Amos but without a doubt linked to him - calls the day of divine punishment a "day of Yahweh" (Am 5.18; Zeph 1.14). Amos, Isaiah and Ezekiel are well versed in the political situations in their own land and in neighbouring states.

A few references will suffice to suppose a general background of knowledge for all the prophets. In actual fact the style and argumentative nature of their speech is marked by extensive - and for all the differences between the individuals - very similar funds of knowledge. These funds can be roughly divided into three areas: national tradition, the prophets' own legacy and politico-historical knowledge. As far as the national story or legend is concerned, the frequent references to the Exodus and the occasional allusions to the forefathers, on the one hand, and the lack of any reference to the Sinai legislation on the other is particularly striking. This so-called prophetic 'concealment of the covenant' can be explained by the fact that the tradition of the Sinai covenant was probably created not before the late monarchy and therefore could not gain a foothold in the repertoire of the prophets. It is especially interesting to see how the prophets utilize the tradition in their message of judgement and salvation. A new wrathful judgement in the desert must come to pass (Ez 20.35-38), a new Exodus to lead the people from the yoke of Babylonian slavery (Isa 43.16-20), a new love between Yahweh and his people in the desert (Hos 2.16). Because Yahweh freed Israel from Egypt and thereby won her, he also has the right to punish her (Am 3.1-2). From time to time the prophets take up old oracles which promise salvation, for instance Yahweh's covenant with Jacob (Ez 37,25) or the election of the Davidic dynasty (Am 9,11; Jer 23,5). It is remarkable that Isaiah does not refer to the Pentateuch tradition of the patriarchs or Exodus, but only to the divine election of Jerusalem (Zion) as the invincible and indestructible city (Isa 14.32; 28.16).

The exclusively prophetic tradition must be distinguished from the national saga. To this tradition belong the ideas connected with the "day of Yahweh". The expression seems to derive from the old political ideology and to refer to the day on which Yahweh gives his army a mighty victory over the enemy (Jer 46.10; Ez 30.3). It is paralleled by the "jour de gloire" sung in the Marseillaise on the day of triumph of the French Revolution. Ever since the expression is introduced (by Amos?) into prophetic tradition it has the opposite meaning of "day of judgement" as well: not a military triumph but a violent defeat is to be expected as divine punishment:

Fools who long for the day of Yahweh,
what will the day of Yahweh mean to you?
It will be darkness, not light. (Am 5.18)

Amos expects the Israelite army to be attacked with all arms, Samaria to be conquered, the town walls to be breached, the palace to be plundered and hardly anyone to be left alive. On the day of Yahweh, which of course must not necessarily coincide with a twenty-four hour day, the upper classes will be led from the land and carried off to a foreign country.

Recurrent mention of the "Day of Yahweh" is made in Isaiah, Zephaniah, Joel, Obadiah, Ezekiel and a few other prophets and marks the prophets' way of thinking about the future. Yahweh will intervene in the course of history more clearly and more drastically than ever before and with his 'coup de force' will give history a new direction. After the "Day of Yahweh" history must take a different path.

In imagining the Day of Yahweh the prophets create a counter-balance to the old retrospective traditions, such as the election of the patriarchs and the Exodus from Egypt.

Whilst Yahweh's past initiative of salvation legitimises the present and the memory of it allows the current state of affairs to appear well-founded, the prophets effect a devaluation of the present. Because Israel is heading for the Day of Yahweh the established tradition loses much of its stabilizing and security-giving power.

The prophets develop series of recurring ideas and formulate detailed themes in the repertoire which can only receive brief mention here. They like to speak of Israel's religious infidelity as 'adultery'. They note the 'remnant of Israel' left over after the expected disaster who, although numerically unimportant, can become a new people of Yahweh. The enemy superior to Israel is called the 'foe from the north'. The people must drink from the 'cup of wrath' and will be cleansed in the furnace like molten metal. Even concrete political ideas become current among the prophets, for instance the rejection of the national foreign policy towards the great powers who may prove to be Israel's undoing. Alongside this pacifism in foreign policy the hope for a strong king of peace from the Davidic dynasty who is superior to the prevailing rulers is audible, a hope which, following the collapse of the monarchy in 586 B.C., changes into an expectation of national restoration which in some circles lives on into the age of the New Testament and can, in the apocalyptic movement, intensify into the expectation of the Messiah.

In addition to these conventional themes from saga and prophetic tradition there is a diversified historical and contemporary knowledge which makes up the third area of the prophets' conventional repertoire. The behaviour of Israel and Judah in foreign policy is chastised in Ezekiel's great portraits of history (Ez 16, 23); the memory of the Davidic empire fades just as little as the knowledge of the northern kingdom of Israel which fell in 721 B.C. From Ez 17.15ff we learn of King Zedekiah's breach of the Babylonian vassel oath, sworn in Yahweh's name (ca. 588 B.C.), of the same king's legation to seek military aid in Egypt. Details of Babylonian military affairs, such as the organization of the army, the war oracle (Ez 21.26) and particular techniques of besieging are also found in Ezekiel. The oracles against foreign nations display surprising familiarity with details about Israel's fellow players on the political stage. Amos not only mentions the war crimes of, for instance, the Aramaeans of Damascus and the Philistines, but he also alludes to the constitutional terminology current among these peoples: some peoples - for example the Aramaeans and Philistines - are ruled by sovereigns, whereas others - the Ammonites and Edomites - have a proper king (Am 1-2). Because the prophets always intervene in concrete national political events and seek to make the word of their god valid, historical and above all contemporary knowledge is indispensable to them.

The Communication of the Message
in Speech, Song, Writing and Theatre /133/

Prophets are continually consulted by groups or individuals and asked for a word from Yahweh. Perhaps they are also asked to take the floor at public worship and make known a message from their god. Research reckons with such a setting, especially in the case of oracles against foreign nations.

According to their written legacy, the prophets rarely have the chance to appear and put across their message in such a way. When they want to follow up their mission they have to search for ways and means of obtaining a hearing for a message which is sometimes less than desirable and frequently far from flattering. Under the pressure and challenge of their mission they develop a new kind of public speech of which Max Weber writes: "The demagogue appears here for the first time historically authenticated."/134/ Prophetic literature reveals a whole repertoire of methods of communication and agitation which, after 'duping' the unwilling to listen, serve to impress and persuade the audience. Five methods can be discerned:

(1) The seeking of listeners at places where many people are circulating, for instance, the town gates, the Temple of Jerusalem, or in Amos' case the Temple of Bethel.

(2) The use of a rhetorical, impressive language which is particularly rich in imagery and easily makes its mark - one thinks, for instance, of the image of Jerusalem as a whore (Ez 16) or of the "cows of Bashan" as an image for the rich ladies of Samaria (Am 4.1).

(3) The use of rhythmic, poetic language. As a glance at any modern translation of the Bible readily shows, a large number of the oracles are given in lines of poetry. These correspond to the reading in rhythmical sing-song which the Oriental loves for the strong impression it makes upon him. A special form of poetic oracle is the rounded-off song that is doubtless sung and not just read. Perhaps we may imagine the accompaniment of a simple string instrument to attract more listeners for a text such as Isa 5, the "Song of the Vineyard".

Chapter Two - What is a Prophet?

It is said of Ezekiel who claps his hands to a sword song (Ez 21.19):

> You are no more to them than a singer of fine songs with a lovely voice, or a clever harpist; they will listen to what you say but will certainly not do it. (Ez 33.32)

Not without good cause is the prophet compared to a street singer around whom the curious people gather. Living in a much more attenuated landscape of media than us, they want to be entertained but they intentionally ignore the serious tones of Ezekiel's message. Such a gulf between attraction and effectiveness, between applause and acceptance of the message must be disappointing for the prophet.

(4) The use of written pieces in which the divine word is recorded. Jeremiah can reach the Judaeans deported to Babylon with a letter (Jer 29). Or he can dictate to his friend Baruch and reach his audience by having his memorandum read out in the courtyard of the Temple without risking the danger of falling into the hands of the Temple police or guards (Jer 36). It is not known to what extent use was made of the opportunity to circulate pamphlets, but Max Weber is probably right when he says of the collections of the prophets' words that they are "the earliest directly topical pamphlet literature known to us"/135/.

(5) The performance of street theatre in which the prophet illustrates his word by game, mime and props. Isaiah warns of an anti-Assyrian league by appearing in the loincloth of a prisoner of war (Isa 20.1-4). Jeremiah buys a big stone jar, smashes it to pieces at Jerusalem's Gate of the Potsherds and throws it onto the rubbish heap with the words:

> These are the words of Yahweh of Hosts: thus will I shatter this people and this city as one shatters an earthen vessel so that it cannot be mended. (Jer 19.11)

Ezekiel acts out the besieging of Jerusalem and enters into a form of hunger strike, eating only bad food in small rations, to demonstrate that a shortage of foodstuffs is to be expected (Ez 4). One should not underestimate the provocative effect of such a demonstration in a society which knows of no mass media. Like Luther's burning of the papal bull threatening excommunication (10 December 1520) or Kruschev's aggressive shoe protest in front of the U.N. Assembly (October 1960), the prophets also mean to cause a sensation and to challenge a wider public to take a stand. It is the street theatre itself which teaches us to understand the prophets not only as theologians of a meditative bent, but also as showmen, as experts in public agitation and propaganda. They reject violence it is true, but they retain all other possibilities of obtaining a hearing and giving weight to the word of their god. The prophets' appearance and desire to communicate is very aptly described by the famous French Orientalist, Ernest Renan, in his 'History of the People of Israel':

> The prophet of the 8th century is a journalist who works in the open air, who reads out his article in person and accompanies it with mime, indeed often converts it into a sign language. Above all it is a question of impressing the people to attract a large crowd. In order to achieve this, the prophet spurns no tricks which modern journalism prides itself upon inventing. He stands at a place where many people are going by, especially at the town gate. In order to win listeners there he uses the most cunning advertising tricks: faked madness, new words and expressions, and carries written posters around him. He taps out his maxims, lets them resound, impresses his audience now in a confidential tone, now with bitter mockery. The figure of the people's preacher has been created. The clownery linked to an uncouth appearance is put into the service of piety. Even the Capuchin of Naples, an edifying variety of fool, had in some respects his predecessor in Israel. /136/

Even if Renan - like Max Weber - is inclined to view the prophets as religious day-dreamers and cranks and misjudges their political concern, yet he does grasp their public appearance correctly. If one expands the picture of Renan's 'prophetic journalist' with the role of 'god's messenger' and places him into the network of social and political powers in Israel, then we can answer without difficulty the question posed at the beginning - 'What is a prophet?'

Appendix to Chapter Two

PROPHECY, SYMBOLIC ACTS, AND POLITICS:
A REVIEW OF RECENT STUDIES

It cannot escape an attentive reader that Israel's prophets
express opinions about political events. Biblical scholarship,
however, must consider the significance of politics in the
framework of prophetic activity and determine the motives
and major ideas which are decisive for prophecy. Max Weber's
presentation is well-known: he invents a vivid picture of the
prophets as pugnacious demagogues, underscoring their basic
and fundamental political orientation in order to present
prophecy and 'Realpolitik' in diametrical opposition. The
political dimension of prophecy is "thoroughly religious and
not politically realistic" (Weber 1920, 295). The impression
that they "were, in the nature of their influence, objectively
political demagogues and in fact above all demagogues and
journalists for world politics" should not lead one to take
them for politicians in reality; they were "subjectively not
political party members. They were not in the least
orientated primarily towards political intersts" (Weber 1920,
288-289). Weber's ideal-typical way of differentiating
between the religious-prophetic and the rational-political
modes seems more applicable to Western societies in the 20th
century than to ancient Israel.

The debate about prophetic politics, i.e., about the
strength of prophets in influencing the conscious decisions
of powerful people and institutions, has been frequently
presented, most recently by Ramlot (1972, 1050-1058,
1096ff), Albrektson (1972) and W. Dietrich (1976, 246-268)
and need not be repeated here. A clear and unequivocal result
cannot be recorded. Albrektson (1972, 55) builds on Weber
and states: "The deepest motives underlying the political
statements of the prophets were not political but religious,
rooted in the holy traditions which formed the religious
foundation of the Israelite state." However, we must question
whether it is right to separate politics and religion from one
another, even if only tentatively. All too quickly one arrives
on this path at the modern misunderstanding in which
Kreglinger (1926, 235) indulges: "The prophets' role in politics

83

is essentially negative; they despise politics (...) The major achievement of prophecy is the discovery of inner religion." In the same spirit Schleiermacher (1850, 209) imparts the following piece of advice to preachers: "Politics is something alien and must take on a subordinate role in preaching. It may be taken as a starting-point for a different issue." A completely different view is taken by Dietrich (1976, 260), who, of his own admission, comes close to Hugo Winckler's writings at the turn of the century. Winckler presented the prophets as realistically-minded politicians. Alongside Dietrich's important study of Isaiah, a number of recent investigations, which may be briefly outlined, point to the same conclusion.

(1) In contrast to a political understanding of Israel's prophets, there exists the opinion developed by numerous exegetes (and rarely without learned comment) that, above all, these men of god have to announce and pronounce god's judgement. Their certainty about the future takes precedence over their criticism of the present. Their critical stance towards contemporary problems must appear as a secondary rationalisation legitimating the coming disaster. The debate on this issue is discussed critically in Lang (1978, 163). Keel (1977) has written the most intelligent contribution to the discussion. He assigns the communication of judgement a very plausible place in the encounter between a prophet and his audience. It serves "to break the opposition of the addressees who trustfully rely on the Lord's will to save them" (Keel 1977, 209). Thus tumbles the thesis of the irrelevance of politics and social criticism. Keel uses Amos, Micah and Isaiah as his examples to illustrate that

> they tried to influence political decisions by expressing their opinions publicly. They fought against certain political solutions and supported others (...) They did not propose an elaborate political programme but supported a policy in which justice and righteousness, which the Lord had entrusted to Israel as a precious possession, have their fixed and firm place (Keel 1977, 215).

(2) Isaiah's political opinions have been known for some time. His pacifistic rejection of a pact between Judah and Egypt or Judah and Assyria can be seen clearly in the biblical text. Dietrich's achievement is to have grasped the exact political circumstances and the prophet's methods of argument in a new and substantiated way. According to Dietrich, Isaiah's prophecy is completely orietentated

towards politics. The prophet involves himself in the political conflicts of his day, particularly those concerning decisions on foreign relations, although he obviously only takes the floor when fundamental issues, important for the fate of his people, are at stake. "Apparently, Isaiah sees himself as a kind of watchman who continuously pursues political events but who only raises the alarm if it is a matter of the being or non-being of the nation" (Dietrich 1976, 258). In such cases he shows a considerable degree of activity. He "appeals to the emotions of the people" (276); he confronts the king himself and, on one occasion (Isa 18.1-6), even confronts an Egyptian legation (227, note 18). If need be, he makes his political judgement known in writing (277, re Isa 30.7). "All this implies the claim to be on a par with the prophets paid by the royal court, namely to partake in the most important decisions and to be listened to by the politicians" (200). According to Dietrich, Isaiah demonstrates, in his opinions and demands, a clear, rationally-founded judgement, a stance "which must be taken seriously by the Judaeans and by the leading politicians in Jerusalem. His stance does not admit of the dismissing label of 'ivory-towered'; at most, one would find it uncomfortable and ignore it. That is what the Judaeans decided to do" (262). By way of comparison, Weber (1920, 295) writes, "The king and the military-political circle really did not know what to make of the purely Utopian admonitions and counsels of the prophets." Dietrich's book, with its thorough bibliographical exposition on the theme of politics and prophecy, will become a standard work on Isaiah's political stance. (In passing, one would like to know Dietrich's opinion on Brunet's provocative theory (1975, 159-189) that Isaiah at least supported, if not initiated, the building of King Hezekiah's water tunnel as a means of defence.)

(3) Swaim (1978) emphasizes not only Hosea's obvious hostility towards a political alliance with the Egyptian or Assyrian kingdom but, above all, deals with the well-known opposition to the king and officials of his Israelite homeland. Proceeding from the assumption that the neighbouring kingdom of Judah and its ruling Davidic dynasty is regarded positively, the author asks whether Hosea does not see the solution to the political problems of his country in the reunion of the two sister kingdoms of Israel and Judah.

Perhaps Hosea's position was that the best answer to both the internal chaos of kingship by brute force and usurpation, and the external threat of Assyria lay in a reunion of all those who truly worshipped Yahweh, i.e.,

Israel and Judah. Hosea saw no one in Israel who could claim any right to the throne. The succession of assassins who followed Zechariah ben Jeroboam apparently did not even bother to claim divine sanction through anointing by a prophet. But Judah still had a Davidic monarch; why not unite under him? (Swaim 1978, 180)

Texts such as Hos 2.2 and 3.5, often taken to be later interpolations because of their pro-Davidic stance and pan-Israelite ideas, can find an easy explanation in the history of the 8th century B.C., and can be attributed to Hosea himself without hesitation. In 1961, Caquot had pointed to the possibility of such an interpretation of the 'political Hosea', but his brilliant essay unfortunately received all too little attention. Recently, G. H. Davies (1980/81) assumes the same pan-Israelite point of view in Amos (cf. Am 1.2; 4.4; 5.4ff; 9.11?). If Zenger (1982) is correct in finding in Hosea the idea of prophetic succession which implies that there can be only one true or major prophet at a time, this would add up to a perfect 'one country, one dynasty, one God, one prophet' ideology.

Caquot (1961, 126) formulates the important principle that additions to the prophetic books require evidence based on language and style and that nothing should be classified as 'secondary' and denied the prophet's authorship solely on the basis of its contents, a principle which, had it been respected, could have spared exegesis many a hypothesis and unbridled speculation. "If there are any interpolations then they can be distinguished by features of language and style, and not by ideology." Cazelles sets similar principles in his essay on 'Bible et politique' (1971, 510 note 22; 513 note 26): "A study of the political context establishes the authenticity of texts which have been disputed in the name of a too linear notion of the evolution of biblical theology"; and, "One often corrects the text instead of making a close analysis of the political situation." These rules, used by Swaim and Caquot independently for a reading of the Book of Hosea, may help us to untangle the mystery of this prophet's political message.

(4) Above all by reason of his arrest in besieged Jerusalem in 586 B.C., Jeremiah is known for his pro-Babylonian, and in those months that means pro-enemy, point of view. But is it politically motivated? Brunet (1968, 87-113) vividly describes the internal party struggles which are raging in Jerusalem at that time, and emphasizes the important political role played by Jeremiah. "After the prophet's break with the king (Zedekiah), we must take Jeremiah to be the head, in the full

sense of the word, of one of the two factions of Judah" (108). The prophet has many adherents, "the masses are on his side" (107 note 1); he is the "mouthpiece of a political party or of a larger part of the masses" (102). Without referring to Brunet, Kegler paints a similar picture of the prophet as "the public mounthpiece of an anti-monarchial faction" (1979, 75). Jeremiah's political practice is to appear publicly as a radical critic of royal policy and its supporters. He expresses criticism verbally, by action (Jer 19; 27; 28), and in writing (Jer 29 and cf. 2 Chr 21.12). He wants to replace the policy of autonomy with a pro-Babylonian policy which he sees resulting in dependence, the only possible way for Judah to continue to exist as a state. Although it is one of his tasks as prophet to pronounce this, to carry it out requires an influential political group. He finds such a group in the circle of reforming-minded politicians who have been active under King Josiah. It is also Jeremiah's political practice to maintain relations with the leading circles of pro-Babylonian politicians, who spare him the fate of the prophet Uriah who is murdered by King Jehoiakim, and enable him to continue to exercise his influence. Because Jeremiah links his prophetic proclamations to his political practice in such an outstanding way, he has to tolerate periods of hiding and, under Zedekiah, even of arrest. These are always symptoms of a political existence which actively opposes the ruling power.

Lohfink (1981, 367), too, portrays the author of Jer 30-31 as a politically active propagandist: "Using a modern term in a distinctly positive sense, we may describe the author of such material as none else but a propagandist of King Josiah and his policy." Lohfink recalls him among a crowd of travelling performers:

> Only by using our imagination can we picture the scene of Jeremiah bringing his text home to his audience. There are no reports of it. The text is such that it could be recited to the accompaniment of music by a minstrel (Jeremiah himself, of course) travelling from village to village and from court to court. But at the same time the text is such that it could form an oratorium to be performed by a whole troup of singers and musicians. A young, gifted Jeremiah, in the service of the king, may well have been engaged in such activities in the latter years of Josiah's reign.

Such a notion does not require an inordinate amount of imagination. See Ez 33.32 and the prophetic street theatre which we will consider next!

(5) To complete the picture I cite my book 'Kein Aufstand in Jerusalem: Die Politik des Propheten Ezechiel' (Lang 1978; cf. 1981a). In this study the prophet, who up until now has been considered a non-political figure, is taken as a politician who lives among the exiles and tries to meddle - as do other prophets mentioned in Jer 29 - in day-to-day politics. Unlike Ahab ben Koliah and Zedekiah ben Maaseiah, he, in 593/586 B.C., does not stir up the anti-Babylonian revolt of the Jerusalem government, but warns of the consequences of the political adventure implied in threatening Nebuchadnezzar. Among the means the prophet employs in broadcasting his warning, the provoking 'one-man street theatre' should be mentioned. It is often misunderstood, categorized under the label of 'prophetic symbolism', as a quasi-magic spell which determines the future by virtue of its "self-fulfilling power" (Paul 1971, 1163).

Speaking of Ancient Mesopotamia, W. von Soden (1955, 165) suggests that "mimical productions played a far greater role in worship as well as in politics and popular entertainment than ancient literature allows us to discern". Israel's prophecy offers striking evidence for this. One should not, however, as frequently happens, lump it together with the harmful spells and magical acts of the prophets (for examples, see Jer 51.59-64; Ez 13.17-21). The basic difference between demonstrative actions and magical manipulation exists in the New Testament as well. On one occasion Jesus acts 'magically' as an exorcist (e.g. Mk 5.1-20) and thus performs a ritual act with a healing purpose. Other times Jesus appears as a teacher; for example, describing the behaviour of the child as exemplary, he places a child in front of his audience and points to him (Mk 9.36-37). Mime is used again when a certain Agabus ties his own feet and hands in order to warn Paul of a journey to Jerusalem (Acts 21.10-11). Such demonstrative acts are unconventional, and, unlike magical manipulation, are neither helpful nor harmful, but are invented ad hoc and pursue an argumentative and illustrative gaol. They come close to such striking demonstrative acts as Luther's burning of the bull threatening his excommunication (10th December 1520) and Kruschev's energetic protest with his shoe in front of the United Nations in New York (October 1960). One can also refer to the widespread practice of burning an effigy of Haman, the anti-Semite, on the day of Purim, an act which has more to do with student demonstration than with magic.

Burning an effigy is a mode of action in its own right - a kind of relief in the midst of frustration. While not conceived as affecting the body of the person caricatured, it may be hoped to influence his mind, as a form of indirect disapproval by those doing the burning - not far from beating the images of saints! (Firth 1973, 114)

As far as the rather infrequent magic acts of the prophets are concerned, it seems to be helpful to divide them into two groups. In this I will take up ideas of John Skorupski (1976, 134-136).

The first group is represented by the 'medicinal' bath in the river Jordan prescribed by Elisha (2 Kgs 5.10), the fig-plaster with which the prophet Isaiah treats his king (2 Kgs 20.7) and by Jesus' use of spittle to heal muteness and blindness (Mk 7.33; 8.23; John 9.6). In these cases a quasi-rational background is provided by the similarity to real, and, in a medical sense, effective methods of healing (or of harming, respectively: Ex 9.8-10). Such a quasi-rational background is lacking in the seemingly automatic curse which Jeremiah had read aloud in Babel (Jer 51.59-64) and by Elisha's war magic which implies that the ritually shot arrow will not miss its target and ensures a future victory (2 Kgs 13.14-19). Here the law of 'mystical participation' (L. Lévy-Bruhl) reigns. 'Pre-imitation' of the future, the magical act (the sinking of Jeremiah's scroll in the Euphrates) paves the way for the historical event (the decline of the Babylonian power). In a mystical way the historical event participates in the magical game and is set in motion by the latter.

(6) The essay to which this note is appended argues that Ezekiel, Jeremiah, Amos and Elisha, and with them the majority of the prophets, belong to the landowning and educated group with a right to a voice in politics. Accordingly, political prophecy must appear as an institution by means of which the free citizens, dignitaries or patricians make use of their right of co-determination. The fact that the prophets do not appear as speakers legitimized by groups, lies in the very nature of 'primitive democracy', in which actual influence and prestige count for more than election and delegation, insofar as it is possible to speak of the latter. The fact that prophets can have a normal function of authority in their society has long been known to anthropology. For instance, Dorothy Emmet (1956, 19) notes, "In a society where religious capacities are venerated, the

office of prophet may be a recognized status alongside other types of authority." Placing the prophets into the social structure and its allocation of power protects us from imagining all of them as similar to John the Baptist, whose position on the edge of, or rather outside, society is described by Mary Douglas (1973, 118) in the following way:

> ... consider the distinctive appearance of prophets. They tend to arise in peripheral areas of society, and prophets tend to be shaggy, unkempt individuals. They express in their bodies the independence of social norms which their peripheral origins inspire in them. It is no accident that St. John the Baptist lived in the desert and wore skins, or that Nuer prophets wear beards and long hair in a fashion that ordinary Nuer find displeasing. Everywhere, social peripherality has the same forms of expression, bizarre and untrimmed.

Such 'symbols of marginality' (Droogers 1980) as recorded in stereotypical biographies, marked occasionally with historical truth for many 'homines religiosi', are not fortuitously lacking in the case of Israel's prophets, but are lacking because only a few of them belong to or associate with the social periphery. Thus Elijah, it is true, wears a skin but is not himself, as some translations of 2 Kgs 1.8 (e.g. the New English Bible) suggest, an uncivilized man with long hair. In fact we only learn in one specific case of a prophet, a member of Elisha's guild, who must have been in financial trouble (2 Kgs 4.1). Normally, Israel's prophets come from solid economic circumstances and so, like the Greek oracular prophets, "from the socially high-placed stratum of the population" and enjoy "social respect" (Krämer 1959, 791).

While some kind of prophets, mostly visionaries preaching repentance and announcing doom, have always appeared in the West, and the category has occasionally been applied to figures such as rain-makers in non-European cultures (Peuckert 1935; Williams 1930, 83-99), native reaction to colonialism and imperialism brought another, and much more dangerous, type of prophet into focus. Neolin, also known as the 'Delaware prophet', an Indian who reported visions, preached return to the pre-colonial way of life and inspired boycott of and war against the whites in 1762-65, was only the first in a long series of decidedly political figures to appear in America, Asia and Africa (Peckham 1947, 98-101; Wallace 1973, 117-121; Frazer 1914, 74ff). The way in which Israel's prophets become politically active can be shown with the help of Dorothy Emmet's study of these figures. Emmet (1956, 17) differentiates the term of prophet and avoids using it exclusively in the sense of Max Weber's sociology of religion. She distinguishes three types: the institutional prophet whose role is prescribed by tradition and who may live in a community of prophets, the charismatic leader who inspires and leads new movements of a revolutionary nature (Weber's ideal-type of prophet), and finally, the moral and spiritual leader, who appears as a critic, reformer or innovator, but does not gather any following among which he enjoys irrational and charismatic authority and respect. As simple, albeit at times influential participants in the field of politics, Israel's prophets belong largely to the third group.

It is not only the author's opinion, but also that the founder of modern research into the prophets (Duhm 1875, 23) that "The discussion of prophetic politics, which should not be missing in any theology of the Old Testament, would reveal an eminently religious dimension and would make some ideas appear in another light". A glance at some recent publications of Israel's prophecy allows us to note a growing interest in a theme which has by no means been discussed in full: the prophet and politics.

Chapter Three

THE MAKING OF PROPHETS IN ISRAEL

N the London 'Times' of May 26th, 1938 on page 7, under the heading 'More Finds in Lachish', there was a short article on the findings of a British archaeological expedition. Referring to the ancient mound of the Judaean town of Lachish it contains the following passage:

The scribblings found on the vertical face of one of the steps of the Jewish Palace, which the expedition is beginning to excavate inside the city, were probably the work of some schoolboy. They consist of a rectangular drawing, with lines across it much after the fashion of a Union Jack, a drawing of a lion, and the first five letters of the Phoenician-Hebrew alphabet (...) From these discoveries it seems clear that the Phoenician-Hebrew script was in general use in the Kingdom of Judah and was being taught in the schools of Lachish before Nebuchadnezzar carried the Jews into captivity.

Attached to the newspaper article is an illustration showing a somewhat simplified fragment of this alphabet /137/. To attribute the scribblings from the eighth century B.C. to a schoolboy must have seemed a journalist's whim to the experts. In the meantime, numerous other written documents, alphabets and attempts at writing have been added to the palaeo-Hebrew letters from Lachish. A few meters from the steps mentioned a potsherd with a part of the palaeo-Hebrew alphabet was found later /138/, so that the assumption that a school of writing existed in this place is at least probable. What the archaeological findings can tell us about the school system in Israel is to be found in André Lemaire's book 'Les écoles et la formation de la Bible' (1981) /139/.

As early as 1938 - when the 'Times' article mentioned appeared - a new conception of Israel's prophecy emerged in the 'Studien über Deuterojesaja' by Joachim Begrich /140/

and in a few other works. If up until then one had taken the prophets to be great individualists and religious virtuosi who helped the Hebrew religion to reach the heights of an ethical monotheism, so now a new, more collective and tradition-bound image of the prophets imposed itself. So-called traditio-historical research worked out an extra-ordinarily far-reaching dependence of the prophets on a set of traditional ideas. A similar if not stronger dependence was discovered by form criticism. Not only the contents of prophetic proclamation are based on prototypes and models, but also the forms and formulae of prophetic speech are broadly traditional and follow well-known patterns. From this point of view it was necessary to say goodbye to the romantic conception of prophets as creative outsiders, although even in 1938 the Tübingen exegete, Paul Volz, in his 'Propheten-gestalten des Alten Testaments' revived this conventional image.

In such research the question of how traditionality actually manifests itself, where it comes from and how it gains its stability, has played a surprisingly small role. How does it come to pass that the prophets always make use of the same clichés and similar contents? Does the school system, which must have existed at least as far as the teaching of writing goes, offer the key to the explanation? It is along these lines that we will be considering and seeking an answer in the following pages if the simple sounding and yet difficult question is posed: How does one become a prophet in Israel?

Prophecy must be learned

The first difficulty we encounter is the multitude of prophetic figures. For how should we pose the question of the genesis of the vocation of prophet in a meaningful way if the term 'prophet' is used in Israelite religious history in different times and in different regional environments to describe thoroughly dissimilar characters and role profiles? The Greek translation of the Old Testament in the third century B.C. from which our English term 'prophet' derives, as well as the Hebrew of the late Judaean monarchy places the multitude of prophets under one single term /141/: without doubt the words nabi' (Hebrew) and prophetes (Greek) express a comprehensive notion, but the prophets thus labelled are really of multifarious type and are hard to grasp in a single word. More recent research has enabled us to distinguish clearly three different types of prophets from one another: the corporative prophets, the temple prophets, and the free prophets. We should attempt to sketch the three prophetic portraits and then ask the question respective of each: how is admission to the group concerned to be reconstructed? It must be emphasised that the following reflections cannot derive from a wealth of results recognised by research but strike cautiously into new territory.

The first type of prophet is labelled the corporative prophet. The Old Testament calls these figures bene hannebi'im /142/, in English 'sons of the prophets', or better still - members of a prophetic guild, corporation or assembly. We learn of three such groups whose heads are named as Samuel, Elijah and Elisha /143/. But according to critical opinion /144/, the only historical one seems to be the group of ecstatics lead by Elisha who lived in or near Gilgal on the river Jordan at the end of the ninth century B.C. The wild dances performed by these characters to the hellish din of simple musical instruments, which makes them, to us, comparable to the dancing dervishes of the Islamic world, are particularly striking /145/. The members of the guild follow what may be termed 'normal' professions, and are therefore peasants and shepherds, but can improve their income from time to time through donations from supporters or remunerations from clients. On request they act as soothsayers or healers for a circle of their clients and supporters, but there is no doubt that they are also involved in politics. Perhaps one can see Elijah, for whom records leave no firm attachment to a guild, as a figure who appears independently in a period of crisis and does not claim group solidarity.

How does one become a member of a prophets' guild? Despite the lack of sources we can make some comments, and 2 Kgs 4.38 provides a convenient starting point. There an Elisha legend begins as follows:

One day, when the sons of the prophets were sitting at his feet, he said to his servant, "Set the big pot on the fire and prepare some broth for the company [lit.: sons of the prophets]!"

The revealing term 'sitting at his feet' is found in a second legend (2 Kgs 6.1-2):

The sons of the prophets said to Elisha, "You can see that this place where our community is sitting at your feet is too small for us. Let us go to the Jordan and each fetch a log and make outselves a place to live in."

Chapter Three - The Making of Prophets

'To sit at someone's feet' (yšb lpny) is translated as 'to be a pupil of' /146/ and one thinks of the lectures which Elisha, as a master prophet, gives for his apprentices. According to the legend mentioned first the tuition lasted such a long time that everyone became hungry; the second text has aptly been called by one commentator /147/ "the first documentary evidence for the building of a new school". Although 'yšb lpny' is not used elsewhere in the Old Testament as an expression for teaching, it seems to suggest the idea of pupils sitting at the feet and listening to the words of a master or 'father' /148/. What is taught is not apparent in the text. According to educated guesses (or, perhaps just to guesses!) everything is imaginable from theology to botany /149/, yet one is most likely to think of the conveying of the prophetic tradition and general practice in meditation and ecstasy /150/. If Elisha needs a minstrel in order to have access to the word of god (2 Kgs 3.15), then that can surely be utilized for the reconstruction of the teaching: playing an instrument has an exciting effect and may lead to the state which is described as being induced by the 'hand of Yahweh'. Alongside the meditative form of ecstasy one surely practises the wild 'dervish' dances, although these are never mentioned in the Elisha legends. Whether further texts can be utilized for reconstructing the life of the prophets' school must remain an open question. If Elijah calls Elisha into his group from working in the fields, by throwing his coat over the young peasant, one may perhaps generalize this: it is possible that the head of the school brings the candidate into the ranks of the pupils by throwing his coat over him (1 Kgs 19.19). Further, in the anointment mentioned once (1 Kgs 19.16) one could recognize the rite of the initial admission of the novices into the order-like company.

All in all one certainly does not go amiss to speak of 'prophets' schools' /151/ and a school entrance to the vocation of prophet.

Old Testament research has found a type of prophet who plays a subordinate role in the Bible, the temple prophet. We only have a few sources at our disposal for examining this type, and if we want to outline his position and function we have to rely largely on assumptions. Yet after the careful studies of A. R. Johnson and Jörg Jeremias /152/ it should no longer be our concern to question the existence of the temple prophets. Along with the priests, these prophets belong to the temple personnel and sometimes seem to perform their office as full-time professionals and sometimes as a part-time occupation. Unlike the priests they are not responsible for the sacrificial cult, but offer advice to the individual supplicant or appear in larger community services of worship, in order to give to the congregation a comforting, promising or admonishing word of god, the contents of which are not or only rarely fixed by tradition. There is evidence that the role of priest and that of prophet are not mutually exclusive. Pashhur, an opponent of Jeremiah, bears the title of priest but a prophetic oracle is ascribed to him (Jer 20.1-6). Perhaps this double role can be explained by his position as supervisor in the Temple; as such he exercises a policing function and can have unmanageable characters such as Jeremiah flogged and put into the 'stocks and pillory' for the night.

It is important for the history of the temple prophets that there are women among them and that all of them, men and women, after the period of the Exile, are absorbed into the temple choir and so lose their individuality and autonomy /153/.

How does one become a temple prophet? The most obvious answer is this: one is trained in this office at the temple; there one learns the basic forms of prophetic speech and comes into contact with the professional tradition. Can these assumptions be supported? Firstly, there is no doubt that the larger temples, such as Jerusalem's, had a school for recruitment to the priesthood at their disposal. Even after such schools had long since disappeared, the Jewish school still maintains part of their curriculum. How else are we to understand the fact that the priests' handbook of Leviticus was the first primer of school children, even in the Talmudic period /154/? Without a doubt the Hebrew script and orthography belong to the subject matter which the pupils of the priests and prophets have to acquire. Contrary to widespread belief, it is hardly to be supposed that the writing of the Hebrew alphabet was effortless without formal tuition and, as John Gray claims /155/, could be learned in a few hours. From Habakkuk, who is seen as a temple prophet by reseach, one word has been handed down to us which echoes his pride in not belonging to the illiterate:

Then Yahweh made answer: "Write down the vision, inscribe it clearly on the tablets, so that one can read it readily." (Hab 2.2) /156/

How does the transfer from pupil of the prophets to appointed prophet, who is allowed to appear in temple service, take place? Some scholars /157/ believe they can find elements of an ordination liturgy in the reports of the callings of Isaiah, Jeremiah and Ezekiel, but such a view remains necessarily hypothetical. Were these scholars correct then the temple prophet would have been called to his office in the course of a service of worship, whereby a prophet already holding the post would have appeared as the spokesman of the appointing godhead.

Another and perhaps more likely view can be taken from a story which vividly portrays the transfer from servant to priest to prophet of the temple /158/. Whilst still a child, Samuel comes to the temple of Shiloh in order to serve his apprenticeship under the priest, Eli. One night, while Samuel is sleeping in the temple, a voice wakes him, calling his name, "Samuel!" Samuel wakes up and answers, "Here I am" and runs to Eli saying, "You called me: here I am." "No, I did not call you", says Eli; "lie down again." When this happens for the third time, the servant is advised by his master as to how he should behave if Yahweh calls him again: "If he calls again, say, Speak, Yahweh; thy servant hears thee."

This story told in 1 Sam 3 is certainly to be labelled as a legend about the famous prophet Samuel who is suddenly called by god to the office of prophet. Yet its meaning is not completely embraced with this classification. Here not a unique but a typical course of events is portrayed. The fact that a young servant of the priest must lie down to sleep in the temple, in order to be called to the role of temple prophet in a nocturnal dream vision, is probably the rule, for which Samuel provides the model. Typically the reception of divine messages in a dream - and indeed on the occasion of a formal incubation - belongs to the characteristic tasks of these prophets (cf. Jer 23.25-32). As our example shows, the actual calling to the office of prophet is preceded by years of training. If this is correct then a sleep in the temple, combined with a dream of calling, marks the transition from servant of the temple priests or temple pupil to temple prophet. Without a doubt the incubation does not take place without preparation, as the Samuel legend portrays it; rather the candidate is acquainted by his master or teacher with what to expect so that the perception of the dream is clearly pre-structured in a state of waking consciousness. In other words, even a 'called' prophet is a 'taught' one.

The numerically smallest but for us most important group are the free prophets. They have released themselves from the temple prophethood and appear seldom or never in services or in the area of the temple. There they run the risk, as in fact Amos and Jeremiah do, of being ordered off by the priestly authorities, of being barred entry or even of being put into the stocks for the night "at the Upper Gate of Benjamin, in the house of Yahweh" (Jer 20.2).

With the exception of Habakkuk, Nahum and perhaps Joel who may be taken to be genuine temple prophets, all the canonical writing prophets belong to this group. They appear unpaid and uninvited and involve themselves in particular in politics, where they often form the anti-monarchical opposition and are often persecuted as shown by the famous case of Jeremiah. It is possible that the term nabi' (prophet) was first applied to this group in the late period of the monarchy /159/. Amos seems to reject the title in the eighth century (Am 7.14). One hundred and fifty years later it is used for Jeremiah and Ezekiel as a matter of course. In Judah, the free prophets, to whom Amos may belong, seem to want explicitly to differentiate themselves from the temple prophets, although they have some features in common. This may have been different for some of the free prophets of the northern kingdom where Hosea /160/, a contemporary of Amos, considers himself to be in agreement with other prophets about whose character and mind we are not informed and whom we can only presume to identify with temple prophets. One must regard the free prophets as 'laymen' by comparison with the temple prophets: unlike them, one can never assimilate free prophets to the official priests; indeed, some of them transcend the inherited role in a truly charismatic way. From the letters found in the Babylonian town of Mari we know that the divinity was accustomed to communicate messages to the West Semites not just through cult personnel; of the thirty oracles a total number of nine comes from laymen /161/ whom we can describe not as prophets, it is true, but as distant relations of Israel's lay prophets.

How does one become a free prophet? Usually one imagines the course of events thus: the vision of calling or in any case an experience of calling comes over someone completely unexpectedly and separates him from what he has thought and done up until then. However, reading the Book of Amos with a critical eye, Klaus Koch gets a different impression: "Carefully arranged poetical sentences and the use of the oracle genre customary among the nabis show that Amos had been through a schooling." He adds to supplement and clarify this: The prophet "did not run straight from his pasture to Bethel in order to express himself spontaneously there. The calling induced him to practise listening to the 'inner voice' and to practise visionary immersion" /162/. Thus Koch reckons with a 'schooling' of Amos in the traditional forms of prophetic speech and a 'practising' of meditation and 'visionary immersion'. Exactly how that occurs Koch does not tell us, but his consideration can probably be carried further. He himself feels that Amos is certainly no "blameless child from the country (...) who has wound up in the capital city and is appalled by the excessive luxury" /163/. Amos is obviously a rich flock owner and thoroughly well-versed in the contemporary world view, has knowledge of the political situation of the surrounding peoples and has an insight into economic abuse. Koch: "This requires an education unavailable for a poor shepherd or a small peasant" /164/. So the only possible conclusion is that Amos enjoyed a school education and mixed in educated circles. At least as a learned man, Amos must have been acquainted before his calling with the mission and the intellectual world of the prophets. As a prophet he could have relied on his knowledge in order to develop his office, in a similar manner to Mohammed who made use of the forms of speech common among the old Arabic soothsayers when he appeared to the public with his message /165/.

One may ask whether Amos went through a prophet school as well. The texts do not tell us but the existence of free groups of prophets with whom he could have received such an education cannot be totally excluded. In any case there is documentary evidence which could point to this. The prophet Isaiah, a somewhat younger contemporary of Amos, speaks on one occasion of his 'pupils' (Hebrew: limmudim) and 'children' (yeladim) to whom he passes on his message (Isa 8.16-18). According to one reading these are not his natural children and also not just supporters of the prophet but men who gather round Isaiah, recognise him as their master and are preparing themselves for the vocation of prophet. With regard to this evidence, some scholars suppose that the prophet school is not only an institution flourishing in Elisha's days but offers, long after the ninth century, an 'intellectual home' to the free prophets /166/. Anyway one must admit that the Isaiah text is not unambiguous and may in fact not speak of the prophet's pupils but first about educated people in general and then about his own children. Apart from Isaiah, formal teaching is also presumed for Ezekiel. W. Zimmerli /167/ imagines this prophet as a master who instructs his adherents in his house in a plainly didactic fashion. The instructive matter-of-factness of Ez 18 and 33 provide the basis for this view. Yet Zimmerli is not thinking of the training of future prophets - he does not even mention this possibility; rather, he looks for a circle of men who, after Ezekiel's death, concern themselves with his written legacy, and to whom we owe the canonical form of the Book of Ezekiel. Zimmerli would not like to mark the start of intensive preoccupation with the words of Ezekiel as after the prophet's death, but anchors it as deeply as possible in his life. Therefore Ezekiel is for him the first reviser of his own words and the disciples later had only to carry on his work.

Because of the lack of adequate sources the following reconstruction must rest on the conventionality of the prophetic mission and on general considerations about the social transmission of particular 'roles'.

The vocational genesis of the free prophet begins with a phase of perception: the candidate lives in Israelite society, learns of the prophets, experiences their public appearance and perhaps reads some of their writings. Thus he takes in the image of the prophets. The phenomenon of prophecy, incluaing its special forms of experience (such as the vision) and methods of communication (for instance so-called symbolic acts) belongs to the unquestioned, self-evident features of his milieu. This phase of perception, which the candidate has in common with his peers, is followed by the phase of learning. Now the young Israelite feels attracted by these men, takes more than a casual interest in their activity, takes up personal contact, studies their public performance, writings and body of thought. He decides to become a prophet himself and absorbs all the information about being a prophet. Perhaps he accompanies a prophet more than once on his public appearances and feels himself to be not only an infatuated adherent of the latter - a 'fan' to use modern jargon - but also to be his pupil. As such he prepares himself for the profession of prophet. But he is not a prophet himself yet. That he first becomes in the phase of breakthrough. One day the candidate hears Yahweh's voice himself or has a vision in which he is called and assigned the office of prophet. He has been waiting and preparing himself for this for months, perhaps years. The meeting with his god is consequently to be understood as a real, inner, psychic occurrence which belongs to the role of prophet and is experienced as really as it is awaited. (The term 'role' which must be used at this point will be examined more closely in the next section, with reference to Sundén's role psychology.)

I would rule out a pseudo-calling by tricksters whose claim to such an experience is without factual basis. With the occurrence of the calling the period of apprenticeship is over; now the candidate is an independent prophet himself. What was previously learned as a role is merged with the core of his personality - the candidate now becomes identified with his role. He does not 'hold' the prophetic role nor does he 'play' it with a certain degree of distance: he is a prophet.

Even if we only possess the calling-reports of three prophets we can still surmise an actual experience of calling for the other (or all!) prophets. The reason to believe this is that the reports of the callings of Isaiah, Jeremiah and Ezekiel are recorded in the most comprehensive prophetic writings; if we had from, say, Amos a more detailed book then we would have more than just the information, "But Yahweh took me as I followed the flock and said to me, Go and prophesy to my people Israel" (Am 7.15) /168/.

After the experience of calling has taken place the phase of prophetic activity begins. Now the prophet appears in public and uses the messenger formula, 'These are the words of Yahweh', or variations of it. (In Ezekiel's report the authorization to use this formula is expressly mentioned: Ez 2.4.) To be in contact and to communicate with his god through auditions and visions belongs to his self-consciousness and his role. It is true that the prophet, as the representative of Yahweh, passes judgement independently, yet he remains in touch with the prophetic tradition, part of which is available in writing. The prophetic records must have remained an important aid to orientation for the activity of the beginner prophet. Jer 28.8-9 provides good evidence for this. In the context of a conflict with another prophet, Jeremiah refers to tradition:

> The prophets who preceded you and me from earliest times have foretold war, famine, and pestilence for many lands and for great kingdoms. If a prophet foretells prosperity, when his words come true it will be known that Yahweh has sent him.

Jeremiah (or if it is a case of a non-genuine word, Pseudo-Jeremiah) refers therefore not to the certainty of his individual experience of god but to the traditional role of the prophet as announcer of doom. This announcement belongs to the utterly conventional prophetic role which Jeremiah wants to play. Perhaps it is also the traditional character of the prophecy of doom that provides the explanation for the

101

curious fact that the early proclamation of Isaiah, as well as Jeremiah, is ruled by a politically imprecise threat of disaster /169/ - both prophets start their career with living from the tradition from which they only gradually free themselves in order to create their own message. The prophet is not the only one to be guided by tradition; his public is too. In the fierce dispute about a particularly sharp word of Jeremiah some of the elders of the land stand up and remind everyone that Jeremiah had not pronounced an unheard oracle but one which a certain Micah of Moresheth had already circulated, and that this had enjoyed citizenship in Israel (Jer 26.16-19).

The prophet is not to be understood as a 'loner' figure. More often contact with prophetic contemporaries as colleagues and pupils is to be surmised, albeit that the prophets act as messengers of their god and never as representatives of a group or as speakers for the group's intention. The prophet must, because he is called as an individual, also appear as an individual. The feeling which is characteristic of Israel's prophets of being a loner also reveals itself in a free, creative relationship to the preceding tradition /170/.

The model of phases is meant, on a trial basis, to present the path of the average Israelite to becoming a bearer of the prophetic role as a learning process. According to its sequence this course of events corresponds to the habituation of almost any other role a new member of society must learn. In the role of the adult Israelite, for instance, the wedding ceremony appears to be as radical as the calling is for the prophet's life. The prophet prepares himself for his calling in the same way as everyone prepares for the day of his wedding. In both cases the longish process of learning and adaptation precedes the decisive event. According to this interpretation the prophetic calling which often has a vision as its climax is a real, psychic event which, however, is prestructured and predefined by the familiarization with the tradition. Convention and actual experience pervade one another and are fused in the event of the calling.

The Psyche of the Prophet

We have tried to answer the question, 'How does one become a prophet in Israel?' in terms of 'school', 'tuition', and 'learning'. The prophet candidate must learn and assimilate his role in the same way as every other activity must be learnt, whether it is exercised professionally or only part-time.

In this examination the psychological side of our question, 'How does one become a prophet?' was left out of consideration. How can one render psychologically comprehensible the prophetic consciousness of vocation, the continual use of the formula, 'These are the words of Yahweh' - that is to say, the claim to be speaking in a god's name - and the manifest experience of a god?

"Moreover it is a useless art", J. G. Herder /171/ writes with respect to this question, "to want to brood or ponder the inner state of the prophets, when times have changed so much", and many theologians agree with him. Yet the posing of the question of psychology has called forth a considerable specialist literature, albeit not always respected by the exegetes. If one casts a glance at this literature then three classical approaches may be discerned.

(1) According to some authors /172/, we are dealing with ecstatics whose altered state of consciousness is produced by fasting, listening to music, constant meditation, wild dancing, etc. Such techniques lead to ecstatic frenzy or, on a more intellectual level, to hypnotic autosuggestion and hallucination - all understood as an experience of the divine. The closest relations of the prophets are consequently the dervishes known in Islam or the Christian mystics and visionaries of the Middle Ages. It was assumed that ecstasy itself does not produce new insights, but furnishes pre-ecstatic knowledge with passion and determination.

(2) A second way of making prophecy comprehensible leads to the area of 'abnormal psychology'. Non-theologians above all favour again and again the view that the prophets - with their visions, auditions and long-distance perceptions - belong to the department of psycho-pathology. The prophet Ezekiel, in particular, proved to be a suitable object of study for psycho-pathological speculation. The best known author in this category is the philosopher, Karl Jaspers, but he is only one of many. Particularly interesting is the view of Jaynes who studied both schizophrenics and thoroughly healthy people who, under stress, had visions and heard voices. He argues that at an early stage of evolution man very much relied on hallucinations that were due to normal communication between the two hemispheres of the human brain. Especially under stress the two hemispheres can function so as to seem like two independent persons - the individual and his god /173/.

(3) A third group of authors attempt to explain the prophetic mind with categories taken from C. G. Jung and S.

Freud, respectively. Whereas it is true that Povah /174/ tries to see the 'Unconscious' as the source of false prophecy only, labelling this "the mere outcroppings of the unconscious mind", Haeussermann /175/ sees the prophetic experience as a whole as having its roots in the unconscious depths of the soul. Another author /176/ believes he can establish supp-ressed and displaced sexuality in Hosea and one last author /177/ describes the prophetic calling as a phase of 'forming the super-ego' which cannot occur without 'narcissistic regression' and 'schizophrenic abandonment of reality'.

Against all three theories refutations have been written - some more and some less successful. In classical Israelite prophecy ecstasy is to be observed at best in passing and therefore cannot form an explanation for the prophetic phenomenon /178/; the theories about prophetic illnesses do not stand up to any serious scrutiny of the sources /179/, and finally one cannot analyse the biblical prophets with the techniques of modern psychology because all too few personal data are available /180/.

After all these objections it is no wonder that standard exegetical literature retreats to talking about the 'secret experience' /181/ of the prophets as the ultimate source of their awareness of vocation and their individual oracles. Koch writes: "One should probably imagine that particular sounds reached the ears of the nabi but his task was the translation of these sounds into another, comprehensible language" /182/. One cannot describe this as an enlightening explanation, and hence can understand L. Ramlot's sigh of despair that psychological research of prophetic ecstasy is 'au point mort' /183/. However, the recent psychology of learning and perception can lead us away from this 'deadlock'. Under the name of 'role psychology' it was applied by the Swedish scholar Hjalmar Sundén /184/ to religious experience and learning, and the same scholar has indeed made some observations about biblical prophets which join the theory presented in the previous section quite well and expand, clarify and deepen it.

Sundén gives an account of how Lewi Pethrus, who at the beginning of our century was the first leader of the Swedish Pentecostal movement, identified himself with the prophet Elijah - not in the pathological fashion of the man who thinks he is the emperor Napoleon or Churchill, but in that he saw both his biography and vocation indicated in the example of the biblical figure. Let us listen to Pethrus' own words:

One evening I sat at home in my house in Storgardskleven, reading the Bible. I began to read about Elijah, whom God had met and armed for his service. He had placed his life in the hands of God. God had answered his prayer, a glowing coal from the altar had touched his lips, and he was a prophet in the service of the Lord. But then God said to him that he should go and settle by the brook Cherith. So I read that after a while the brook dried up, that Elijah had to go to a poor widow in Zarephath, where in poverty and want he saw wonders of God. After these experiences Elijah was permitted to see the fire fall upon his sacrifice and reveal God to Israel. This spoke to me. It became quite clear to me that even if this should be my experience, that the activity God commanded to me should dry out like the brook Cherith, and if I were to go in the most barren and poorest circumstances, yet should God be able to reveal himself even there. I understood that this was the way to greater spiritual experiences and the path to becoming of greater blessing for others. /185/

It would not be entirely correct to say that Pethrus identifies himself just with Elijah; for him, Elijah, whom he somehow mixes with Isaiah, epitomizes a biblical prophet. Through his identification with this model, Pethrus acquires the possibility of seeing God at work in his own fate: he expects that God will deal with him as God dealt with the prophet(s). Pethrus therefore does not only adopt the external role of the prophet but enters into the 'dual role situation', which includes, besides the human role, that of god as well, and so constitutes the religious situation in general (i.e., man standing vis-à-vis god). "From a psychological point of view," writes Sundén, "the god of the Bible must be termed a role which man anticipates by identifying himself with some figure of the biblical tradition." And he continues summarizing the result of his analysis:

> If a man identifies himself with a human figure of the biblical tradition, we say, he adopts this role; but at the same time he 'takes' the role of god, that is, he can, by virtue of the biblical story, anticipate god's way of acting and can perceive all that is yet to happen in his life as god's action. /186/

This statement, stressed (italicized) by Sundén, contains three main points: <u>Firstly</u>, the adoption of a given human role; <u>secondly</u>, the 'taking' of god's role which belongs in a constellation with the traditional human role; <u>thirdly</u>, the formation of a readiness to perceive god's actions. With no effort we can transfer these elements of role psychology to the situation of Israel's prophets portrayed in our previous section.

(1) The first element of Sundén's statement does not require further explanations. The fact that an Israelite who becomes a prophet adopts a given human role, has already been established. In contrast to Sundén's example, the Israelite had to let himself be guided, not by an individual figure provided by literature, but by prophethood which he knew as a well-established institution and whose function he could experience in numerous people and on numerous occasions. His adoption of the role is not partial and limited, as it is in Pethrus' case who, of course, could not become a man speaking god's words because he lived in Sweden in the 20th century and not in biblical Israel. The Israelite does not need to make any reductions in the conventional role nor replant it in another milieu. If a European of our century identifies himself with a biblical prophet, through whom god's wonder comes to pass and is not satisfied with the general role of a person before god, then one may describe this as an exceptional case. Not, however, in the case of an Israelite in whose society the vocation of prophet is not exactly rare: adopting the role of prophet is doubtlessly easier for him than for one of us.

(2) Taking up a phrase of the Swedish religious historian, Tor Andrae, Sundén writes:

> The personal inspiration of the prophets with their direct experience of god who speaks and appears to them, the communion with god in an ordinary life of piety which consists of the heart to heart conversation with god in prayer, and the willingness to accept inspiration from god through the words of the Scriptures, the Psalms and devotional writings - these are all points on one and the same scale of disposition which imperceptibly merge into one another. /187/

The prophet experiences the role of god more intensively than the normal believer and also more than the average Israelite. What the person at prayer experiences as the silent presence of god, becomes for the prophet, who is awaiting it, an experience of god speaking in the audition which can rise to a vision, embracing all his senses and capacities - alongside seeing and hearing, also taste, being moved, speaking and acting /188/.

Sundén establishes that:

Visions seen in the light of role psychology, have no pathological character at all, which is characteristic for them if considered as isolated phenomena. Seen in this light they mean that the devotional life of a person is very sincere, and that he has absorbed himself so deeply into the situations and roles of, e.g., the Bible, that a disposition of the brain has developed which is of a similar type to that brought about by practice of a foreign language. Not until such a disposition has been fixed in the brain can the different collections of sounds of the foreign language be so processed that meaningful descriptions of experience emerge. Only if practice in role-playing and role-taking has preceded, do visions occur, but only under certain conditions. /189/

Unfortunately we do not know to what extent Israel's prophets make use of a particular 'technique' to hear their god's voice and experience visions. The fact that certain techniques must be at their disposal can be recognised from Elisha's harp player and Daniel's fasting before the experience of a vision (2 Kgs 3.15; Dan 10.3). More important than such external technique must be the observation that the prophets expose themselves to prophetic literature and absorb its manifold motifs which open the possibility for their own perceptions. Thus Miller can prove that Ezekiel is very intensively preoccupied with the words of his older contemporary, Jeremiah; similarly, Amos' influence on Isaiah is established /190/.

Writing about prophetic charactes in Christian history, the German enlightenment philosopher, Leibniz, notes their dependence on tradition:

Melancholy, mixed with pious devotion, and a high degree of self-confidence has always led some people to believe that they were on much more familiar terms with God than others. (...) They admire themselves and have others admire that fertility which is taken to be divine inspiration. This merit derives for the most part from a strong imagination animated by religious passion, as well as from a good memory which has retained the style of prophetic literature familiar from personal reading or listening to others. /191/

That extraordinary religious experience presupposes both knowledge of tradition and a stimulating atmosphere is the theme of a painting by Paul Gaugin which is called 'Vision after a Sermon' (1888, Edinburgh National Gallery): It shows a man who, half sleeping and half awake, sees, in a vision, Jacob wrestling with God's angel. Many students of religion have already known what Sundén elaborates as a theory.

(3) In the 'dual role situation' in which the prophet experiences the presence of his god, the normal field of experience is restructured. The prophet looks at the world with different eyes; he sees it as a space in which god acts. Whatever the prophet experiences is involuntarily associated with his religious frame of reference which is stronger than any other frame such that he can never avoid it. If, for instance, he hears of an advance of enemy troops, then for him that means Yahweh's punishment of his disobedient people, not an opportunity for military trial or an occasion for diplomatic action. Sundén describes the usual, that is to say non-visionary, nature of the prophetic experience of god in an especially detailed fashion:

> What confronts the human race in epiphanies is not a throughly unrecognizable and unclear being which only moves the unworldly soul, but the world itself as a divine figure, as the wealth of divine configurations. /192/

What Sundén, quoting W. F. Otto, says of the experience of god in nature is even more true for the experience of god in human fate and history:

> The profane, technical form of multitude in which the world usually meets man can disintegrate at any moment, another figure steps forward, the whole universe individualizes and differentiates itself as a person acting out roles. Thereby, man feels completely passive in the way which is characteristic for any metamorphosis of form. /193/

As an appropriate example Sundén quotes Luther's reading of Jonah 2.2,

> in which he very much stresses the fact that here it is said that God and not just the crew of the ship threw the prophet into the sea, and that not only the waves of the sea but also the waves of God washed over him (...) For Jonah, who of his own accord fled from God and his will, the seamen, the storm and the waves become the expression of God, God's actions and tools for the attacking of conscience. This means that the external world and normal events may represent God to man or are 'masks of God', larva dei. /194/

This same nature of the field of experience becomes evident when the prophets portray the relationship between Yahweh and Israel and thereby describe god with different images: as father (Jer 3.19), as mother (Isa 66.13), as husband (Hos 2.16), as friend (Jer 3.24), as shepherd (Ez 34.31), as peasant (Am 7.7), as potter (Jer 18.16), as fisherman (Hab 1.14), as midwife (Isa 1.2), etc.

What one usually calls 'images', is better described as roles. With this terminology we can see more clearly how the prophet's field of experience is organized. There are situations in the life of the people of Israel which befall the prophets as dual situations, in which only Yahweh and Israel are in interaction with one another, i.e. Yahweh here coincides to a certain extent with everything that Israel is not. The whole world manifests itself against Israel as an activity structured by roles. /195/

Without a doubt the understanding of the prophetic psyche can be led into a new direction by Sundén, a direction free from unnecessary suppositions and distortions. "The role is the only psychological term," writes Sundén, "which, in describing religious experience, does not pervert it, but takes heed of the demand of the pious to meet God as a person" /196/. Let us stay with psychology for a while!

Readiness to Perceive God's Action, from a Psychological Point of View

As Sundén emphasizes, the prophet develops a readiness to discover god's action in the human and natural world: without such an attitude, he could neither experience him in fact nor enter into any relationship with him. Because the prophets, unlike 'normal believers', do not only meet god casually, but their life and work is characterised by continual union and communication with him, it is important to look at the structure of perception and its prerequisites more closely.

The prophet is distinguished by a particularly structured field of perception and experience. The fact that, by reason of a mental disposition, restructuring of the area of experience is not only possible but ensues involuntarily, can be proved from many examples - one needs only to think of the well-known picture puzzle whose figures can only be recognised if one is prepared to see such things. The naive-realistic assumption that perception is a 'copy' of the environment reduced to an experience of the senses, approaches the problem from the wrong angle. "One must not ask whether we really perceive a world, but on the contrary one must say: the world is what we perceive" /197/. Perception is not only determined by impressions of the senses, but by a whole range of other factors, too.

There is more to perception than meets the eye or ear (...) For our perceptions reflect not only the information brought to the brain by the sensory nerves, but also certain information (beliefs, feelings, and memories for instance) previously stored in the brain.

Moreover, what you perceive is conditioned by

your particular sense organs, your individual history, your enduring personality traits, your present expectations, moods and general feeling tone ... /198/

and we may add, "by your or your society's world view". There can be no doubt that one's beliefs, feelings, expectations, etc., are largely determined by a given society's 'culture' and assimilated in both formal and informal education:

The public symbolic system which has been set up by social intercourse puts its controlling stamp on individual perception and restricts understanding to the possibilities admitted in its own construction of the universe. /199/

An enlightening theoretical consideration and presentation of the cognitive process comes from F. H. Allport /200/ and is known as 'hypothesis theory'. Allport describes the behaviour of perception as a process of testing hypotheses, whereby a hypothesis is made up of personal experiences, values and motives. If one transfers Allport's statement to Sundén's psychology of religious experience, the result is that the religious frame of reference, proportioned by the biblical pattern of experience and expectation, consists of an inventory of such hypotheses or mental dispositions. Information from the environment can now verify or refute hypotheses which already exist. This means for a prophet that he proceeds from his inner attitude (turning to his god) and his professional knowledge, in order to measure the stimuli of the environment. The result of his perception is therefore a product of hypotheses and additional stimulus-information from his surroundings. At the same time, there is no compulsion to evoke a particular hypothesis: not all the environmental influences are interpreted from the start with a view to god's action. The probability that a particular hypothesis is asserted in fact depends on the quantity of suitable and supporting stimulus-informations, that is, the larger their number, the weaker a hypothesis can be and vice-versa. Similarly, the sum of contradicting information which is used in order to abandon an hypothesis must be larger, the stronger the hypothesis is.

Because of his training and attitude, a prophet will be able to understand the signs of his time and announce divine punishment earlier than is possible for the average believer; he will perceive god's will more clearly because he is 'pre-programmed' for this.

Now the question is, on what the strength of the hypothesis or the extent of a disposition depends. In the first place, one must refer to the frequency of endorsements in the past. For the Israelite audience the fulfilment of an oracle is an important criterion for distinguishing a true from a false prophet /20/. For the prophet himself, it is the certain knowledge of proclaiming and receiving the will of god which has a strengthening effect on the formation of his disposition.

In second place comes the number of available alternative hypotheses. A prophet, especially, has at his disposal by means of his training, a large store of knowledge of both tradition and contemporary political affairs. He has specialised in this and therefore has a greater number of hypotheses at his disposal which point to god's action, so that other patterns of explanation and interpretation become less important.

The third relevant factor in this connection relates to motivation. The result of a particular perception is heavily influenced by the value it has for the person concerned. (If you are actively searching for a lost key in a cluttered drawer you have a strong set to see that key - and for a second, you may even take some unidentifiable small object for that key, given some superficial similarity.) If one characterises the prophet as a person who is ready for god's word in a particular way, who therefore approaches god, psychologically speaking, with a high self-participation, then one may suppose that a large strength of hypothesis has developed within him.

Fourthly, one must mention the cognitive agreement with the perceptions of other people which are especially useful if the testing of a hypothesis is rendered difficult. This is true for a prophet in so far as he is part of a particular tradition

111

and belongs to a guild or community with which he knows himself to be allied, even in difficult situations /202/.

Additional security is provided by the prestige of prophetic foretelling which "rests on a few, but for their contemporaries tremendously impressive cases in which they were unexpectedly confirmed by success" /203/.

Finally one must emphasize that it is, of course, not only religious roles which determine the individual structure of the field of experience. For this we can refer to a psychologist's /204/ own report which portrays how the countryside changed for him as he had to experience front-line action in the First World War. What previously seemed to be open country now has limits and breaks off at the front; if up until then fields, woods, houses and equipment were to be perceived, so now they are fighting objects - the field is a field of firing, the houses are cover, domestic belongings are lawful possessions which must be freely at the soldiers' disposal. This change in the environment is based on the new system of norms which accompanies the role of soldier and the war situation, and now gives way to the predominant frame of reference for experiencing the environment.

A New Image of the Prophet

The end of the investigation must consider the question of how the image of the prophet outlined by role psychology relates to the traditional one.

Moses was alone during the Exodus from Egypt, Elijah was alone in the time of King Ahab, Elisha was alone after him, Isaiah was alone in Jerusalem, Hosea was alone in Israel, Jeremiah was alone in Judea, Ezekiel was alone in Babylon, and so on.

These sentences are to be found in the reply which the reformer, Martin Luther, wrote after receiving the bull of damnation in the winter of 1520/21. He continues:

Saint Ambrosius was alone in his age, St. Jerome after him, and St. Augustine after them. /205/.

The eightfold repetition of alone makes it abundantly clear that Luther saw himself to be one of the great saints and prophets: he comprehends them all to be religious solo fighters whom god himself had called to their task and who appealed to their conscience as opposed to the great mass of people who thought differently from them.

Chapter Three - The Making of Prophets

The sociologist, Max Weber, has seen in the prophets thus understood a classic example for his differentiation between charisma and office, which he takes to be constitutive for human society in general. Office means institution, continuity, consolidation, and the exclusion of the new; this is what the priests and the king stand for in Israel. Charisma, on the other hand, means the creative outsider who renounces all security and means the power of innovation - see the prophets. /206/

Even if this quotation only gives one side of Weber's view and does not mention the common interests of Israel's priests and prophets emphasized by him, yet Koch expresses a wide-spread opinion. The most recent research into the prophets, from traditio-historical research and form criticism to the learning model outlined here, can be read as a single refutation of the orthodox image of the prophets. However, it would be wrong to interpret the great figures of the Old Testament - such as Isaiah, Jeremiah or Ezekiel - as people who are completely trapped in conventional imaginings. Rather one has every reason to point out their freedom and even independence in relation to their own prophetic tradition. As surely as there are examples for the isolated case of charisma, unhindered by any tradition or office, so it is certain that Israel's prophecy cannot be a valid example for this. The prophets are neither lone wolves nor bearers of an absolutely anti-traditional and anti-institutional charisma; rather, charisma and tradition are bound to one another and permit no more than theoretical differentiation. The prophetic charisma is to be understood as a power of renewal which breaks out in the middle of traditional structures that are transcended without being destroyed.

Chapter Four

THE SOCIAL ORGANIZATION OF PEASANT POVERTY IN BIBLICAL ISRAEL

Where the means of production are fragmented, usury centralizes monetary wealth. It does not change the mode of production, but clings on to it like a parasite and impoverishes it. It sucks it dry, emasculates it and forces reproduction to proceed under ever more pitiable conditions. Hence the popular hatred of usury, at its peak in the ancient world (...) In Asiatic forms, usury can persist for a long while without leading to anything more than economic decay and political corruption.

Karl Marx, Capital, III, ch. 36
(1981, 731-732)

Introduction

MOS, a prophet active in eighth century B.C. northern Israel, remains an elusive figure. Possibly he tried to instigate a coup d'état against the king, Jeroboam, whom he knew to be unwilling or unable to carry through social reforms such as a general remission or reduction of peasant debt or a restriction of debt bondage. Like his younger contemporary, Hosea, he may have thought that a re-union of the two kingdoms, Israel and Judah, under leadership of the Davidic dynasty would solve political and social problems. He enforced his programme - if that is the right word for it - not only by making it the explicit will of Yahweh, the god of the state, but also by announcing a military invasion of the Assyrians who would destroy the urban centers and thus 'punish' the élite for its social crimes. Whether this prophet's activity had any impact on society we do not know. Possibly he left the country after having cursed the priest of Bethel who had denounced him at the royal court, as well as his wife whose fate as a city prostitute he angrily announced (Am 7.17).

Chapter Four - Peasant Poverty

Though partly based on a statement made by an upper-class contemporary of Amos (i.e. priest Amaziah) and on comparative evidence /207/, this reading represents no more than an educated guess. Scholarly imagination is indispensable, yet a poor substitute for lacking sources and evidence not available.

Whereas the aim of Amos and the precise nature of his activity must remain a matter of conjecture, his literary legacy provides us with much evidence for the economic and social situation that obtained in his society.

Wealth and poverty, townsmen and peasants are contrasted with one another in a harsh manner.

(Shame on) you who loll on beds inlaid with ivory
and sprawl over your couches,
feasting on lambs from the flock
and fatted calves ...

reads chapter 6.4. And from chapter 5.11 we can guess at the source of the luxury:

You levy taxes on the poor
and extort a tribute of grain from them.

Whether one speaks of economic classes or social strata does not make any difference - the contrast cannot be overlooked, and the words of Amos made him famous as an early social critic if not as a people's tribune. It is, of course, much more difficult to analyse the background of the obvious class differences. How did such an economic stratification come about?

The older commentators did not see any problem here. For biblical Israel as well as for their own society they took poverty and wealth for granted - as facts that could not be altered. However, what could be changed was the conduct of the rich - and thus the prophet was understood. Egotistic exploitation was to give place to the patron's solidarity: The rich were to soften the harshness of poverty through well-directed gifts and thus to recreate some kind of social balance.

Another view, arguing from social history, was taken by the last generation of scholars and is still to be found in the standard literature. According to his view, the contrast between poor and rich is a Canaanite feature and belongs to the urban culture of ancient Palestine. The background of the prophetic protest - so it was argued - is provided by an egalitarian ideal which implies the basic economic equality of the whole Israelite peasant population. But from the era of David and Solomon onwards there has been a progressive "Canaanization" of the economic system which created the situation attacked by Amos. The prophet launched his protest as a spokesman for the old partly nomadic, partly agrarian ideology of brotherhood that knows of no classes: 'égalité' implies 'fraternité' ! Egalitarian Israel versus Canaanite classes provided the key to almost everything in Israel's social development. Recently, however, it has become clear that things are not to be explained so easily, and that an originally classless and egalitarian society is rather more wishful thinking than characteristic of the earliest Israel. But even if some Canaanite influence in the formation of a stratified society is admitted, the 'Canaanite vs. Israelite systems' approach never explained how the exploitive system actually worked.

Peasants and Landlords
in Near Eastern Economic History

For these reasons it seems more promising to proceed from agrarian societies as studied by social anthropology. Such 'peasant societies' as they are called are usually characterized by the following three traits /208/:

(1) A peasant is not a farmer or an agricultural entrepreneur but rather maintains a household. Instead of earning a profit, he wants to feed his family which is the basic economic unit. As for biblical Israel I may add that we are dealing with a nuclear family consisting of parents and unmarried children; as is the rule with us the newly married couple resides neolocally - it builds its own house /209/.

(2) Peasants do not form a complete and independent society; in fact, they are only one half of it, the other half being a propertied, educated and merchant élite often resident in towns and always monoplizing control of public affairs.

(3) The ruling class makes permanent charges on the agricultural production. There are different titles to do so: The right to taxation may be placed in the hands of a lord who inherited a village as his patrimonial domain (patrimonial system); or a lord may be paid by peasants in return for the exercise of some ecclesiastical or civil office (prebendal system). A third system does not involve a general rule over and taxation of peasants but rather leaves this to free business in the market. In this case, the peasant may run into debt and become dependent on an urban money lender or

merchant - or he may be forced to cultivate the soil of others on a share-cropping or tenant basis.

In the Near East, this last arrangement between peasantry and élite which may be christened the mercantile system has found a particular expression in which is called rent capitalism /210/. The urban propertied class skims off the largest possible portion of the agricultural produce as a regular income or "rent" claimed on the basis of liabilities or full urban ownership of land. As a rule, there are dyadic contracts between an urban landowner or merchant and individual peasants.

I will proceed to illustrate and elucidate several aspects of this general description.

(1) The small peasant living on his plot does not produce for the market but for his family and himself (subsistence economy). Given the existing productive techniques, crop yields are determined by factors outside the control of the producer - principally by variations in rainfall. The climatically conditioned crop failures can be balanced more or less by keeping a few cattle. If no more than every fourth harvest fails, the present-day peasant of Iraq breaks even /211/, thus achieving a stability which, however, fluctuates on the edge of disaster. If crop failures occur more frequently (e.g. caused by locusts or several successive droughts) then the peasants have to make use of credit. Equally, illness, payment of the bride wealth etc. may force them to incur debts. Taking a loan almost automatically leads to long-term or even permanent dependence because of the high interest rates - in antiquity as today. Interest at the rate of 40-60% per six months and 5-8% per month are quoted for Syria in the 1960's /212/. According to documents from the fifth century B.C., the Jews of Elephantine in Egypt were expected to pay 5% per month, unpaid interest being added to the capital, which equals at least an annual interest rate of 60% /213/. In one passage the Bible tells us with all desirable accuracy how a free peasant becomes more and more dependent on a creditor: Genesis 47.13-26. It is reported that in a time of famine the Egyptians had to convey everything to the Pharaoh - first their cattle, then their land and even themselves, so that they were in bondage, owing to the king 20% of their annual yield. It is known that this passage does not fit in with the Egyptian economic system; rather, it reflects how the poor Israelite peasant becomes dependent on a rich lord /214/.

(2) As a rule, credit is taken from a rich townsman who often becomes the actual owner of the cultivated land. Thus ownership of land and labour are separated: whereas the agricultural production remains with the small family, the land is entirely or in part property of a landlord. Not always /215/ but very often and typically, the landowner is a townsman so that the dualism of rich and poor corresponds to the country's dependence on the city. As an indebted peasant or small tenant the poor man is the landlord's bondsman and sometimes a kind of serf or even slave - especially when he has to render regular or occasional services in addition to the payment of rent.

> The rich lord it over the poor;
> the borrower becomes the lender's slave (or serf) ...

says Prov 22.7 /216/. While a serf is working, the creditor or landlord draws an income without actually working for it, enjoying the pleasant life of the leisure class.

(3) The wish to lead such a life rests on the disdain for any physical work - compare the attitude of the patricians of classical Athens. People want to earn their living as great merchants, major civil servants or big landowners. Manual work is considered to be menial and degrading, and hence for the lower classes. Exemption from labour is the only true criterion of distinction: he who is at the lowest level of the economic and social scale has to work with his hands; he who belongs to the 'better classes' gives proof of it by disdaining manual labour. This ethos of the Eastern economic mind is often noticed by Western visitors, and not very flatteringly styled as oriental laziness /217/.

(4) The relationship between the poor and the rich may be organized in a variety of ways - including arrangements not entirely unfavourable for the peasant /218/. At the cost of some over-simplification one may distinguish three different types of characteristic peasant-landlord relationships: patronage, partnership and exploitation. The idea of patronage implies a mutual relationship between the wealthy and influential patron and the peasant. The patron protects his client and feels responsible for the survival of his client and his client's family; in return, the peasant pays a certain portion of his crop. Thus, the landlord shares part of the risk, since in years of a bad harvest he will get only a small payment or none at all or may even be put in the position of being like Job in the 29th chapter - a distributing "father to

the needy". One passage in Deuteronomy suggests that poor people who own no land travel very far - even by sea - in order to find a wealthy patron who would 'buy' their labour and give them food and shelter (Deut 28.68). In a partnership arrangement the merchant provides materials, e.g. a weaving loom and wool, so that the peasant or his wife may produce for the urban bazaar and have some extra income. Or sharecropping contracts may stipulate a 50:50 distribution of the yield, thus leading to village prosperity in times of good harvest.

The third type is exploitation, based on the landowner's or creditor's interest in profit-making which excludes any personal loyalty to or reciprocity with the tenant or debtor. This estrangement is favoured by the landowner's urban residence ('absentee landlordism') as well as by the situation of the upper class which provides both for social prestige and political influence independent of any clientele support.

The consequences are reported by Lambton in her book on 'Landlord and Peasant in Persia':

> Between the landowner as a class, no matter what his origin, and the peasant there is a wide gulf. In no sense is there a spirit of co-operation or a feeling of being engaged in a mutual enterprise. The attitude is on the whole, though not without exceptions, one of mutual suspicion. The landowner regards the peasant virtually as a drudge, whose sole function is to provide him with his profits and who will, if treated with anything but severity, cheat him of his due. It is widely believed in landowning circles that anything above the barest consideration of the well-being of the peasant would be taken by the latter as a sign of weakness, and as a result he would not pay the dues of the landowner /219/.

The different arrangements - patronage, partnership, exploitation - alternately have had their impact on the economic history of the Near East. Urban entrepreneurship invites partnership; rural residence of the rich and democratic or quasi-democratic political constitution favour a patron-client-relationship, because a patron may be dependent on entourage, co-operation and support. As soon as the market is able to provide luxury goods and gives rise to a corresponding urban life-style - which was the case in Antiquity and has been true especially after the middle of the previous century - then exploitation may be a consequence.

In biblical Israel we can distinguish between two different

systems of credit available to the small peasant. According to the first, the peasant goes to a kinsman to borrow some money or he sells him a plot of land, perhaps to get it back with the duty to pay some regular rent. Thus, the better-off kinsman takes over a patron's role as, e.g., does the urban resident Jeremiah, who buys a field of one of his village kinsmen /220/. The other credit system is based on the market and does not make use of any kinship connections. In this case the creditor may be extremely merciless and, as we know from Nathan's famous parable, may take the poor man's only sheep out of the fold/221/. Unfortunately, we cannot say under what circumstances the one or the other credit system was resorted to; both systems seem to operate at the same time. One may suggest that Jeremiah's kinsman uses the seventeen silver shekels he gets from the prophet to pay for his debts in the market and thus changes the credit system. Be this as it may - the two systems and their consequences are quite different for the debtor, as the generosity and amity usually shown toward a kinsman have no place in the market and are supplanted by pure calculation of profit.

(5) Rent capitalism has left its imprint on the Near East and the results are still visible today: there is a marked contrast between the splendour of the cities and the misery of the countryside /222/. To be sure, you can see beggars in town, but there are no urban proletarians as in classical Athens or Rome. The poor live in the country as fellaheen or hired labourers, but not in urban slums (which are a rather recent phenomenon in the Near East) /223/. As the parasites, living off the countryside, the cities skim off a substantial portion of the proceeds of agricultural production leaving for the pauperized fellaheen hardly the means for their bare existence. We have a stagnating traditional culture and society at a very low ebb, in fact in a state of decadence not witnessed before. The philosopher, Oswald Spengler, took the 'fellah people' of Egypt to illustrate what comes after the decline and final breakdown of a major civilisation /224/. However, the decline does not affect everything: technology and the economic system become more and more nearly static and sterile, while in the urban culture the fine arts, literature, philosophy, religion and law - to name but a few disciplines - are fostered and often flourishing. The contrast between the primitive rural culture and the sophisticated urban civilisation can hardly be exaggerated. It was only the advent of rent capitalism's younger brother, 'productive capitalism' with its organization of labour in factories,

national insurance and rural development which could provide the basis for technolgical progress and new (not always better) social conditions.

Rent Capitalism and the Book of Amos

Now I will try to show how these social and economic conditions are reflected in the Book of Amos. The prophet accuses Israel, or, more precisely, its upper classes, of exploitation and oppression of the peasant population. According to him, their behaviour deserves a punishment of the most severe kind. Amos threatens them with a political disaster mentioning mass-deportation to a foreign country. Israel was situated on the periphery of the Assyrian empire and was becoming more conscious of the growing influence and claims of the Assyrians. Already one hundred years before Amos, in 841 B.C., the Israelite king Jehu was paying tribute to the Assyrian overlord - see the famous black obelisk of Shalmaneser on display in the British Museum /225/. In 1967, an Assyrian inscription was found that mentions an Israelite payment dating from 797 /226/, and with this document we are almost in the generation of Amos whose prophetic activity is around 760. However, we are not going to deal with Israel's foreign and military policy, but with its domestic situation as it is sharply criticised by the prophet.

(1) Quite often the rich are townspeople, who indulge in drinking and lead a life of shameless luxury.
For urban residence one can refer to Am 6.1-8:

Shame on you who live at ease in Zion,
and you, untroubled on the hill of Samaria ...
I loathe the arrogance of Jacob [i.e., Israel],
I loathe his palaces [or, magnificient houses]:
city and all in it I will abandon to their fate.

The poetic text requires some explanation. The passage speaks of the capital of the northern Israelite kingdom, Samaria. It is situated on a small mound justifying the expression 'hill of Samaria'. The parallel term 'Zion' does not refer to Jerusalem as it does elsewhere, but is metaphorically applied to Samaria /227/. The prophet's 'shame on you' (the 'woe' of the older translations) is directed towards the rich who either live permanently in the capital or have an extra residence in town where they spend most of their time, far off from their landed property. (We know that Jeremiah was living in Jerusalem but had landed property at Anatot.) Another text which mentions the city is Am 4.1, where the prophet addresses the women; he says to them, "You cows of Bashan who live on the hill of Samaria, you who oppress the poor, and crush the destitute (etc.)". Comparing women to the well-fed cows of the Bashan region seems impolite as it violates our notion of female beauty, but in fact, even in the contemporary Near East, some well-to-do women do not care much for a slim body.

Open the book of Amos and you will find urban luxury and extravagance in almost every page: The rich have separate residences for winter and summer (3.15), built of fine ashlar stones (5.11); their furniture is decorated with beautiful carved work of ivory, now well-known from archaeological finds (3.15; 6.4). Amos 6.4 - "Shame on you who loll on beds inlaid with ivory and sprawl over your couches" - does not only attack wealth, but also 'la dolce vita'. On the later subject see also Am 2.7: "Father and son resort to the same girl." According to Amos, the rich spend most of their time feasting; their luxuriant parties are in temples (2.8) or private houses (6.4ff.). As for the temple parties, the expression "in the house of their god" is of particular interest: The parties take place in the temple of the clan's patron deity who is not necessarily identical with Israel's national god, Yahweh. This does not imply any prophetic criticism of some unorthodox cult; to be sure, Amos speaks in the name of Yahweh, but he does not encourage Yahweh-alone worship, the promotion of which rests with a small minority, possibly led by Hosea. What is needed for feasting is almost always referred to more than once. Wine takes the first place: 2.8; 4.1; 6.6. The last-named passage refers to the big cups used for drinking - the 'bowls' of the English translations imply some mild understatement. Am 4.1 quotes the command, "Bring us drink" addressed to husbands thus suggesting female dipsomania. In addition to wine we hear of "fatted calves" (5.22; 6.4), perfume (6.6), music and singing (5.23; 6.5). This refined banqueting, drinking and feasting culture is not confined to Samaria, of course; in the late eighth century it has its firm place in Isaiah's Jerusalem /228/. In this context Isaiah gives us a list of female jewelry and attire precious not only to the historian of culture; among its twenty-one items you can find familiar fancy articles such as ear-rings and necklaces but also lesser-known ones such as nose-rings and anklets. These women must have loved to load themselves with ornaments literally from head to foot! Some

122

commentators have suggested that Isaiah, the townsman, was more familiar with the details of luxury than Amos, the villager.

As for the provenance of luxury goods no more than an informed guess is possible. The fine ivory carvings of this period found at Samaria by archaeologists may be local work but reveal Phoenician style, and it is self-evident that the expensive ivory was imported /229/. Most probably, the craze for precious ornaments never died out in Israelite towns and was often influenced by foreign fashion. Nobody wants to be inferior to other countries' upper classes, and capable dealers succeed in selling their stock. Palestine, and especially its northern part, is very fertile and gets enough rain; since time immemorial wheat and olive oil have been exported to Tyre in exchange for timber /230/ and, possibly, all kinds of fashionable and beautiful smallware. One generation after Amos, when Israel finally loses the rest of its political independence, its crop goes to Assyria - now of course as a regular payment and hence without a corresponding economic return. Nothing but successive locust plagues prevent wealthy Samaria from paying its tribute - as a document of the Assyrian state archives reports /231/.

The upper class of the days of Amos and Isaiah shows all the features of Thorstein Veblen's 'Theory of the Leisure Class', a book originally meant to criticize the American aristocracy of money by revealing its affluent life style and preference of meaningless activities (such as sports, hunting and academic study) and unproductive professions (such as merchant and diplomat). The members of the leisure class or - to use an expression of the German Middle Ages - 'honourable idlers' (ehrbare Müßiggänger) do not produce anything, but rather consume according to the standards of conspicuous consumption, conspicuous waste and conspicuous leisure and pleasure. Consumption, extravagance and leisure are unlimited and constitute features of prestige or status symbols to be publicly displayed. The leisure class lives parasitically at the expense of the working class and does nothing but feast night and day. See Isa 5.11-12:

Shame on you! You rise early in the morning
to go in pursuit of liquor
and draw out the evening inflamed with wine,
at whose feasts there are harp and lute,
tabor and pipe and wine ...

And see Isa 56.12:

"Come", says each of them, "let me fetch wine,
strong drink, and we will drain it down;
let us make tomorrow like today,
or greater far!"

And again Amos:

Assemble on the hills of Samaria,
look at the tumult seething among her people ... (3.9)

(2) Landed property is often cultivated by small tenants
liabable to tax who are ruthlessly exploited by their landlords.
Amos reports more than once that the rich are taking
advantage of their debtors or tenants /232/, their poor
clientele. Am 2.8 must be translated as follows:

Men lie down beside every altar on blankets
seized in pledge,
and in the house of their (clan) god
they drink wine got by way of exaction.

Fine blankets and wine - basic requirements for temple
parties - are taken from debtors or tenants. Amos 4.1 - the
oppressive women's categorical "bring us drink!" - seems to
point to the same source of supply. Equally, Amos 5.11 refers
to payments of crop. According to the New English Bible, the
passage says: "Because you levy taxes on the poor and extort
a tribute of grain from them (etc.)", but a more accurate
translation may be, "Because you make tenants out of the
weak, and take tribute of corn from him" /233/. The same
passage explains what the landlords do with the extorted
riches: They build beautiful "houses of hewn stone" and plant
"pleasant vineyards" - possibly for letting them out on lease.
Investing income to open up new sources of gain is known
from the capable wife of Proverbs (Prov 31.16) and belongs to
the business of rich capital owners living on rents.

(3) Peasants overburdened with debts have to sell
themselves into bondage to work off their liabilities. The
bondsmen become serfs liable to tax - or they are even sold
and thus become real and permanent slaves.
This can be demonstrated on the basis of Am 2.6 and 8.6;
however, both texts have to be analyzed very carefully as the
standard translations are misleading. But as I have presented
the cultural background involved and all the arguments
elsewhere /234/, let me just state the results.
In an imagined speech the wealthy upper class people are

made to say, "Let us buy the poor because of silver (i.e., debts of money), the needy because of a pair of sandals" (Am 8.6). Two details require some explanation: How can you actually 'buy' a debtor, and what is the matter with the sandals? They are the reason for buying the debtor. The symbolic action of giving a sandal is a feature of concluding an agreement or a transaction; this is understood from Ruth 4.7 which says, "It was the custom for a man to pull off his sandal and give it to the other party. This was the form of attestation in Israel". The sandal given to one's partner is the pledge for transferred property. Hence, the Hebrew word 'na^{c}alayim' 'a pair of sandals' acquired the meaning of 'bond'. Applied to our passage of Amos: the poor man is being 'bought' because of a bond or obligation.

But what is the meaning of 'to buy'? The context states quite clearly how the poor met the rich: as customers of the grain merchants. Viewed from outside, the poor buy the merchant's grain, but actually it is the merchant who buys his clients, that is to say: he makes them dependent on him, so that they become his permanent debtors and bondsmen. In fact, this was felt by Luther who translated, "wir wollen die Dürfigen unter uns bringen", i.e, "Let us subjugate the needy". The text suggests just this. The poor cannot pay for the grain bought for consumption or sowing, run into debt, pile up interest payments, and end up with that slave-like bondage which is so characteristic of rent capitalism.

Moreover, the relationship between creditor and debtor attains its full harshness only in the exploitation-variety of rent capitalism. As long as the rich feels a patron's responsibility, such harshness does not arise. To have to borrow because of poverty is always humiliating, but under the patronage-system debtor and creditor stand within a network of mutual obligation and solidarity - the client being cared for by his patron, at least being prevented from starving. Once this network is broken, the creditor no longer acknowledges any responsibility for his debtor and uses him as a source of income. The debtor, always in a precarious situation, is now even more estranged and becomes a depersonalized object to be exploited. Since the law prohibiting the taking of interest belongs to the social legislation of the period of the exile, and thus to early Judaism /235/, it was incapable of protecting the debtor during the Israelite monarchy. Deut 23.21 - a passage attesting the prohibition - reveals the actual relation between creditor and debtor: originally, interest is not taken from someone who happens to be a stranger, but rather the person from whom one extracts interest is considered a stranger. Later, the practices used to get around the condemnation not only of usury but of any kind of interest are legion.

In Am 2.6 we can see how far the estrangement can go. The prophet reproaches his contemporaries for "selling the innocent because of silver (i.e., debts of money) and the poor because of a pair of sandals". In this case the poor are not bought but rather sold, cleared away by selling. They are not just reduced to being serfs or bondsmen but become slaves disjoined from their kinsmen who cannot buy them back any more /236/. What is the legal basis for such a sale? As a matter of fact, Israel's law as transmitted in the Bible does not provide any grounds for taking such action. On the other hand, exporting debtors to foreign countries is known from classical antiquity, namely from Rome and Greece. Its basis is easily understandable: to prevent the development of a poor and dependent class of proletarians in the community, debtors are disposed of by selling them abroad. Such deported persons are called 'innocent' by our prophet, the Hebrew 'ṣaddiq' possibly implying a legal context. Granted this assumption we may infer a court order and consider the deportation as a legal measure. The prophet seems to reproach a legal yet unfair and unjust sentence, which bestows material advantages on the wealthy demandant and does away with the insolvent and perhaps insubordinate bondsmen. The court pronouncing such sentence must not be imagined as a centralized royal institution of superior authority, for the Israelite legal system has always been decentralized and local, with the adult male members of village or town forming the forum for the administration of justice. Hence, the poor were at the mercy of the landed proprietors themselves.

(4) Along with rent and interest, the corn trade is another important source of income of the upper classes and strengthens their position in the economy.

Having repeatedly referred to one aspect of Am 8.4-6 we are now in the position to understand this passage as a whole. It reads:

Listen to this, you who grind the destitute
and plunder the humble,
you who say, "When will the new moon be over
so that we may sell corn?

When will the sabbath [i.e., full moon] be past
so that we may open our wheat again,
giving short measure in the bushel
and taking overweight in the silver
tilting the scales fraudulently,
and selling the dust of the wheat;
that we may buy the poor because of silver
    [i.e., debts of money]
and the destitute because of a pair of sandals?"

Amos is secretly listening to a (fictitious) speech which reveals the corn dealers' brutality and fraud. New moon and full moon - the latter not to be understood as the weekly sabbath of the exile period - appear to be days where shops are closed and no transactions possible. Impatiently thinking of their usurious and fraudulent business the corn dealers can hardly await the end of the holidays. In years of hard harvest the peasants are likely to buy grain to survive. Likewise, day labourers depend on buying corn. Prov 11.26 alludes to the practice of hoarding grain in seasons of scarcity in order to sell it at a high price:

He who withholds his grain is cursed by the people,
but he who sells his corn is blessed.

This proverb praises corn dealers who do not hold back their stock until starving customers are willing to pay any price demanded even for the worst quality - for they need food: for their family, themselves and perhaps for their cattle /237/.

In saying all this I am well aware that I am going slightly beyond the information given in the biblical sources. But read in the light of anthropology, the scattered bits of economic and social information fit into a definite and clear picture known as rent capitalism. Everything finds, so to speak, its natural place.

Chapter Five

THE MAKING OF MESSIANISM

S Solomon was anointed king by Zadok the priest and Nathan the prophet, so be thou anointed, blessed and consecrated Queen over the peoples whom the lord thy God hath given thee to rule and govern" /238/.

As the Archbishop of Canterbury pronounced these words in Westminster Abbey, he dipped his thumb into sweet-smelling oil /239/ and made the sign of the cross on the palms of both hands, the breast and the crown of the head of Princess Elizabeth seated before him. The presentation of the royal insignia, the crowning and the enthroning followed. In this way, on June 2, 1953 the twenty-seven year old Princess became Queen Elizabeth II of England.

There are other features besides the words solemnly pronounced at the anointing of a British monarch which show that this coronation closely corresponds to the consecration of Israelite kings. Both rituals also contain the presentation of the royal insignia, the new monarch's oath to maintain and defend the law of God, seating the monarch on the royal throne, a solemn blare of trumpets and roll of drums, and finally the people's shout of acclamation and assent, "Long live Queen Elizabeth" or "Long live King Solomon", respectively /240/.

The Hebrew word 'mashiach' is better known in its Greek transcription, Messiah, and literally means 'the anointed (or perfumed) one'. Referring to this ritual of royal coronation it is the solemn designation for an Israelite king.

A Messianic Monarchy

Israel's history begins with several centuries which lack even the idea of a messiah. During the periods of the nomadic or semi-nomadic patriarchs, Exodus, the conquest and Judges, dating perhaps from the 15th through the 11th centuries B.C., there is an ever-growing consciousness of solidarity among the Israelite tribes but no central and integrative political power. There is not even evidence of a wish or plan to create such an institution, or to sacralize it by a ritual of anointment. Judging from subsequent history there must have been some opposition to the idea. In the period of the Judges, when Abimelech claims the title of a kind of Shechem he is a petty monarch of a small town and a limited area who tries to imitate an established Canaanite pattern. This monarchic episode, however, seems to have lasted for no longer than three years (Jdg 9.22). A much larger territory centering in the tribal lands of Ephraim and Benjamin is governed by King Saul (ca. 1030-1000 B.C.). Later tradition takes Saul to be the first king of Israel, calling him by the title of messiah and reporting his solemn anointment /241/. Without doubt, this is legendary embellishment. Saul is neither king of all the tribes of northern Palestine nor does he claim any sacred status for his position.

The appearance of David (1000-970) marks the end of the pre-monarchic and early monarchic periods. He is the actual creator of a centralized political power in Palestine. A successful military leader, he first becomes king of Judah in southern Palestine, and, shortly thereafter, of Israel in northern Palestine as well. The report about David's accession to kingship mentions a ritual of anointment which seems, however, not a religious ceremony but a feature of solemn etiquette, carried out by the landed nobility and not by priests (2 Sam 2.4; 5.3). If a ritual framework is provided by the temple of Hebron, scene of the accession, it is not explained by the source. Solomon's accession to the throne of David (ca. 970) carries the reference to an elaborate ritual led by a priest. This occasion may be called the hour when messianism is born. The climax of the ritual (the details of which are indicated in 1 Kgs 1) is the anointment with aromatic oil. This anointing is thought of as an act of consecration that establishes a special relationship between the king and Israel's national god. According to one biblical view, the anointment bestows the spirit of god ("breath of Yahweh") upon the king and thus endows him with particular vitality and talents of leadership /242/. The formula employed in the ritual says, "I anoint you king over Israel (or Judah)" or "Yahweh anoints you prince over his inheritance", and may be continued by phrases such as, "You shall rule the people of Yahweh and deliver them from the enemies round about them" (2 Kgs 9.3; 1 Sam 10.1). These phrases indicate what is expected from the new messiah. Scattered passages, which may reflect the coronation liturgy of Jerusalem, give us more information about the anointed king's prestige, his position in theology and the way in which royal office is understood. The messiah is taken to be immune and tabooed and hence neither to be judged nor touched by anyone (1 Sam 24.7). He is his people's "breath of life" and source of blessing (Lam 4.20). He should be a gifted military leader and victor in the battle against Israel's enemies (Ps 2.8-9; Isa 9.3ff), and in his own kingdom, there should be an impartial and effective administration of justice (Ps 72.2.12ff; Isa 11.3ff). His government is expected to bring prosperity and peace portrayed as follows:

> The people of Judah and Israel were countless as the sand of the sea; they ate and they drank, and enjoyed life. Solomon ruled over all the kingdoms from the river Euphrates to Philistia and as far as the frontier of Egypt; they paid tribute and were subject to him all his life. (...) and he enjoyed peace on all sides. All through his reign Judah and Israel continued at peace, every man under his own vine and fig-tree, from Dan to Beersheba. (1 Kgs 4.20-21.24-25)

The king can even be called 'god' or 'son of god', expressions which are rather irritating to scholars who favour a monotheistic reading of Ps 2.7 and Isa 9.5. Unfortunately, the precise meaning of these terms in the framework of Hebrew mythology escapes us. How can it be that the king is the son of Yahweh, a god without a consort? Does the king in some mystical way come forth from Yahweh's mouth as is the case with the figure of Hokhmah (Wisdom) in Sir 24.3? Or is divine kinship a pre-existent form created in the remote past and realized in each individual monarch (cf. Ps 110.3)? Whatever its background such rhetoric is deeply rooted in polytheism, and obedient theologians, poets and prince-pleasers of the court never hesitate to use it for the greater glory of their lord. Yahweh-aloneists, of course, either oppose such rhetoric or prefer a different reading. To them it is an ornate and grand court style which does not imply the king's divine nature but rather his adoption by god, his status as Yahweh's vassal, his kingship 'by divine grace'. Mono-yahwistic orthodoxy can only conceive of a king who is strictly subordinated to god. Without altogether abandoning the rhetoric of polytheism, they 'sterilize' the ideology from which it is derived. The old vocabulary survives - in the form of cut flowers which are beautiful but without life.

The psalms quoted may reflect, or even form part of, the coronation service, whereas Isa 8.23-9.6 is Isaiah's political 'cradle song' presented either at the birth or at the coronation of King Hezekiah of Judah, who ascended the throne while still a child (733 or 728 B.C.) /243/. All texts mentioned are from the southern kingdom, Judah, and give evidence for a messianic theology accompanying the Davidic monarchy until the destruction of Jerusalem in 586 B.C. Whether or not the northern kingdom of Israel, which ends in 721, practices anointment in its (assumed) coronation ritual, is difficult to decide. There is only one report of anointment of a northern monarch, but it is legendary and historically doubtful (King Jehu: 2 Kgs 9.6). Although the kings of northern Israel may not have been bearers of the messianic title, there can be no doubt about the existence of a royal ideology comparable to that of the south. The kings of Israel must have been thought of as no less divine or divinely elected than their southern colleagues.

The ambitious messianic theology outlined thus far implies that the king consecrated in a ritual of anointment and actually reigning is 'the messiah'. Even though texts which speak of the messiah as the reigning monarch were often read as prophecies of the Christ, their royal character has never been forgotten. In late antiquity and in the early Middle Ages, ritual anointing became the climax of royal coronations both in Byzantium and the West. Moreover, the idea of kingship by divine grace was made one of the foundations of a political theory that was to be influential until the 20th century, and is still alive in countries which adopt a royal constitution.

In order to assess the value messianic theology had in biblical times, we must look at ancient political reality. As is often the case, claim and reality do not coincide. Time and again, royal Israel enjoys brightest periods, even national revivals. However, the Israelite and Judaean kingdoms lead a comparatively humble and unpretentious life in the shadow of the much stronger Aramaean empire and the even more impressive Assyrian and Babylonian superpowers. It is from control by these larger powers that they try to liberate themselves through endless political maneuvering. Even if the idea of the messiah's universal rule is taken to imply the more realistic aim of a peaceful and unmolested political existence, it generally remains wishful thinking. The oldest representation of an Israelite king, now on display in the British Museum and available as a postcard, shows King Jehu kissing the dust in front of his Assyrian overlord, Shalmaneser (841 B.C.) /244/. Yet we are not solely dependent on extra-biblical sources for facts. The biblical authors must be praised for not messianically glorifying the kings of Israel. For facts of political history, the Bible is generally quite reliable. On the other hand, accounts of religious history, in which biblical writers take much more interest, must be as carefully evaluated as any other party document.

The Messianic Politics of the Royalist Party

In the summer of 586 B.C., the era of the monarchy (and hence, messianism) comes to an end. For a long time, the petty kingdom of Judah had to be content with the modest role of a tribute-paying vassal. Now, even domestic kingship becomes a victim of foreign rule. Babel puts an end to home rule and integrates the territory of its former vassal into its system of provinces. The biblical account of the Judaean monarchy ends with a proudly told, yet humble scene, bare of any messianic pretensions. The last living ex-king of Jerusalem is released from prison and made the honorary chairman of the petty kings deported to Babel (2 Kgs 25.27-30). How modest have they become! And what a poor rehabilitation of a king who had to atone for a rule of three months with thirty-seven years in jail! The dream of a messiah's universal rule, so convincingly sung in Psalms 2 and 72, is over, unmasked as unrealistic enthusiasm, forever refuted by firm political facts.

The unrealistic expectations of the royalist restoration party include the return of the exiles soon after the destruction of Jerusalem, and an immediate resurrection of the monarchy. To this group belong anonymous circles to

132

whom we owe such additions to prophetic literature as Jer 33.14-26 (and possibly Am 9.11), and especially prophets Ezekiel and Haggai. Writing in exile in Babylonia, Ezekiel develops a royal constitution for the resurrected state, which will be ruled by a figure without actual political power, thus filling the position of a mayor and a patron of the cult. While one hesitates to call Ezekiel's imagined king a messiah, Haggai is too explicit to allow for such scruples. He is a contemporary of Zerubbabel, a Persian governor of Davidic descent who, in 520 B.C., lays the foundation stone of the new temple of Jerusalem, which was to be completed within a few years' time. Like many other Jews, the prophet is not satisfied with a Persian governor, though a native and even of royal lineage. The upheavals which follow the death of the Persian king, Cambyses, prompt the prophet's expectation of a cataclysm which would restore Israel and the house of David to unchallenged pre-eminence. He takes Zerubbabel, the governor, to be qualified to ascend the throne. Haggai does not apply the messianic title to him but calls him the chosen servant of Yahweh and god's own "signet ring" (Hag 2.23) which, however, amounts to very much the same /245/. Unfortunately, the biblical documents do not tell us what happened to the messianic movement of the year 520 B.C. The only thing we know is that Judah did not become a monarchy nor Zerubbabel a king.

Zerubbabel disappears from the scene, leaving no line of Davidic kings, but only the restored temple as the legacy of his short leadership. Judah remains in Persian hands, and a note of disappointment is heard in the statement that "the whole world is still at peace" (Zech 1.11). Two generations later, the royalists seem to have another candidate for the messianic office, again a member of the Davidic lineage. His office of governor, however, seems to offend their sense of pride rather than satisfy it. This governor's name is Nehemiah /246/. Around 440 B.C., he denies any basis to rumours of his royal ambitions, or of prophets hired to proclaim his accession (Neh 6.6ff).

The royalism of the exilic and post-exilic periods, which must have flourished, although hardly represented in our sources, is the second type of messianism. This movement of dissatisfied conservatives has precise yet unrealizable objectives: to restore Judah as a state, to re-establish political independence, to re-introduce monarchy, and to give the royal office, if possible, to a descendant of the Davidic dynasty dethroned in 586 B.C. (Such descendants seem to have been available until the fourth century B.C. when the royal lineage disappears /247/.)

The Non-Messianic Idea of Religion

While royalism does not succeed, another movement does. Indeed, by renouncing political ambitions, the 'ecclesiocrats' /248/ are the most successful of all groups, and their approach shapes even the modern concept of religion. This group rejects the idea of an independent Jewish state governed by a native ruler, in order to conserve and maintain the traditional (or supposedly traditional) Jewish way of life. Jewish identity should be safeguarded by a flourishing ritual life at the Jerusalem temple, by common holy days, customs and, not least, by the office of the high priest conceived of as a religious rather than a political institution. The Jewish religious community, dicovered, or indeed, created by the ecclesiocratic movement, seems to provide enough protection against the threat of disintegration, assimilation and absorption into the pagan way of life. They make their peace with the heathen over-lord and his political régime, and as loyal subjects they are willing to 'pay Caesar what is due to Caesar', as long as he grants the free practice of Jewish religion. The ecclesiocrats are so loyal that they can distinguish the high priest of Jerusalem with both royal anointing and the traditional vestments of the king /249/ without being accused of illegal royalistic machinations by non-Jewish authorities. Unlike a king, a priest cannot be dangerous to imperial power. The most extreme expression of ecclesiocratic loyalty toward the régime is Deutero-Isaiah's use of the messianic title for the Persian overlord, Cyrus (Isa 45.1). For a Jewish royalist, it would be utterly impossible to call a non-Jew, and indeed someone who does not worship Yahweh, the messiah! /250/

The Apocalyptic Renaissance of Messianism

After 586 B.C. there is no longer a royal messiah in Israel. There are, it is true, royal or quasi-royal episodes. In the second century B.C., the Hasmoneans establish themselves as a ruling Jewish dynasty and, between 104 and 63 B.C., claim the title of king. The succeeding dynasty of the Herodians owes its rulership to the Romans, yet is able to determine the fate of Palestinian Judaism for almost a century. The famous founder of this house, Herod the Great (37-4 B.C.), is proud of his royal title bestowed upon him by the Senate of Rome in

40 B.C., several years before he succeeds in actually ruling his people. Some of his successors maintain the royal title though ruling over no more than small sections of the kingdom divided by Herod between his sons. In short, there are kings of Israel after 586, but none of them enjoys full support of all subjects and none of them receives the traditional messianic consecration.

None of these kings is able to live up to the now developing new model of messiah and the exaggerated expectations it implies. Now, a Jewish messiah is not only expected to be the royal head of a re-established separate state for the Jews, but also the head of a real universal kingdom. To found such an empire is far beyond the powers of Jewish rebels, of course, who form anti-Seleucid or, later, anti-Roman leagues. This leads to expectations of divine intervention which, by angelic help in war, should lead to victory and establishment of a universal and eternal empire. This ideology, which implies the end of the prevailing political régime in the very near future, emerges in the second century B.C. and is known as apocalypticism. This period sees the rise of a completely new messianic idea.

The earliest sources for this 'apocalyptic messianism' are some manuscripts belonging to a Jewish sect whose library was discovered in the neighbourhood of Qumran at the Dead Sea. Sometime between about 140 and 120 B.C., a number of pious Jews defect from the Hasmonean rulers, form a sect, and withdraw to the desert to prepare themselves for the expected new order. One of the reasons for its segregation and its uncompromising opposition to Hasmonean rule is the dynasty's apparent desecration of the high priestly office. One one hand, the Hasmoneans have liberated the office from heathen (Seleucid) influence, but on the other hand, they do not restore it in a manner many Jews consider legitimate. The Hasmoneans commit the crime of keeping this office in their own hands, combining it with political leadership so that Hasmonean rulers are political and religious leaders at the same time. The Qumran people do not object to a royal arrogation of priestly functions as such, but rather to an arrogation of a priestly office by a dynasty which is not of the line of Zadok. The sectarians are not the only ones challenging royal policy /251/, it is true, but it is their criticism which has left its mark on the earliest design of apocalyptic messianism. The imaged universal empire would not be ruled by one, but by two persons who share in the messianic office /252/. In other words, they expect two messiahs instead of one. One messiah will be responsible for the restored temple ritual and will be head of the priesthood and the whole nation as well. The other messiah will be a layman responsible for administrative and military matters. As bearer of the royal title he would not be subordinate to the high priest, but the sources indicate that he is conceived of as a messiah of slightly lower rank. In certain situations, e.g., at benediction before a solemn meal /253/, even the common priest is of higher rank than the royal (i.e. lay) messiah. Without a doubt, this extremely high esteem of the priestly office is due to the fact that the anonymous founder or reformer of the sect, known as the 'Teacher of Righteousness', was himself a high priest.

One of the most important and certainly most difficult problems of Qumran doctrine is finding the proper incumbents for the two messianic offices. For the pre-eschatological period, i.e. the present, the sect renounces messianic leadership and leaves decision-making to a council of members. But how can the beginning of eschaton and universal empire which require messianic leadership, be determined? The sectarian theologians' answer is that a prophet would have to appear. He would present two men, without doubt members of the community, for the messianic offices and probably anoint them as well. The first element in the series of eschatological events would be the awaking of prophetic charisma, which should hoist the flag of messianism. Many sectarian rules apply only "until there shall come the prophet and the messiahs from Aaron and Israel" /254/; however, a Utopian constitution for the messianic age was found among the Qumran parchments /255/.

It should be evident that there is a great difference between the apocalyptic expectation of a messiah and the older royal messianism with its strong political orientation. Certainly, both have their roots in pre-exilic royal ideology, building their own ideologies on its textual repertoire. Yet, while messianic politics pursues aims which seem within reach, at least theoretically, apocalypticism hopes beyond realism and expects a future for Israel which will, in the eschatological process of events, blend with the future of mankind. Later and less enthusiastic forms of messianism remain within the apocalyptic, i.e. universal, pattern. When Church and Synagogue incorporate the apocalyptic expectation of a messiah into their creeds, they renounce the ambitions of the royalist as well as the short timetable of the apocalyptic movement. By doing so, they transform the messiah from a figure of political debate, passion and hope into one of dogmatic reflection and speculation, which loses much of its former vitality. Apocalyptic messianiam develops into what may be called dogmatic messianism. Dogmatic messianism's central figure is pale and shadowy and is far removed from the present. God's judgement, along with the ending of this world, is no longer imminent. It is an event veiled in the darkness of a distant future centering around a figure reached only by dogmatic imagination /256/. As is clear from Christian and Jewish history, messianic belief can, however, always change from dogmatic assertion into vital if not violent political practice, as witness the Jewish messiahs, Bar Kochba and Sabbetai Zwi in the 2nd and 17th centuries A.D., and the impressive number of Christian sects which live in expectation of an imminent end of the world and the Christ's advent.

Chapter Six

FROM PROPHET TO SCRIBE:
CHARISMATIC AUTHORITY IN EARLY JUDAISM

The Eclipse of Prophecy

IN the religious history which is reflected in the Bible we can observe how an older religion gives birth to a younger one and how the younger system gradually supplants the other. Since the beginning of the nineteenth century critical scholarship has been preoccupied with differentiating between what is called Israelite religion and Judaism and with describing both their dissimilarities and partial continuity. A short account may read as follows: Israelite religion, documented mainly from the tenth to the sixth centuries B.C., is characterized by polytheism and prophecy. Besides the state deity, Yahweh, the 'god of hosts', a host of other gods and goddesses are worshipped, some of whom, including Yahweh, have their human spokesmen who, whether convenient or inconvenient, comment on current affairs in oracular form.

Judaism, on the other hand, is monotheistic and soon replaces the old personal name of its god by 'the Lord' or simply 'God'; as the only existing divinity he does not need a proper name any more. This deity no longer communicates its will in the form of oracles that deal with concrete and specific issues of the day which hardly lend themselves to generalization. Now, the will of god consists of a body of doctrine, the timeless nature of which is soon acknowledged. In some cases, this doctrine is not explicitly laid down in sacred literature but can be identified by exegetical technique. The most prominent feature of worship at the synagogue is recitation of biblical texts followed by an exposition which explains Jewish doctrine and practice and relates them to contemporary issues and day-to-day life. Polytheism and prophecy are replaced by monotheism and 'scribes' or scholars. The historical watershed is the

Babylonian Exile of the sixth century. It is then that the proto-Jewish doctrine of an earlier minority, the best representatives of which are Hosea and the book of Deuteronomy, gains influence and becomes the nucleus of a developing new religion.

The formative phase of Judaism, so-called Early Judaism, extends from the Babylonian Exile of the sixth century B.C. to the first century A.D. During these six-hundred years that Judaism emerges which still flourishes in our days. In the earlier years of that period, prophets are still very active, and Deutero-Isaish's first unequivocal statement of monotheism is decisive for the development of doctrine. Later, when belief in a future Kingdom of God, resurrection and eternal life emerges, there are no more prophets at work but scholars, who find evidence for their new teachings in the old Scriptures. They have no new word of god, and no one expects it. In the sixth century B.C., Jeremiah and Ezekiel are approached by people asking them for a 'word of Yahweh'; in the first century A.D., Paul is asked to explain Scripture in the Synagogue /257/. Jeremiah and Ezekiel are prophets, Paul is a doctor of law.

Unfortunately, our fragmentary sources do not permit us to see even the outlines of a history and sociology of scriptural scholarship in Early Judaism. Likewise, no satisfactory account of the eclipse of prophecy is available. However, a possible clue is the book of Deuteronomy which dates from the seventh and sixth centuries. In this document, the proto-Jewish or Yahweh-alone movement sets up its statutes in the form of a textbook which is a catechism and a legal code at the same time. Morton Smith's view is as follows:

> Malachi is the last of the preserved books of the prophets, therefore much has been written about the cessation of prophecy at this time. However, it was not prophecy which ceased. There were still prophets in Nehemiah's day and in the days of the Maccabees. What ceased was the preservation, by the Yahweh-alone party, of new collections of prophecies. The party had begun preserving prophecies as documents in support of its position during its battle for control of the Judean government in the Assyrian period. The fulfillment of the political prophecies of Jeremiah, Ezekiel, and Second Isaiah had doubtless been used as 'proof' of their theological pronouncements, so their prophecies were collected and preserved as propaganda to further the

growth of the party in the diaspora. Now, however, the essential position had been formulated in deuteronomic law and its consequences worked out in the deuteronomic histories. The works of the prophets already preserved gave these ample support. What was needed now was not further prophecy but practical application. /258/

This is plausible, but perhaps one can even go beyond the view of Morton Smith in saying that prophets are not only irrelevant, but inconvenient and undesired. The programme of Deuteronomy is modelled on the political bureaucracy developed by the Assyrians and Babylonians who managed to control a vast empire with a network of vassal treaties /259/. Deuteronomy translates political loyalty into religious belief in general and into acknowledgement of the only god in particular. Further, what has been determined by bureaucracy will hardly allow for prophetic manipulation and intervention. As the Assyrians suspect prophets to be inciters of political rebellion, so Deuteronomy treats them as possible agents of foreign gods /260/, making it almost a norm that 'the only good prophet is a dead prophet'.

It is therefore hardly surprising to see that the latest prophecy which achieves canonical status in Judaism - namely Malachi and Joel - is ideologically close to Deuteronomy /261/. Before prophetic charisma dries up, it bows to the Law - in order to disappear soon. It seems that temple prophecy, which still flourishes in the days of Jeremiah, is not successfully re-established after the exile. One day, temple prophecy disappears or, rather, loses its distinctive features by being incorporated into the temple choir /262/. The place of the prophets is taken by figures standing, as it seems, closer to bureaucracy - the scribes /263/.

Unfortunately, we know only two scholars active in pre-rabbinical times, Ezra and Jesus Sirach. We have many questions concerning these men: (1) To which social stratum do they belong? (2) Which area of learning is the focus of their interest? (3) Do their activities, besides studying, also include writing and publishing? (4) Are they interested in political leadership? (5) Do they form a distinctive professional group or 'class'? (6) Can we say anything about their particular theology? (7) What kind of religious authority do they claim or actually wield? With these questions in mind we will now turn our attention to Ezra and Jesus Sirach.

Ezra and the 'Community of Exiles'

Ezra is the first Jew our sources call a scriptural scholar or 'sofer', i.e. a 'scribe'. The traditional date of his appearance in history is 458 B.C., a year which also figures in the annals of a people living at the other end of the ancient world. In that year a certain Cincinnatus, while working in his fields, was surprised by the call to Roman dictatorship. While the early Roman republic was striving for political and military identity, another people, living at the opposite end of the same world, was creating a quite different kind of identity, that of a religious community, Judaism, which looks back to the eclipse of its political commonwealth. Cincinnatus is a farmer and a statesman, Ezra is priest and scholar.

The sources available for Ezra's story are the books of Ezra and Nehemiah which close the long series of Hebrew historiography. Chronologically, this history writing ends with the account of events that happen in the fifth century B.C., events which establish a new cultural and religious situation for which modern authors introduce a new name, that of Judaism. Thus we read about the temple community of Jerusalem, hear of immigrants and donations coming from the diaspora, of protection and privileges granted by Persian authorities, of a public service of worship anticipating features of the later synagogue, of a legal code brought by a scribe, of the prohibition of mixed marriages with non-Jews, of a strict observance of sabbath, and of Jewish holy days. The protagonists who often autobiographically report in the first person are Ezra and Nehemiah. They both come to Jerusalem from the Babylonian diaspora, their missions being authorized by royal Persian authorities. Despite the institution they find in full function - a restored temple with a priesthood celebrating the daily ritual of sacrifices - they appear to be the great reformers if not actual 'founders' of post-exilic Judaism.

Looking for the historical Ezra, the scribe, we must, however, free ourselves from the exaggerations and misrepresentations of both biblical and modern authors. Basing their views on Jewish apocryphal literature, Muslim polemicists and writers of the European Enlightenment have often taken Ezra to be the compiler or redactor of the Pentateuch; thus again Ernst Bloch in his 'Atheism in Christianity' who counts Ezra among whose who shaped Judaism by deliberately suppressing older and anti-theocratic traditions, some traces of which can be detected by rigorous criticism /264/. Yet, there is no such information in the Book of Ezra; it simply reports that Ezra, coming from the diaspora, brings a legal code, possibly some edition of the Book of Deuteronomy /265/, and is an expert on Jewish religious law. Of a younger date is the assumption that Ezra must have been a Persian 'secretary of the state in charge of Jewish affairs'. This reading of Ezra's official title as 'scribe' (sofer) or 'scribe of the Law of the God of Heaven' goes back to H. H. Schaeder's work published in 1930, and enjoys some circulation still today; it has recently been repeated by Siegfried Herrmann in his 'History of Israel in Old Testament Times' /266/. Most authors rightly reject this interpretation as improbable as there is no evidence for such a position in the Persian government. In order to advance to Ezra as a historical figure we must say good-bye to the functionary of the Persian Empire as well as to the editor of the Pentateuch.

Yet even then we have not arrived at our destination. Rather, we have to remove another layer of misjudgement and distortion, due not to modern authors but to the compiler of the biblical account. The Chronicler's Ezra is characterized by at least three traits which are unhistorical:

(1) The Chronicler makes him a contemporary to another important figure of early post-exilic Judaism, Nehemiah. By interweaving and editing his sources, he creates the image of two independent characters whose periods of activity in Jerusalem alternate and intersect, yet on one occasion he even joins them together in a scene of public worship (Neh 8). Modern critics prefer to place Ezra and Nehemiah in two different generations of the fifth century.

(2) The Chronicler makes Ezra appear to be the great reformer of the temple community of Jerusalem and Palestinian Judaism as a whole. He invents the image of a Jewish Martin Luther who reforms or, indeed, creates the community on the basis of God's Word, the Torah. True Judaism is where the Torah is properly preached and its precepts realized in practice. The sources at the Chronicler's disposal, however, do not lend themselves to such interpretation. In fact, there is clear evidence for the limited nature of Ezra's mission and influence. Far from addressing all the Jews living in Jerusalem or Judea, he is concerned with a small group occasionally referred to as the 'bene haggolah', the 'sons of the exile' or members of the Jerusalem Association of Exiles /267/. Whereas the Chronicler presents a monolithic Jewish community, the unedited text knows of a

greater variety and mentions at least two distinct groups, the community of those who had returned from Babylonia, and those natives and residents of Jerusalem who never had left their home country. The community of families who had been living in Babylonia forms a separate group with a spirit of solidarity and an organization which, according to evidence, is lacking or less developed in the native community. One of the arguments for this view is philological: just as the Book of Nehemiah calls the members of certain professional guilds the 'sons of the goldsmiths' or 'sons of the perfumers' /268/, the designation 'sons of the golah' is the name of the Association of Exiles, without doubt a kind of ethnic community /269/ of Jews formerly living in Babylonia.

(3) More than once the Chronicler associates Ezra, the priest, with Levites as his associates; they are, in fact, presented as his assistants in teaching the Torah. For the Chronicler, the Levites are religious instructors; long before the exile, and quite anachronistically, he has King Jeho-shaphat send these men like apostles to the towns of Judah to instruct the people in the Torah: "They taught in Judah, having with them the book containing the law of Yahweh; they travelled through all the cities of Judah and taught among the people" (2 Chr 17.9). However, such operation is unlikely to have occurred in the ninth or fifth century B.C.; rather, it seems to reflect an event or institution of the Chronicler's own time, i.e. the third century. For the subject of the present chapter, early Jewish scholarship, these preaching experts of the Law would certainly be of great interest; yet the history and function of the Levites belong to the unsolved riddles of biblical research.

After these introductory remarks about Ezra as seen by some scholars and as seen by the Chronicler, i.e. about some misrepresentations of this figure, I will be dealing with what can be historically ascertained with some confidence.

(1) Ezra belongs to the Jewish priestly aristocracy and is introduced with a genealogy of seventeen generations (Ezra 7.1-5). His high position in society is underscored by the fact that he has a firman issued to him by the Persian government. On the other hand, he seems to be boasting when he assures us that he would have been able to claim military escort from Babylonia, where he resides, to Palestine:

> I would have been ashamed to ask the king for troops and horsemen to protect us against enemies along the way, since we had said to the king, "The favouring hand of our

God is upon all who seek him, but his mighty wrath is against all who forsake him". (Ezra 8.22)

Saying this he wants to underline his position in an effective way - and, indeed, succeeds in misleading those modern scholars who take him to be a high functionary of the Persian Empire.

(2) Ezra is an extremely learned man who speaks both Hebrew and the official language of the Persian empire, Aramaic. He is introduced as a "scribe, well-versed in the law of Moses which was given by Yahweh the God of Israel", and instead of 'scribe' we can translate 'scholar'. The Aramaic firman he bears repeats and acknowledges this title by calling him "Ezra the priest, scribe of the law of the God of Heaven" /270/. This title suggests his status as a scholar and an authority on Jewish law which clearly underlies all his activities in Jerusalem. According to Ezra 7.10 he is a distinguished teacher: "Ezra had set his heart on the study and practice of the law of Yahweh and on teaching statutes and ordinances in Israel." The Persian document as well as the whole account presuppose that Ezra is armed with a legal code, that is to say that a scroll is part of his luggage. He is a man of letters.

(3) Moreover, he is a writer, author of an autobiographical report about his mission to Jerusalem. We do not know how long this document was and how to account for the alternation of passages in the first and third person; perhaps it is due to some literary convention. While one has to allow for some editing by the Chronicler, there is no reason for doubting the authenticity and general reliability of the document.

(4) Writing is, however, not Ezra's main concern. In the first place he is a man of action who is an outstanding organizer and impressive charismatic leader. In Babylonia, he raises a caravan of some 1,500 returnees, women and children left uncounted - if this figure is not exaggerated. This caravan transports huge treasures which include, among other things, a hundred talents of gold (i.e. at least 300 kgs), as a donation to the Jerusalem temple. Upon arrival in Jerusalem and at the local 'golah' community, he almost immediately succeeds in establishing a kind of personal charismatocracy, while the actual leaders of the community figure only on the periphery and even as delinquents. In Jerusalem, one has never seen anything like this. Taking up a phrase of the New

Testament one may somewhat anachronistically say that Ezra 'teaches with authority and not like the scribes'. He preaches and admonishes in a way that makes his audience burst into tears on more than one occasion; he succeeds in dissolving more than one hundred marriages with non-Jewish women, the names of the men guilty of the crime being written down in a list (the problem is not so much the mixed marriage itself but rather the 'dangerous' and possibly 'corrupting' relations with non-Jewish families); he has people celebrate holy days hitherto unknown; on a large square outside the Water Gate he builds a wooden platform from which he reads the Law to the congregation, possibly for hours. Omitting, with the New American Bible, the Chronicler's additions, the report on the latter event, a landmark in the history of liturgy, reads as follows:

> On the first day of the seventh month Ezra the priest brought the law before the assembly, which consisted of men, women, and those children old enough to understand. Standing at one end of the open place that was before the Water Gate he read out of the book from daybreak till midday, in the presence of the men, the women, and those children old enough to understand; and all the people listened attentively to the book of the law. Ezra the scribe stood on a wooden platform that had been made for the occasion; at his right side stood Mattithiah, Shema, Anaiah, Uriah, Hilkiah, and Maaseiah, and on his left Pedaiah, Mishael, Malchiah, Hashum, Hashbaddanah, Zechariah, Meshullam. Ezra opened the scroll so that all the people might see it (for he was standing higher up than any of the people); and, as he opened it, all the people rose. Ezra blessed Yahweh, the great God, and all the people, their hands raised high, answered, "Amen, amen!" Then they bowed down and prostrated themselves before Yahweh, their faces to the ground. (...) Ezra read plainly from the book of the law of God, interpreting it so that all could understand what was read. Then (...) Ezra the priest-scribe (...) said to all the people: "Today is holy to Yahweh your God. Do not be sad, and do not weep" - for all the people were weeping as they heard the words of the law. He said further: "Go, eat rich foods and drink sweet drinks, and allot portions to those who had nothing prepared; for today is holy to Yahweh. Do not be saddened this day, for rejoicing in Yahweh must be your strength!" (...) Then all the people went to eat and drink, to distribute

portions, and to celebrate with great joy, for they understood the words that had been expounded to them. (Neh 8.2-12)

This is the first 'liturgy of the word' on record in history. Ezra imports this kind of worship from the diaspora where it must have been practised for many years. Unfortunately, the text gives no information about the regularity of such events, but it makes sense to suppose that they were more frequent than is prescribed by Deuteronomy, i.e. every seventh year (Deut 31.9-13). One particular feature is worth noting: the 'interpretation' of the law. The Hebrew term is ambiguous and may refer to either translation or explanation. I do not think that Ezra was preaching in the way it became customary in the later synagogue. There was another, and more elementary, problem. The people belonging to the exilic community were speaking Aramaic, a language they had adopted in Babylonia, rather than the Hebrew spoken by the Jews of Palestine which was also the language of the Torah. Thus it seems more likely that Ezra translated the Hebrew text into the Aramaic vernacular of the exilic community. The concluding statement that the people were pleased "for they understood the words" echoes both the interpreter's pride of his achievement and the joy of listening to Aramaic spoken in public, which cannot fail to strengthen the feeling of belonging together.

(5) Is it possible to speak about Ezra in terms of an established role which he represents or an office he holds? The best approach to this problem is to analyze the final passage of Ezra's royal Persian firman. It reads:

As for you, Ezra, in accordance with the wisdom of your God which is in your possession, appoint magistrates and judges to administer justice to all the people in West-of-Euphrates, to all, that is, who know /271/ the laws of your God. Instruct those who do not know these laws. Whoever does not obey the law of your God and the law of the king, let strict judgement be executed upon him, whether death, or corporal punishment, or a fine on his goods, or imprisonment. (Ezra 7.25-26)

The correct interpretation of these lines, viz. that they are not referring to the 'golah'-community of Jerusalem, was first suggested by Hugo Mantel. Throughout Babylonia and in Jerusalem there are Jewish 'golah'-communities which enjoy certain privileges granted by Persian authorities, such as limited self-government and autonomous jurisdiction. Mantel compares and even assimilates these communities to the guilds of weavers, merchants, boatmen, potters, bakers etc. of the Babylonian and Achaemenid world, guilds which have their own magistrates and leaders and determine the political, social and religious life of their members. This comparison may not be valid /272/. However, there is evidence for the relative autonomy and self-government of some ethnic minorities living in a foreign environment /273/. The constitution of the golah-communities seems to reflect an ordinance of the Jewish legal tradition, viz. Deut 16.18. This passage reads:

> You shall appoint judges and officials throughout your tribes to administer true justice for the people in all the communities which Yahweh, your god, is giving you.

Other texts such as Deut 13.1-19 and 17.1-7 indicate how Deuteronomy conceives of the local court's main task: as the control of religious orthodoxy, control which should even penetrate into marriage and family. This is the beginning of a development which involves far-reaching consequences such as the formation of the concepts of orthodoxy, religious discipline, control of belief and practice, which again lead to and are embodied in institutions such as church visitation, inquisition, censorship of books, eccelesiastical permission to teach, etc.

While Ezra is authorized to establish autonomous Jewish communities in West-of-Euphrates and furnish them with a magistracy, he cannot claim any legal authority nor pass sentence in Jerusalem. There, he can only 'investigate', because there is an autonomous 'golah'-community already, which, however, does not follow the strict pattern of Babylonian Jewry - at least according to people such as Ezra. For the Babylonian communities, this is intolerable as diaspora Judaism (unto this day) considers Jerusalem to be the symbolic centre of the Jewish world. Hence, corrective measures must be taken - and Ezra is the self-appointed reformer who will set things in order.

In Jerusalem, he lacks the authority of a judge who could give orders, but he can claim the charismatic authority of a teacher and leader, that is, he depends entirely on the power of persuasion and personality, never on compulsion. When informed of the intermarriages, he does not report that he 'summoned the guilty and asked them for an explanation', but rather:

When I had heard this thing, I tore my cloak and my mantle, plucked hair from my head and beard, and sat there stupefied. Around me gathered all who were in dread of the sentence of the god of Israel on this apostasy of the exiles, while I remained motionless until the evening sacrifice. (Ezra 9.3-4)

This is not the way a judge or an official, backed by a mandate, behaves, but the manner of a charismatic whose success depends on the creation of dramatic scenes.

Unfortunately, the Chronicler leaves out the story of extra-Palestinian Judaism; that is why we do not know whether and how Ezra fulfills the second part of his mission, the establishment of other 'golah'-communities outside of Palestine. Apparently, he leaves Jerusalem after a short visit of no more than a few months, in order to disappear in that dark of history which is not illuminated by documentary evidence.

While Ezra's further fate escapes us, the final passage of his Persian firman quoted earlier tells us something about his office and origin. He comes from a Babylonian 'golah'-community which is administrated by office-holders such as magistrates, judges and - this is not explicitly mentioned, but may be conjectured - 'scribes'. What this office involves can only be described tentatively, since the ordinary 'scribe' is unlikely to share the charismatic qualities of an Ezra. There can be no doubt that he is 'well-versed in the law of Moses', qualified for teaching that law and perhaps active in the developing synagogue worship by reading or chanting Scripture. Whether any formal preaching, that is exposition of biblical texts to the congregation, existed at that time or represents later development, is unknown. Although we do not know anything about his training, involvement in regular instruction, professional pride or class feeling, and are dependent on conjectures about his activities, it seems justified to compare him to the later rabbi. In his capacity as an expert on the written and perhaps unwritten religious tradition, the 'sofer' or 'scribe' of the early 'golah'-community is a precursor of the rabbi.

The Scholar as an 'Honourable Idler': Jesus Sirach

Two centuries after Ezra, around 180 B.C., Jesus Sirach writes his book, and we must immediately add, his curious book, or how else shall we call a work which, in beautiful classical Hebrew poetry, deals with the following subjects the arrangement of which reflects no logical sequence: how to protect your daughter against male approaches, table manners, reflections on the transitory nature of life, a patriotic prayer, an outline of Israel's history, impressions of a solemn service at the Temple, a praise of friendship, generosity and stinginess, and much more. There is also a long passage on professions such as the peasant, the engraver of seals, the smith, the potter - professions of which the author admits that "without them no city could be lived in". However, the place of honour is given to the 'scribe' who does not get his hands dirty. And now I quote:

> The scribe's profession increases his wisdom;
> whoever is free from toil can become a wise man.
> How can he become learned who guides the plow,
> who thrills in wielding the goad like a lance,
> who guides the ox and urges on the bullock,
> and whose every concern is for cattle? (...)
> How different the man who devotes himself
> to the study of the law of the Most High!
> He explores the wisdom of the men of old
> and occupies himself with the prophecies.
> He treasures the discourses of famous men,
> and goes to the heart of involved sayings.
> He studies obscure parables
> and is busied with the hidden meanings of the sages.
> He is in attendance on the great,
> and has entrance to the ruler.
> He travels among the peoples of foreign lands
> to learn what is good and evil among men.
> His care is to seek the Lord, his Maker,
> to petition the Most High,
> to open his lips in prayer,
> to ask pardon for his sins.
> Then, if it pleases the Lord Almighty,
> he will be filled with the spirit of understanding.
> He will pour forth his words of wisdom
> and in prayer give thanks to the Lord,
> who will direct his knowledge and his counsel,
> as he meditates upon his mysteries.
> He will show the wisdom of what he has learned
> and glory in the law of the Lord's covenant.
> Many will praise his understanding;
> his fame can never be effaced.
> Unfading will be his memory,
> through all generations his name will live.

Peoples will speak of his wisdom,
and in assembly sing his praises.
While he lives he is one out of a thousand,
and when he dies his renown will not cease.

(Sir 38.24-25; 39.1-11)

Analysing this poem and some information given elsewhere in his book, we can arrive at a fairly clear profile of Jesus Sirach, author, scholar, scribe.

(1) He belongs to the rich urban class and is in solid economic circumstances. An 'honourable idler' (to use an expression of the German Middle Ages), he has leisure to engage in activities unrelated to gaining one's livelihood. He is an intellectual, and has the means to travel abraod and to study. Unlike Ezra, Jesus Sirach is a layman and not a priest, and his genealogy lists no more than three generations (Sir 50.27). Or is he, as one author has recently argued, a member of the priestly aristocracy living by taxes paid to the Jerusalem temple /274/?

(2) For him, being educated means being well-read in the Scriptures. Most probably, biblical literature is his only field of competence. He writes about 'the superiority of the scribe over peasants and artisans', a theme popular in ancient Egyptian literature, and alludes to a passage of Homer that compares human life to a falling leaf (Sir 14.18). Of course, he may have picked up the metaphor from someone quoting the Iliad to him /275/; but isn't it more probable that he, as an educated man, knew as much Greek as his grandson? One who does not know the language is not able to enjoy travelling in a Greek-speaking world as much as Sirach did and is less likely to be able to cope with its vicissitudes (Sir 34.11-12). Or did the wealthy traveller rely on an interpreter as did Herodotus, the Greek historian of the 5th century?

(3) Jesus Sirach writes a book, and is proud of being able to do so. According to chapter 24, his work is a kind of supplement to the Torah, the Pentateuch. He refers to this in metaphoric language: the Torah is an overflowing river, the scholar's book a rivulet channelling the waters. He continues as follows:

Thus do I send my teachings forth shining like the dawn,
to become known afar off.
Thus do I pour out instruction like prophecy
and bestow it on generations to come.

(Sir 24.30-31)

150

Sirach speaks plainly: I am a prophet and I am writing for generations! In fact, he was not alone to consider his book to be so important and, indeed, a Scripture. The preface to the Greek translation tells us the story of the book: One day, the author's grandson comes to Alexandria where the Bible is read in Greek translation, but people do not know his grandfather's work. The grandson produces and promotes his own translation which apparently wins approval. The translator, too, must have enjoyed some derived prestige. Thus the book eventually finds its way into the Greek Bible.

(4) Jesus Sirach is one of those intellectuals for whom writing is not the ultimate satisfaction. He endeavours to exercise social, if not political influence, to be a judge, to speak up in public assemblies, to give advice to princes. He warns, it is true, of holding an office - but his very words indicate that he is not against such aspiration:

Seek not from the Lord authority,
nor from the king a place of honours (...)
Seek not to become a judge
if you have not strength to root out crime,
or you will show favour to the ruler
and mar your integrity. (Sir 7.4.6)

Our author does not tell us whether he was ever in such a position. What he says sounds like a wish. 'Scribe et impera', write and rule!, has always been the secret motto of intellectuals, but most of them never went beyond writing.

Nevertheless, there is some evidence for the assemblies in which Sirach wants to speak up and have his word appreciated. 1 Maccabees reports about assemblies which play a certain role in the political troubles of the generation after Sirach. In 160 B.C., when a commission of some sixty scholars (in Greek: synagoge grammateon) approaches a new high priest of doubtful legitimacy to offer him co-operation, it is deceived and murdered (1 Macc 7.12). Twenty years later, "a great assembly of priests, people, rulers of the nation, and elders of the country" (1 Macc 14.28) celebrate Simon the Maccabee and make him their permanent leader and high priest. The resolution adopted is written down on bronze tablets that are publicly displayed. Sirach, however, can only dream of such important occasions for conspicuous display of judgement and learning.

(5) Jesus Sirach is no longer a prophet, and not yet a rabbi. For a prophet, he is too much teacher. He pronounces

not a single topical word of god and neither thematically nor stylistically imitates prophetic literature; rather, he takes the book of Proverbs as his model. For a rabbi, he lacks interest in controlling religious life and lore, and there is no evidence for exegesis governed by rules, for explicit scriptural proof, and for the master-student relationship. As a child and a young man, Jesus Sirach went to school, but his special interest in religious literature leads him to private study rather than to joining an established authority. There is no evidence for rabbinical training. Jesus Sirach is a private scholar and an author of devotional literature, no head of school.

The Scholar's Charismatic Authority

When looking at the two scholars, Ezra and Jesus Sirach, can we perceive anything of the development leading from the topical oracle to 'doctrine' and 'theology'? It is immediately clear that neither of them pronounces prophet-like oracles. As regards doctrine, the incomparability of our two sources has to be taken into account: Sirach's book, although no statement of doctrine, teaches wisdom as a way of life; Ezra, on the other hand, reports on his mission to Jerusalem in autobiographical form. Referring to a liturgy of the word, this report nevertheless includes an element of teaching and doctrine which is also presupposed in the reforming activities. Asking our two authors what their specific doctrine or message is, we discover some common ground, i.e. the Torah of Moses, and both scholars write and work in order to support and promote it. But how different is their way of interpreting the Torah! For Sirach, the Torah is a source of wisdom. This notion relates to a cosmopolitan tradition, well-known from ancient Egypt and Mesopotamia, which teaches the ability to cope with life and shows the way to social success. That Sirach, in one passage (Sir 24.22), equates this wisdom with the Torah, shows how easily he moves from the specifically Jewish to the general human which, indeed, form one single unity. Throughout his book he is indebted to the universalist way of thought which is echoed in other Early Jewish wisdom writings, viz. the book of Job (5th century) and Ecclesiastes (ca. 200 B.C.).

Although the law of Ezra can be called the wisdom of his god which is in his hand (Ezra 7.25), the sapiential notion of wisdom does not apply to Ezra's understanding of the Torah. Sirach's wisdom is human and humane, while Ezra's is divine and stern. His activities are guided by a spirit which may be taken to be characteristic of the Babylonian 'golah'-communities of his time. It can be called <u>discipline</u>. Ezra is determined to re-establish what he considers to be the true Jewish way of life in the 'golah'-community of Jerusalem, and he brings a legal code which is the basis of his mission. Both Jesus Sirach and Ezra travel, but how different are their notions of it! According to Sirach, the scholar "travels among the peoples of foreign lands to learn what is good and evil among men"; elsewhere he adds that "one never put to the proof knows little, whereas with travel a man adds to his resourcefulness" (Sir 39.5; 34.10). The travels of Ezra, on the other hand, are not valued as a cultural experience, but are comparable to the missionary travels of Paul which aim at establishing and controlling religious communities.

Mary Douglas' description of the sectarian attitude obtaining in small and tightly controlled communities reads like a commentary on Ezra's mission. According to this view,

all human beings are divided into insiders and outsiders, the latter hostile and the former continually disappointing expectations.

A need to control admission and to strengthen the boundaries against outsiders will be apparent to members of the group wishing to avoid its disintegration.

The small sequestered community (...) will see no need or reason to travel to strange places: abroad may be interesting because of the group's historical origin there, and travel for the sake of missions or visiting shrines. /276/

As soon as men of Ezra's kind gain wide influence, one is likely to fear them. In the first century B.C., the Jewish scholar, Simeon ben Shetach, not only demands compulsory school education for all children, but also has hanged eighty women, probably accused of witchcraft, at Ashkelon /277/. It is well known that such a spirit was passed on to Western societies. Not without good reason writes H. H. Schaeder:

The contribution Judaism (he implies Ezra) was assigned to make to humanity was not another aesthetic dimension, but order, intellectual and moral discipline. /278/

Wisdom /279/ and discipline, with more emphasis on the latter, was also prominent during the final phase of Early Judaism in 150 B.C.-70 A.D. However, two more features emerge: an exegesis which is governed by a set of rules, and the never-ending dispute about the true meaning of Scripture and the proper way of Jewish life. The generation following Jesus Sirach sees a proliferation of sects and movements: apocalypticians, Pharisees, Sadducees, a list which soon includes the Essenes, the people of Qumran and various Christian groups, too. All these have their own way of reading Scripture and hence their own body of doctrine.

When looking at our two scholars, Ezra and Jesus Sirach, can we perceive anything of the emergence of a new religious vocation, that of the scriptural scholar? Negatively, it is clear that neither of them is, or wants to be, a prophet. Are they scriptural scholars in the sense of the proto-rabbis characteristic of the period 150 B.C.-70 A.D., that is, are they figures like Simeon ben Shetach and St. Paul? Without doubt, Ezra conforms better to the proto-rabbinical pattern than Jesus Sirach. Both of them, however, belong to the same sociological category of 'brain-workers' or intellectuals as these terms are used today. This general category, as well as the culturally specific traits of the Jewish scriptural scholar (from Ezra and Jesus Sirach to Simeon ben Shetach, St. Paul and Yohanan ben Zakkai) can be characterized as follows /280/:

(a) The intellectual is required to master a complex body of specialist knowledge and related skills which are basically intellectual in nature. - As regards the scriptural scholar, this is knowledge of biblical literature, Jewish tradition and their relevance for, or application to, a wide field of ritual practice. These rituals extend from festival liturgies of the Jewish year to everyday matters such as the ritually correct slaughter of animals, and female menstruation.

(b) Such specialist knowledge cannot be acquired quickly even by persons of ability. - The scriptural scholar acquires his knowledge either privately or studies under an acknowledged authority. We find, however, no official arrangement of training and no regular system of promotion, although from the late first century onwards there are 'schools' (those of rabbis Hillel and Shammai) in which certain patterns of transmission emerge. A figure like the famous Yohanan ben Zakkai (ca. 1-80 A.D.) is not integrated into any hierarchy and is not the head of a school or an alumnus of one /281/.

(c) Intellectuals may be engaged in any type of employment, but they are concentrated in teaching, preaching, and the arts. - In ancient Judaism scriptural scholars are not religious 'officials' but private scholars who depend on agriculture or, less frequently, on trade or handicraft for their livelihood. Most of them refuse the idea of using their learning as a source of income. The ideal is to combine study of Torah with the practice of a trade - compare the two aspects of St. Paul's life, tentmaking and missionary preaching. While the priest is likely to have some form of income from his activity at the Temple, scriptural scholarship is a leisure time activity that lacks an economic dimension.

(d) Though intellectuals often have considerable influence over others, they seldom have much formal authority. They are like ministers without portfolio, experts without the power to translate their ideas into public policy. - Jewish scholars do not lead the retired life of people who are 'wise for themselves', but share freely their wisdom and advice. The mind of the sage is not dedicated to merely theoretical concerns; there is also a will to power. As individuals they seek public influence without aspiring to political leadership. They conceive of themselves as advisors rather than actual leaders, although there is some evidence for scholars pursuing public careers or working in governmental institutions /282/. Unlike Greek and Roman philosophers from Plato to Mark Aurelius who placed themselves on the emperor's throne, the more modest Jewish sages rest content with being consulted in their study. Accordingly, their authority has no basis in institutions such as local synagogues or the Temple, but rests in their own personality and performance as scholars. (This may explain why Ezra was authorized to appoint magistrates and judges, but no scribes; these stand outside the institutional hierarchy.) In Weber's terminology: their authority is of a 'charismatic' nature /283/.

The impact of scribal charisma on contemporaries can be studied in Ezra as well as in later figures. Consider Simeon ben Shetach who, as already noted, hanged eighty witches, and the influential Gamaliel whom the New Testament describes as "a teacher of the law, held in honour by all the people" (Acts 5.34). The scriptural scholar's authority is charismatic, and it may be remembered that Weber adopted the term of charisma from Rudolf Sohm who introduced the concept to describe the authority of early Christian teachers active in a non-institutional context /284/. At this point we can come back to the prophets with whom we started our discussion. They, too, are charismatic personalities. But there is an important difference in their influence. However tradition-bound a prophet's oracle may be, it is a new revelation. For the scribe, the living spirit has crystallized into a book which permits of no new revelation. Although the charisma is embodied in a book and thereby 'tamed', it still retains its supernatural quality. One is not surprised, then, to hear that some of the scriptural scholars act like prophets /285/. On the other hand, the difference is characteristic: the oracle religion becomes a book religion, the direct experience of revelation becomes the knowledge thereof /286/, the place of the charismatic prophet is taken by the charismatic teacher.

It should be clear that Ezra's and Jesus Sirach's contribution to the formation of early Judaism should not be exaggerated. They were not selected for analysis because of the impact they made but because their literary legacy provides us with at least a glimpse of the kind of people who became the fathers of Judaism. They were intellectuals, and just as the intellectuals of all times, they loved and studied their books, wrote, and, last but not least, wanted to put their ideas into practice. By thus concentrating on the formation of the scribe as a social type we had no occasion to speak about his contribution to the formation of Jewish institutions. These institutions include the Bible as a canon of holy writings, the synagogue service featuring scriptural recitation and preaching, and Jewish schools which use the Bible as their textbook.

NOTES
BIBLIOGRAPHY
INDEXES

ABBREVIATIONS

AGJU	Arbeiten zur Geschichte des antiken Judentums und des Urchristentums, Leiden
BASOR	Bulletin of the American Schools of Oriental Research
BZAW	Beiheft zur ZAW, Berlin
EJud	Encyclopaedia Judaica, Jerusalem
FRLANT	Forschungen zur Religion und Literatur des Alten und Neuen Testaments, Göttingen
HAT	Handbuch zum Alten Testament, Tübingen
HUCA	Hebrew Union College Annual
JAOS	Journal of the American Oriental Society
JBL	Journal of Biblical Literature
JPSt	Journal of Palestine Studies
KAT	Kommentar zum Alten Testament, Gütersloh
MDOG	Mitteilungen der Deutschen Orient-Gesellschaft
OBO	Orbis biblicus et orientalis, Fribourg
RB	Revue biblique
ThB	Theologische Bücherei, München
ThWNT	Theologisches Wörterbuch zum Neuen Testament, Stuttgart
VT	Vetus Testamentum
VTS	Supplements to VT, Leiden
WMANT	Wissenschaftliche Monographien zum Alten and Neuen Testament, Neukirchen
WUNT	Wissenschaftliche Untersuchungen zum Neuen Testament, Tübingen
ZAW	Zeitschrift für die alttestamentliche Wissenschaft, Berlin

NOTES

1   Herbert of Cherbury 1967: 218; cf. 158-168.
2   Lafitau 1974: 96-99.
3   Voltaire 1967: 360 (entry on 'Religion').
4   Cf. Pajak 1978.
5   Cf. Müller 1911; Nikiprowetzky 1975; Lang 1980: 149-161; Keel 1980: 11-30.

6	Kuenen 1877: 585.	7	Nikiprowetzky 1975: 86.
8	Kuenen 1883: 118-119.	9	Nikiprowetzky 1975: 80f.
10	Von Rad 1966: 39.		

11   Herrmann 1971: 156, 168. The author even dares to make the statement that "Theology of the Old Testament, however different-iated, will be, in the final analysis, a theology of Deuteronomy" (167).

12	Keel 1980: 24.	13	Von Rad 1938.
14	Maag 1980: 111-169, 256-299.		
15	Stolz 1980; Henninger 1981.	16	Oldenburg 1969.
17	Renan 1958: 147-148. Cf. Patai 1977: 347-351.		
18	Lawrence 1962: 40.	19	De Vaux 1971.
20	Gottwald 1980: 616.	21	Gottwald 1980: 693.

22   Cf., however, Spieckermann 1982: 307-372 who argues that the Assyrians have their vassals worship Assyrian gods on a regular basis.
23   Tracing back customary law to nomadic ancestors such as Jonadab (Jer 35) may have been widespread and be implied in, or have given rise to, the idea of Mosaic law.
24   Jer 7.18; 44.25. Baking-molds in the shape of a goddess were found at Mari, see Rast 1977.
25   Num 21.29; Jer 48.46.
26   Micah 4.5. Cf. also the list of local gods in 2 Kgs 17.30-31.
27   1 Kgs 20.23,28 (cf. Jdg 1.19); Am 9.17. Yahweh's domain is co-extensive with the land of his people, Israel. Any divine activities beyond the confines of this area are based on Israel's kinship connections with neighbouring peoples or on political treaties, see Wright 1965: 236-237. For a similar reading of Hab 3.3 and the epigraphically attested "Yahweh of Teman" see Emerton 1982: 9-13. The narrow geographical perspective of Ex 19.5; Deut 7.6; Am 3.2 is often obscured, viz. enlarged, by modern translations, see the com-ments of Wildberger 1960: 74-77.

28	Lemaire 1977.	29	Zeph 1.5. Cf. 2 Kgs 17.33.
30	Gen 14.19. Cf. Miller 1980.		

31   It is possible that, as creator, Yahweh is the monotheistic god, see the comments below ('Phase 5') and the following Septuagint addition which seems to imply a monotheistic reading of Hos 13.4: "I am the Lord your God [LXX: who established the heaven and created the earth, whose hands created all the host of heaven, and I did not show them to you in order that you might follow them. And I brought you up] from the land of Egypt."
32   Pfeiffer 1926; Obbink 1929; Dus 1961.

33   Lemaire 1977. The 'asherah' which I interpret as 'sacred tree' is not the personal name of a goddess as is assumed by modern translations. Cf. below, note 70.
34   Ps 63.1-2. Cf. Lang 1980: 144-146.
35   Dan 3.2-3. For the priestly presentation see Ex 32.4; for parallels: Smith 1925 (Mesopotamian statues); Krairiksh 1979: 220-224 (statues of the Buddha).
36   Ps 2.7 (cf. 110.3); Isa 9.5.
37   Diodor 20.14 on the Carthaginians (310 B.C.): "In their zeal to make amends for their omission (i.e. to honour their gods), they selected two hundred of the noblest children and sacrificed them publicly; and others who were under suspicion sacrificed themselves voluntarily, in number not less than three hundred."
38   Cf. the polemical statements Micah 1.7; Deut 23.19.
39   Brichto 1973; Loretz 1978 and 1982.
40   Ez 43.7,9; 1 Kgs 1.10; 11.43.
41   See above, note 33.
42   Hoffmann 1980: 91. 'Gebirah' ('mistress') is the Hebrew title of the queen mother who enjoyed an important position at the royal court.
43   Würthwein 1977: 187.
44   1 Kgs 16.31. For Jezebel's Sidonian (rather than Tyrian) origin, the 'Baal of Sidon' as god of her home town, and her legendary rather than actual involvement with the prophet, Elijah, see Timm 1982: 224-231, 235-236, 295-303.
45   Pritchard 1969: 655b; Shea 1979.
46   Yadin 1978; Mazar 1978.
47   Mattan, priest of Baal in 9th century Jerusalem (2 Kgs 11.18), has a Phoenician name. Levin 1982: 62-64 argues that the passage is a late addition that cannot be used as a source for pre-exilic religion in Judah.
48   Astour 1959.
49   Hofmayr 1925: 160. In times of crisis (drought) one is inclined to think that one is left or neglected by one's own gods and hence has to turn to foreign or new ones; see also below, note 55.
50   Donner 1977: 405.
51   Ahab's immediate successor, Ahaziah, reigns for no more than two years (853-852): 1 Kgs 22.52.
52   Ahlström 1977.
53   Cf. below, note 244.
54   Von Soden 1955: 162ff.
55   Livy 4.30 = Foster 1922: 353-355.
56   Cf. "Yahweh alone" Deut 6.4; "Yahweh and no other" 1 Kgs 8.60.
57   It is not quite clear whether Amos, whose activity is in the northern kingdom, is a native of the south as is generally assumed. His northern origin is advocated by Koch 1978: 81-82.
58   Rudolph 1966: 112.   59   Rost 1950.
60   For the secondary nature of Hos 8.5-6; 13.2; 14.4; see Willi-Plein 1971.
61   See above, note 32.   62   Van Selms 1973.
63   Atrahasis I 376-383, 409-413 = Lambert/Millard 1969: 69, 71; Von Soden 1979: 24-25.

64   For pre-Islamic gods 'without a son' see Winnett 1938; Mooren 1981: 555-557.
65   For Micah 1.7; 5.11ff see Jeremias 1971; for Isa 2.7-22; 10.10-11 see Stolz 1980: 178 note 85.
66   Hoffmann 1980: 154.
67   For this translation see Rudolph 1975.
68   Scharbert 1982. However, the authenticity of Zeph 1.1-6 is not beyond doubt and it may well be that date and oracle are the work of a Yahweh-aloneist editor: Levin 1981: 437-439.
69   Herrmann 1971: 170 note 32.
70   See above, note 33. For the 'pieces of cloth for "asherah"', mentioned below, cf. the sacred trees of traditional Arab Palestine to which rags of cloth are frequently attached: Curtiss 1902: 90-92 (with plate facing p. 90); Frazer 1919: 45-51; Elan 1979 (esp. plate 2).
71   Wellhausen 1878: 419.   72   Ez 14.1-11; 20.
73   Holladay 1976: 470-471. The case of an earlier career of Jeremiah, starting in 627 B.C., is argued by Albertz 1982.
74   Hermopolis no. 4.1 = Bresciani/Kamil 1966.
75   Comprising the Books of Deut, Josh, Jdg, Sam and Kgs.
76   "You must not add anything to my charge, nor take anything away from it." Deut 4.2; cf. 13.1.
77   2 Kgs 23.32; cf. 23.37; 24.9, 19.
78   1 Kgs 11.41; 14.19, 29; 15.23 etc.
79   Hossfeld 1982.
80   In the early 6th cent. B.C., Ezekiel knows no sabbath as the seventh day - Ez 46.1 clearly contains an addition, see Lemaire 1973: 182-183.
81   Ex 23.12; 34.21. Babylonian workmen have every tenth day off (Lautner 1936: 129-133). According to Von Soden (1979: 9) Mesopotamian rulers used to decree release or relief of debts and to increase free days at the beginning of their reign; "one has, however, to keep in mind that in those times a day off did not necessarily imply that there was no work to be done; in many cases a leave of absence was granted to allow men to do work in their own houses that was necessary and could not be coped with by the women alone."
82   Am 8.5.   83   Hos 2.15; cf. 2.13.
84   Ex 20.10; Deut 5.14.
85   Ex 16.23, 25; 31.15; 35.2; Lev 23.3, 38; 25.2, 4.
86   This 'spirit of control' is modelled on the control system of the Assyrian and Babylonian empires; see Weinfeld 1972: 91-100.
87   Mt 10.35ff; 19.29; Koran: Surah 9.23-24.
88   Deut 7.3; Josh 23.12.   89   Ez 40.1.
90   Isa 45.1.
91   For the translation see Peter 1980.
92   Isa 46.6-7; cf. 44.9-20; 48.5.
93   Deut 6.4.   94   bMegillah 13a.
95   Cf. Wellhausen 1921: 152.   96   Lohfink 1969.
97   Lohfink 1969: 58.   98   Lohfink 1969: 63.
99   Vorländer 1981.   100   Kittel 1898.
101   Smith 1963.
102   See esp. Boyce 1982: 43-47, 62-66, 188-195.

103 Saggs 1978: 41-44.

104 Several inscriptions of King Nebuchadnezzar combine motifs of creation with those of world dominion, e.g.: "I [Nebuchadnezzar] am the prince who is ready to serve you [Marduk], the creature of your hand. You have created me, you have given me kingship over the totality of the peoples" (Langdon 1912: 122-125). Other Mesopotamian texts universalize and symbolize royal power by calling the king Lord of the Animals; thus Shalmaneser II: "Ninurta and Pali, who love me as their high priest, handed over to me the animals of the fields and ordered me to hunt them" (Michel 1947/52: 473). The 'owner of animals' motif is found elsewhere in the Bible (Ez 19.8-9; Dan 2.38; Judith 11.7) in passages with Mesopotamian echoeš. That Jeremiah should take up Babylonian ideas is likely from the historical setting of his oracle: it is addressed to the members of an anti-Babylonian meeting held in Jerusalem in 594 B.C. who were planning to rebel against Nebuchadnezzar. The prophet sides with the Babylonian overlord.

105 Koch 1980: 109.

106 Cf. Job 31.24-28. For the 5th cent. dating see Lévêque 1981; Albertz 1981.

107 Koch 1976: 316. Cf. also Eerdmans 1936 (and 1942); Vorländer 1975: 215-224.

108 Gen 17.1; 28.3; 35.11; 43.14; 48.3; 49.25; Ex 6.3.

109 The view presented here is a revision of Lang 1975.

110 See his religio-philosophical and apologetical study Kitāb al-Fiṣal, treatise 1 (ch. 15, no. 208) = Asín Palacios 1928: 367.

111 Kramer 1949: 207, 215; Haussig 1965: 115-116; Sjöberg 1976: 174-175.

112 One scholar takes the goddess Anatyahu to be Yahweh's daughter (Kraeling 1953: 91); according to Porten 1968: 171 she is rather his consort.

113 Prov 9.10 in the context of the final passage 9.7-12 (which is displaced in the present text). For 'qedoshim' 'gods' see Deut 33.2; Job 5.1; 15.15; Ps 89.6ff.

114 Lang 1975: 149ff.

115 F. Schiller, Die Götter Griechenlands (poem).

116 Isa 45.21; cf. Hos 13.4; Dan 3.29.

117 Wallis 1935: 7.   118 Gressmann 1913: 477.

119 Pettazoni 1960, 117.

120 Keel 1980: 21: "The model of a chain of revolutions in relatively rapid succession, leading towards monotheism, seems inevitable."

121 Holladay 1970; Scanlin 1978; cf. also Weinfeld 1976: 392ff. For the general situation in Palestine, the following entry in Sennacherib's Annals, referring to an incident of ca. 700 B.C., is particularly revealing: "The officials, the patricians and the common people of Ekron had thrown Padi, their king, into fetters because he was loyal to his solemn oath sworn by the god Ashur" (Pritchard 1969: 287b).

122 Mettinger 1976: 111-130; Halpern 1981: 187-249.

123 Weber 1947: 341.   124 Weber 1947: 346.

125 Weber 1947: 347.   126 Weber 1947: 358-359.

127 Jer 32. Cf. Long's assessment of the evidence and his conclusion: "Jeremiah may have been born a rural non-Jerusalemite, but his blood and social relationships are anything but lower class" (Long 1982: 47).

128 In the second chapter of his biography, Josephus mentions a certain Bannus "who dwelt in the wilderness wearing only such clothing as trees provided feeding on such things as grew of themselves, and using frequent ablutions of cold water, by day and by night, for purity's sake". The Jewish historian relates that he had been a "devoted disciple" of this character.

129 Douglas 1973: 118ff.

130 Hag 2.21-23; Zech 6.9-15 (read "Zerubbabel" instead of "Joshua"!); Neh 6.7.

131 Annals of Sennacherib: Pritchard 1969: 288a.

132 2 Kgs 3.15; Dan 10.2ff. One text dating from the post-exilic era, Zech 13.2-6, gives revealing evidence for a dervish-type of ecstasy which obtains even in the late period: An ex-prophet who abandons this no-longer prestigious profession apologizes for his ecstatic delirium and the wounds of his ravings by calling it the effect of wine-drinking, see Ginsberg 1978. We do not know, however, to what extent ecstasy was believed to be a prerequisite for receiving an oracle. For the 'ecstatic of Byblos' it was clearly the case. The Egyptian 'Report of Wen-Amon' (Pritchard 1969: 25-29) dating from ca. 1076 B.C. tells about a young man who went into an ecstatic frenzy and uttered an inspired oracle, addressed to the ruler of Byblos. The oracle rescues the travelling Egyptian out of a precarious situation and helps him to fulfil his mission on behalf of the high priest of Thebes. As can be argued on the basis of this incident, Israel's prophecy has its roots in Canaanite culture, and there is neither nomadic legacy nor peculiar to Israel (Schmitt 1977).

133 Lindblom 1962: 152ff; Lang 1978: 166-188 (language of propaganda, street theatre).

134 Weber 1920: 283.　　　　135 Weber 1920: 285.

136 Renan 1953: 574. According to this author, a prophetic poster seems to be mentioned in Isa 8.1 where the prophet is told to "take a large tablet and write on it in common (readable?) writing, Maher-shalal-hash-baz (Speed-spoil-hasten-plunder)". - Burke (1978: 101) vividly describes how the Christian preachers of early modern Europe entertained and provoked their audience: "Prominent among the Catholic preachers are the friars. St. Francis had described his own order as 'god's minstrels' (joculatores Domini), and the parallel was in fact a close one in many respects. Like the minstrels, the friar wandered from town to town and often performed in the market-place - for the churches were not big enough to hold every one who came to listen to them. Contemporaries estimated some of the crowds at 15-20,000, and some people came the night before to be sure of a place. The friars seem to have learned a trick or two from the minstrels in whose steps they followed, for disapproving references can be found to preachers who, 'in the manner of buffoons, tell silly stories and make the people roar with laughter'. Bernardino da Feltre took his sandal off and threw it at a man who was sleeping

during his sermon. Some Franciscans certainly acted on the pulpit; even St Bernardino had been known to imitate the sound of a trumpet or the buzzing of a fly. Roberto Caracciolo, preaching a crusade, was said to have thrown off his gown in mid-sermon to reveal a suit of armour underneath. Barletta's sermon-notes frequently say 'shout' (clama). Olivier Maillard wrote himself the following stage-directions in the margin of a sermon: 'sit down - stand up - mop yourself - ahem! ahem! - now shriek like a devil'."

137 See now: Tufnell 1953: 118 fig. 10.

138 Lemaire 1976.

139 See also the present writer's 'Schule und Unterricht im alten Israel' in Lang 1980: 104-119.

140 Begrich (1938) 1963: 90: "It is striking to what extent Israel's religious tradition emerges in the words of Deutero-Isaiah."

141 Bernhardt 1972: 27, 30, 38.

142 1 Kgs 20.35; 2 Kgs 2.3, 5, 7, 15; 4.1, 38; 5.22; 6.1; 9.1.

143 Samuel: 1 Sam 19.18-24; Elijah: 2 Kgs 2.1-18; Elisha: 2 Kgs 4.1-7, 38-41; 6.1-7, et al.

144 Jepsen 1934: 113-114; Schmitt 1972: 162-172; Porter 1981.

145 1 Sam 10.5-13; 19.18-24.

146 Baumgartner 1974: 424a; cf. the Jewish Yeshiva, i.e. the Talmud school, and Acts 22.3.

147 Herner 1926: 66.   148 1 Sam 10.12; 2 Kgs 2.12.

149 Van den Oudenrijn 1925: 166.

150 Keil 1875: 162; Schmitt 1972: 165-166; Koch 1978: 35.

151 The first to draw attention to this feature of biblical prophecy was J. Alting in his 'Historia academiarum Hebraearum' (1647), printed in this author's 'Operum tomus quintus' (Amsterdam 1687), who relied on the targumic renderings of texts such as 2 Kgs 4.38 and 1 Sam 19.18-23.

152 Johnson 1962 and 1979; Jeremias 1970. See also Neumann 1979: 24-32.

153 Bernhardt 1972: 23 note 2, 25 note 2; Jeremias 1970: 6-7.

154 Bacher 1903: 67. For the temple school see Hermisson 1968: 129ff.

155 Gray 1962: 177.

156 Jeremias 1970: 189: "Perhaps one may take Hab 2.2 as evidence for this prophet's education at the temple school of Jerusalem."

157 Gunneweg 1967; Reventlow 1963: 24-77.

158 For 1 Sam 3 see Bernhardt 1972: 46n; one scholar reads this text as a tradition current among the temple prophets of Ramah: Willis 1971.

159 Jepsen 1934: 132-142; Bernhardt 1972: 26-27; Koch 1978: 26.

160 Wolff 1964.   161 Noort 1977: 73-74.

162 Koch 1978: 49.   163 Koch 1978: 60-61.

164 Koch 1978: 60. Cf. Renan's remark on Isaiah's style: "une telle perfection suppose l'école" (1953, 609).

165 Gibb/Kramers 1974: 207.

166 Bernhardt 1972: 42-43 note 1. However, it seems unlikely to assume with Mowinckel 1935: 265 that "most of these men came, perhaps, from the guilds of the nebi'im. Some of them, at any rate,

accepted the title nabi', and we are expressly told that Jeremiah belonged to the organized body of temple nebi'im (Jer 29.26f). They observe the forms of nebi'ism in their actions, and they express themselves in its language."

167   Zimmerli 1979: 70-71. In an earlier study, Zimmerli calls Ezekiel a "cult prophet" (1957 = 1963: 128-129).

168   Rudolph 1976: 61-62: "Zechariah belongs to the prophets whose calling is not on record (...), but that he must have had such an experience follows from the way he acts."

169   Zimmerli 1974: 88-91. Whereas the early Isaiah relies on Amos (Fey 1963: 145), Jeremiah seems to follow Hoseanic tradition (Rudolph 1968: 17: "in a young prophet who just starts his career such dependence is not surprising").

170   Fohrer 1969; Zimmerli 1978. Cf. Gal 1.16-24 where Paul asserts his independence of the Jerusalem apostles.

171   Herder 1880: 53.

172   Kurtz 1904; Hölscher 1914; Lindblom 1962; Wilson 1979.

173   Jaspers 1947; (cf. Lang 1981a, 57-74); Jaynes 1982: 84-125, 293-313.

174   Povah 1925: 105.   175   Haeussermann 1932.

176   Allwohn 1926.   177   Arlow 1951.

178   Seierstad 1965; Langkammer 1965.

179   Howie 1950: 69-84; Cassem 1973; Bron 1981. In fact, Ezekiel may have been ill (Lang 1981a: 57-74) but anthropologists of religion warn us to generalize pathological traits in individual prophets and shamans (Lewis 1978: 179-186; Wilson 1980: 44-46).

180   Klein 1956.

181   The expression goes back to Gunkel 1917: 1-31 and is still used, e.g., by Koch 1978: 16.

182   Koch 1978: 31.

183   Ramlot 1972: 914. Cf. Von Rad 1965: 69: "The methods of recent psychology have not produced a satisfactory account of what goes on in the prophet's psyche."

184   Sundén 1966: 28-29, 77, 93, and 1969. For an English summary of Sundén's psychology of religion see Unger 1976: 9-31, and for a related view of authors belonging to the American 'culture and personality' school see Spiro 1953, Spiro/D'Andrade 1958. - For a different yet comparable use of the concept of 'role' in prophetic research see Petersen 1981.

185   Sundén 1966: 28-29.

186   Sundén 1966: 29. - A role-psychological analysis of nordic shamanism is Honko 1969 who defines 'role-taking' not as "the overt enactment of what one conceives to be one's own appropriate role in a given situation" (this would be 'role-playing') but rather "the imaginative construction of the other's role" (37 note 39). He outlines the following elements which may elucidate biblical prophecy: The shaman passes through a long noviciate under an old and skilled master; he gets acquainted with his role "through intentional instruction and incidental learning" (38); in the process of instruction, the 'role-taking' of the roles of gods and spirits is mediated by the telling of myths; the spirits manifest themselves to the novice in

visions and auditions; the spirit roles structure the shaman's perceptual set and form his frame of reference for understanding what he feels, sees and hears. That gods fall under the category of role was already seen by the American social psychologist, G. H. Mead, who referred to gods represented in ritual drama. Children 's playing with an imaginary companion seems to provide as easy access to the concept of 'dual role situation'. See the stage-play 'Harvey' by Mary C. Chase (1950), and Mead 1934: 150-153.

187 Sundén 1966: 77.   188   Ez 3.3; 37.7; Isa 6.7.

189 Sundén 1969: 136. The 'conditions' are, of course, those of stress, cf. Jaynes 1982: 93: "During the eras of the bicameral mind, we may suppose that the stress threshold for hallucinations was much, much lower than in either normal people or schizophrenics today. The only stress necessary was that which occurs when a change in behavior is necessary because of some novelty in a situation. Anything that could not be dealt with on the basis of habit, any conflict between work and fatigue, between attack and flight, any choice between whom to obey or what to do, anything that required any decision at all was sufficient to cause an auditory hallucination."

190 Miller 1955; Fey 1963.   191   Leibniz 1961: 617, 623.
192 Sundén 1966: 89.   193   Sundén 1969: 139.
194 Sundén 1966: 93.   195   Sundén 1969: 139.
196 Sundén 1969: 140-141.   197   Merleau-Ponty xi.
198 Krech 1976, 184, 205.   199   Douglas 1973: 182.

200 Allport 1955. Cf. the related 'constructionist' approach to perception which suggests that we add remembered residuals of previous experiences to here-and-now stimulus-induced sensations and thus construct a percept: Krech/Crutchfield 1974: 302-304.

201 Deut 18.21-22; Jer 28 (see esp. 8-9, 16-17).

202 Carroll 1977: 146: "The coenobia of the earlier prophets and the disciples of the canonical prophets provided the prophetic movement with adequate social support to shield them from the onslaught of their critics and the worst ravages of dissonant experiences."

203 Weber 1920: 322.

204 Müller/Thomas 1976: 127. The same point is made by Antoine de Saint-Exupéry who concludes that the 'believer' and the 'non-believer' inhabit a totally different world (Citadelle, Paris 1949: 26): "Car j'ai découvert une grande vérité. A savoir que les hommes habitent, et que le sens des choses change pour eux, selon le sens de la maison. Et que le chemin, le champ d'orge et la courbe de la colline sont différents pour l'homme, selon qu'ils composent ou non un domaine. Car voilà tout à coup cette matière disparate qui s'assemble et pèse sur le coeur. Et celui-là n'habite point le même univers qui habite ou non le royaume de Dieu."

205 Luther 1897: 311, 317.   206   Koch 1978: 34.

207 For the politics of Amos and Hosea, see (above) the Appendix to Chapter Two - 'Prophecy, Symbolic Acts, and Politics'. The Hebrew term for 'to conspire', 'qashar', generally used for activities resulting in the murder of a king (1 Kgs 16.16; 2 Kgs 12.21), is central to Amaziah's denunciation: Am 7.10. For the practice of remission of

debts by royal decree see Jer 34.8-22 (minus the secondary verses 13b-15a); Pritchard 1969: 526-528; Lemche 1976.
208   Redfield 1956: 35-66; Wolf 1966: 2ff, 48-57; Dalton 1972.
209   Gen 2.24; Deut 5.14 (to be understood of unmarried children); 28.30. The extended family called 'the father's house' is a patrilineal lineage of three to four generations (Lev 18.6-18; Josh 7.17-18); it is no economic unit but may extend help to members in need.
210   Bobek 1962, 1974, 1979; Loretz 1975. See also Weulersse 1946: 121-132.
211   Wirth 1962: 20-21.
212   Wirth 1971: 219. For 'mechanisms of growing indebtedness' see Ehlers 1980: 235-236. Cf. Marx, 'Capital', vol. 3, ch. 36 (1981: 734): "When considered in detail, the preservation or loss of the petty producers' conditions of production depends on a thousand accidental circumstances, and each such accident or loss means impoverishment and is a point at which the parasite of usury can seize hold. The peasant only needs one of his cows to die and he is immediately unable to repeat his reproduction on the old scale. He falls prey to usury, and once in that position he never recovers his freedom."
213   Papyrus Cowley 10 and 11: Grelot 1972: 78-84. Further evidence is quoted by Maloney 1974.
214   Janssen 1981: 70. - For the 'downwards mobility' of peasants see Kippenberg 1982: 54-77 and Cardellini 1981: 323-334 on Neh 5.1-13, and Aristotle, 'Athenaion politeia' 2.
215   See Lutfiyya 1966: 32ff, 106-107 for classes within a village.
216   Debt bondage and slavery are, of course, not the same thing. In the Bible debt bondage is much more prominent. (cf. Lang 1981d; Kippenberg 1983). Finley, speaking of classical antiquity, insists that "slavery was a late and relatively infrequent form of involuntary labour, in world history generally and in ancient history in particular. (...) The common pattern until the [sc. Roman] Empire seems to have been one of urban slavery and rural dependent, rather than slave, labour" (Finley 1980: 77, 79).
217   Wirth 1969.
218   Wirth 1973; Scott 1977; Robertson 1980; Ennew 1981. That exploitation in terms of the rent capitalist system correlates with the political stability (Wirth 1973: 328ff) and the emergence of a domestic market bound to foreign exports and based on money as the medium of exchange, and a centralized bureaucracy (Harik 1972) since the mid-nineteenth century may be true, but it seems that rent capitalism as such antedates the nineteenth century. Equally, situations lacking stability may lead the rent capitalist to exploit peasants as long as he is able to do so (Wolf 1966: 56). Usury, taking of high interest and the peasants' dependance on urban credit facilities and landlords is, e.g., characteristic of the Near East in the eighteenth century as well (Volney 1787: 372-379; Hourani 1957).
219   Lambton 1953: 263.
220   Jer 32.6-15 according to Kippenberg 1982: 33.
221   2 Sam 12.1-4. Job 24.3 implies similar conditions.
222   Wirth 1973: 332.   223   Radin 1929: 113.
224   "That which follows a Culture we may call - from its

best-known example - fellah-peoples." Spengler 1928: 169.
225 Galling 1979: no. 20.   226 Page 1969.
227 Fohrer 1964: 294.   228 Isa 3.16-4; 1; 5.11-12.
229 From the Sudan: Crowfoot 1938: 54-55.
230 1 Kgs 5.20-25; Ezra 3.7; Ez 27.17. Some statistics for 19th century Palestine is given by Buheiry 1981, Schölch 1981.
231 Pfeiffer 1935: no. 97 (read in the light of K. Deller in Orientalia 31, 1962: 234-235).
232 This is, however, not without problems. Land tenure is well-known from both the New Testament and post-biblical Jewish legal sources, but its existence cannot be demonstrated for the Old Testament period. The first unquestionable attestation is a contract document found in Egypt dating from 515 B.C., see Grelot 1972: 71-75. For tenure in general see Kreissig 1970: 28f, 39f, 54; Prenzel 1971; Ries 1976.
233 Mays 1969: 90.   234 Lang 1981d.
235 In Deut 23.20; Lev 25.36; Ez 18.17 the exilic period asks for an exceptionally high measure of national solidarity. The older legislation in Ex 22.24 seems to forbid nothing but too high rates of interest, not interest taking as such; the second part of the commandment forbidding to take interest at all seems to be a secondary addition, see Beer 1939: 117.
236 Steiner 1954. In classical antiquity, too, slaves were denied the most elementary of social bonds, kinship: Finley 1980: 75-76.
237 Examples from a later period of Jewish history are given by Kreissig 1970: 37-38.
238 'The Coronation Service', in: 'The Times' (London) of June 1, 1953, p. iii.
239 The oil is made up according to a special formula which includes orange flowers, roses, cinnamon, jasmine, sesame, musk, civet and ambergis. The chronicler adds a note about the chemist: "In order to improve his sense of smell, he gave up smoking for a whole month before starting work" (Lacey 1978: 234-235). An ointment recipe is given in Ex 30.23-25. For the production of perfume in antiquity see Forbes 1955, Beck 1978.
240 Cf. 1 Kgs 1.32-40; 2 Kgs 11.4-20.
241 1 Kgs 15.1. - For the history of the anointment ritual see Mettinger 1976: 185-232; Weisman 1976; Schoors 1977; Kutsch 1980; Halpern 1981: 125-148; Levin 1982: 91-94.
242 1 Sam 16.12; Isa 61.1.
243 This is how traditional Jewish exegesis reads the passage (Rashi, Ibn Ezra, Qimchi). For the chronology see Pavlovsky/Vogt 1964.
244 The figure showing a scene on the 'Black Obelisk' found in Nimrud in 1846 (British Museum no. 118885) is from Haag 1968: 809.
245 Cf. 2 Sam 3.18; 1 Kgs 11.13, 32-38; Ps 89.4 etc.
246 Kellermann 1967: 154ff; In der Smitten 1975. Another view is taken by Grosheide 1978.
247 Liver 1971.
248 In order to have a name for the Jewish religious community which is no 'state', Josephus coined the term 'theocracy' (Against

Apion 2: 165) which later, however, developed a quite different meaning due to the influence of Voltaire's pejorative use of the term. Faced with this dilemma, Albright (1964: 188) coined the related term of 'ecclesiocracy'. The phenomenon as such is dealt with by Plöger 1968; Hanson 1975: 209-279; Fischer 1978: 212f; Schäfer 1978: 20f, 214-243; Becker 1980: 48-53, 68-82.

249   Lev 21.10; de Vaux 1961: 400-401.

250   The problem of foreigners ruling in Israel, such as Queen Athaliah (2 Kgs 11), Tabeel (Isa 7.6), the Herodians, is faced by Deut 17.15 with an unambiguously patriotic decision: "You must not appoint a foreigner, one who is not your brother."

251   Cf. the resistance of the Pharisees mentioned by the Jewish historian, Josephus (Antiquities 13.288-298). Further: Beck 1959.

252   Van der Woude 1957. - Caquot (1978), followed by Laperrousaz 1982, distinguishes three stages in the development of the sect's messianic doctrine: Bi-messianism which implies a priestly and a lay figure, dates from the days of Alexander Jannaeus (103-76 B.C.) and reflects opposition against the Hasmonean fusion of secular and religious leadership (1 QS 9.11; 1 QSa 2.11). In the time of Alexandra or Aristoboulos (76-63 B.C.) only a priestly messiah was expected (Dam A 12.33; 14.9; B 1.10; 2.1), and in Herodian times only a royal one (4 QPatr, 4 Q 174 = 4 Qflor), the latter being accompanied by priests or an "Exegete of the Law" (4 Qflor, 4 Q 161). See also Donaldson 1981.

253   Cf. the Messianic Rule (1 QSa 2.17b-22): "And when they shall gather for the common table, to eat and to drink new wine, when the common table shall be set for eating and the new wine poured for drinking, let no man extend his hand over the first-fruits of bread and wine before the priest; for it is he who shall bless the first-fruits of bread and wine, and shall be the first to extend his hand over the bread. Thereafter, the messiah shall extend his hand over the bread, and all the Congregation of the Community shall utter a blessing, each man in the order of his dignity" (Vermes 1968: 121). Cf. van der Woude 1957: 105-106.

254   1 QS 9.11 (Vermes 1968: 87). The correct interpretation is given by Hengel 1976: 246.

255   The so-called Messianic Rule (1 QSa), an appendix of 1 QS, the Community Rule.

256   An early example for the displacement of an immediate religious expectation by translating it into petrified dogma is Ez 12.27-28; see Zimmerli 1979: 284: "God's announcement of his action, given at a particular time, here suffers an apparently pious form of rejection by his people. The word of God is not completely dismissed, but is removed from the present and applied to a distant date. Obedience is changed into a pious view of the world which even has room for judgement - only a far off judgement some time, finally at the end of time. Examples of the putting off of the immediate threat of God's judgment in what was perhaps a very elaborate 'eschatology' could easily be multiplied in Synagogue, Church, and Islam." Thus the religions mentioned tend to become more moderate in their immediate claims without giving up what may be called their

totalistic pretensions or long-term expectations. By avoiding concrete claims, religion insulates itself from empirical testing, and hence is able to survive as a dogmatic system or ideology.
257 Jer 37.17; Ez 20.1-2; Acts 13.15.
258 Smith 1971: 118. The post-exilic spirit of anti-prophetism found a belated spokesman in Delitzsch (1921: 86-87) according to whom the prophets' "incessant intervention in political life heavily contributed to the fact that Israel and Judah can be called the most disorganized states that ever existed on earth". A penetrating study of the eclipse of prophecy is Blenkinsopp 1977.
259 Weinfeld 1972.
260 The model text of Asarhaddon's vassal-treaties announces the severe punishment of any subject who hears anything that is detrimental to the crown without immediately denouncing it; possible sources of such evil speech are, besides "sons, daughters, brothers, father's brothers, cousins", "a prophet, an ecstatic, a dream-interpreter" (Pritchard 1969: 535). - For Deuteronomy, see Deut 13, 6. Cf. also 18.9-22 where v. 15-19 seem to be an addition in favour of prophecy, which is, however, tempered by v. 20-21 (another addition?). Perhaps the issue of prophecy divided the Yahweh-aloneists. Those in favour of the prophetic institution could refer to Hos 12.14 (see Zenger 1982). The issue is discussed by Blenkinsopp 1977: 39-46.
261 Kellermann 1968: 383-384. For the subordination of prophecy to law see also the postscript to the book of the minor prophets, Mal 3.22.
262 This seems to be the implication of 1 Chr 25.1-3. Cf. Johnson 1962: 69-74.
263 Bousset/Gressmann 1926: 162-171; Urbach 1968 and 1975: 564-648; Hengel 1969: 143-152, 241-275; Schürer 1979: 322-380. For specifically theological notions of the 'eclipse of prophecy' and the sages or scholars as the true 'successors' of the prophets see Leivestad 1972/73; Stadelmann 1980: 266-270.
264 4 Ezra 14 (Charles 1913: 622-624); Bloch 1972: 72-73; Lang 1981e.
265 Kellermann 1968.
266 Schaeder 1930; Herrmann 1981: 309.
267 Ezra 8.35; 9.4; 10.6-8; cf. Mantel 1973. For the difference between Judaeans and the minority of returnee clans listed in Neh 7.7-69 = Ezra 2.2-67 (ca. 20% of the population?) see also Weinberg 1972.
268 Neh 3.8, 31. Cf. the 'sons of the prophets' of 2 Kgs 2.3, 5 etc. who are generaly understood, and in the New American Bible of 1970 translated, as 'guild prophets'. See below, note 272.
269 For the self-government of displaced ethnic minorities see Ephal 1978.
270 Ezra 7.6, 12. 21.   271 I.e. acknowledge.
272 The existence of Mesopotamian guilds of labourers and artisans is widely acknowledged (Mendelsohn 1940a and 1940b; Weisberg 1970), though not without problems. Mendelsohn argues from Mesopotamian and biblical designations such as 'son of a shepherd (shepherds)' which

he translates as 'member of the shepherd's guild'. That the relevant Mesopotamian names bear such interpretation is questioned by Weisberg (1970: 80-85) whose own translation reads 'of the shepherd family'. Lambert 1970 doubts the existence of guilds.

273 Ephal 1978.

274 Stadelmann 1980: 4-26; cf. Sir 7.29-31.

275 Iliad 6.146ff. Isa 64.5 provides no real analogy; the fallen leaves of autumn seem to be more characteristic of Greece than of Palestine. According to Mishna Yadayim 4.6, certain Jewish circles were acquainted with Homer, the 'pagan' equivalent of the Torah.

276 Douglas 1978: 22, 20, 25.

277 Mishna Sanhedrin 6.4. Cf. Mishna Pirqe avoth 2.8: "The more women, the more witchcraft."

278 Schaeder 1930: 3   279 Cf. Mishna, Pirqe avoth.

280 For the intellectual/professional as a general social category (underlined in the text) see Lenski 1966: 70, 365; for the scriptural scholar, Urbach 1968: 47-48.

281 Urbach 1968: 54.   282 Urbach 1968: 41.

283 Weber 1920: 409: "from a typological point of view, rabbinical teachers [enjoyed] charismatic authority".

284 Sohm 1892: 26-66. Recent authors assert that Paul's authority in the Christian communities founded by him is 'charismatic' in Weber's sense: Schütz 1975: 249-280; Holmberg 1978. How Paul, the charismatic, seeks to establish his authority and manipulates his readers, is discussed by Shaw 1983: 26-185.

285 Simeon ben Shetach assumed more than one facet of prophecy, namely to intervene in political life, to reprove rulers and men of power openly, and to wage war against corrupt conduct. Urbach 1975: 573-574.

286 "By almost exclusively focussing on content modern theology understands the 'word of God' different from its original meaning. Accordingly, the word of God is something God has said, something that exists already, and an object of rational analysis. The word of God is separated from the 'word event' and hence open to learned manipulation" (Westermann 1978: 11). This is not only an apt characterization of the difference between the prophetic dimension of the Old Testament and 'modern theology', but also of the oracle religion as opposed to book religion in general.

BIBLIOGRAPHY

Ahlström, G. W.
1977 "King Jehu - A Prophet's Mistake", in: Scripture in History and Theology (Pittsburgh): 47-69.

Albertz, R.
1981 "Der sozialgeschichtliche Hintergrund des Hiobbuches und der 'Babylonischen Theodizee'", in: Die Botschaft und die Boten - Festschrift für H. W. Wolff (Neukirchen): 349-372.
1982 "Jer 2-6 und die Frühzeitverkündigung Jeremias": ZAW 94: 20-47.

Albrektson, B.
1972 "Prophecy and Politics in the Old Testament", in: The Myth of the State, ed. by H. Biezais (Stockholm): 45-56.

Albright, W. F.
1964 History, Archaeology, and Christian Humanism (New York).

Allport, F. H.
1955 Theories of Perception and the Concept of Structure (New York).

Allwohn, A.
1926 Die Ehe des Propheten Hosea in psychoanalytischer Beleuchtung (BZAW 44, Giessen).

Arlow, J. A.
1951 "The Consecration of the Prophet": The Psychoanalytic Quarterly 20: 374-397.

Asín, Palacios M.
1928 Abenházam de Córdoba, vol. 2 (Madrid).

Astour, M.
1959 "Métamorphose de Baal. Les rivalités commerciales au IXe siècle": Evidences 10: no. 75, 34-40; no. 77, 54-58.

Bacher, W.
1903 "Das altjüdische Schulwesen": Jahrbuch für jüdische Geschichte und Literatur 6: 48-81.

Baumgartner, W.
1974 Hebräisches und aramäisches Lexikon zum Alten Testament, vol. 2 (Leiden).

Beck, L. Y./Beck, C. W.
1978 "WI-RI-ZA Wool on Linear B Tablets of Perfume Ingredients": American Journal of Archaeology 82: 213-215.

Becker, J.
1980 Messianic Expectation in the Old Testament (Philadelphia).

Beek, M. A.
1958 "Hasidic Conceptions of Kingship in the Maccabean Period", in: The Sacral Kingship (Studies in the History of Religions 4, Leiden): 349-355.

Beer, G.
1939 Exodus (HAT).

Bibliography

Begrich, J.
1963 Studien zu Deuterojesaja (ThB 20).
Bernhardt, K.-H.
1972 "Prophetie und Geschichte": VTS 22: 20-46.
Blenkinsopp, J.
1977 Prophecy and Canon (Notre Dame).
Bloch, E.
1972 Atheism in Christianity (New York).
Bobek, H.
1962 "The Main Stages in Socio-economic Evolution from a Geographical Point of View", in: P. L. Wagner and M. W. Mikesell, eds., Readings in Cultural Geography (Chicago): 218-247.
1974 "Zum Konzept des Rentenkapitalismus": Tijdschrift voor economische en soiciale geografie 65: 73-77.
1979 "Rentenkapitalismus und Entwicklung im Iran", in: G. Schweizer, ed., Interdisziplinäre Iran-Forschung (Wiesbaden): 113-124.
Bolkestein, H.
1939 Wohltätigkeit und Armenpflege im vorchristlichen Altertum (Utrecht).
Bousset, W./Gressmann, H.
1926 Die Religion des Judentums im späthellenistischen Zeitalter (3rd edn., Tübingen).
Boyce, M.
1982 A History of Zoroastrianism (Handbuch der Orientalistik), vol. 2 (Leiden).
Bresciani, E./Kamil, M.
1966 "Le lettere aramaiche di Hermopoli": Atti Della Accademia Nazionale dei Lincei, Cl. di Scienze Morali, Memorie 8/72: 357-428.
Brichto, H. C.
1973 "Kin, Cult, Land and Afterlife - A Biblical Complex": HUCA 44: 1-54.
Bron, B.
1981 "Zur Psychopathologie und Verkündigung des Propheten Ezechiel": Schweizer Archiv für Neurologie, Neurochirurgie und Psychiatrie 128: 21-31.
Brunet, G.
1968 Les Lamentations contre Jérémie (Bibliothèque de l'Ecole des Hautes Etudes, sciences religieuses 75, Paris).
1975 Essai sur l'Isaïe de l'histoire (Paris).
Buheiry, M. R.
1981 "The Agricultural Exports of Southern Palestine, 1885-1914": JPSt 10/no. 40: 61-81.
Burke, P.
1978 Popular Culture in Early Modern Europe (London).
Caquot, A.
1961 "Osée et la Royauté": Revue d'histoire et de philosophie religieuses 41: 123-146.
1978 "Le méssianisme qumrânien", in: Qumrân. Sa piété, sa

Bibliography

théologie et son milieu (Gembloux): 231-247.
Cardellini, I.
1981 "Die biblischen 'Sklaven'-Gesetze im Lichte des keilschrift-
lichen Sklavenrechts (Bonner Biblische Beiträge 55,
Königstein).
Carroll, R. P.
1977 "Ancient Israelite Prophecy and Dissonance Theory": Numen
24: 135-151.
Cassem, N. H.
1973 "Ezekiel's Psychotic Personality", in: The Word in the World.
Essays in Honor of F. L. Moriarty (Cambridge, Mass.): 59-70.
Cazelles, H.
1971 "Bible et politique": Revue des sciences religieuses 59:
497-530.
Charles, R. H.
1913 The Apocrypha and Pseudepigrapha of the Old Testament,
vol. 2 (Oxford).
Crowfoot, J. W. and G. M.
1938 Early Ivories from Samaria (London).
Curtiss, S. I.
1902 Primitive Semitic Religion To-day (London).
Dalton, G.
1972 "Peasantries in Anthropology and History": Current Anthropology 13: 385-415.
Davies, G. H.
1980/81 "Amos - The Prophet of Re-Union": The Expository Times
92: 196-200.
Delitzsch, F.
1921 Die grosse Täuschung, vol. 1 (Stuttgart).
Dietrich, W.
1976 Jesaja und die Politik (Beiträge zur evangelischen Theologie
74, München).
Donaldson, T. L.
1981 "Levitical Messianology in Late Judaism": Journal of the
Evangelical Theological Society 24: 193-207.
Donner, H.
1977 "The Separate States of Israel and Judah", in: J. H. Hayes/J.
M. Miller, eds., Israelite and Judaean History (London):
381-434.
Douglas, M.
1973 Natural Symbols (2nd edn., London).
1978 Cultural Bias (Royal Anthropological Institute, Occasional
Paper 35, London).
Droogers, A.
1980 "Symbols of Marginality in the Biographies of Religious and
Secular Innovators": Numen 27: 105-121.
Duhm, B.
1875 Die Theologie der Propheten (Bonn).
Dus, J.
1961 "Das zweite Gebot": Communio Viatorum 4: 37-50.

174

Bibliography

Eerdmans, D. B.
1939 Studies in Job (Leiden).
1942 "On the Road to Monotheism": Oudtestamentische Studiën 1: 37-50.
Ehlers, E.
1980 Iran (Wissenschaftliche Länderkunden 18, Darmstadt).
Elan, S.
1979 "Der Heilige Baum - ein Hinweis auf das Bild ursprünglicher Landschaft in Palästina": MDOG 111: 89-98.
Emerton, J. A.
1982 "New Light on Israelite Religion": ZAW 94: 2-20.
Emmet, D.
1956 "Prophets and their Societies": Journal of the Royal Anthropological Institute 86: 13-23.
Ennew, J.
1981 Debt Bondage. A Survey (London).
Ephal, I.
1978 "The Western Minorities in Babylonia in the 5th-6th Centuries B.C.": Orientalia 47: 74-88.
Fey, R.
1963 Amos und Jesaja: Abhängigkeit und Eigenständigkeit des Jesaja (WMANT 12).
Finley, M. I.
1980 Ancient Slavery and Modern Ideology (London).
Firth, R.
1973 Symbols (Ithaca).
Fischer, U.
1978 Eschatologie und Jenseitserwartung im hellenistischen Diasporajudentum (Berlin).
Fohrer, G.
1963 "Sion", in: ThWNT 7: 291-318.
1969 "Tradition und Interpretation im Alten Testament", in: id., Studien zur alttestamentlichen Theologie und Geschichte (BZAW 115): 54-83.
Forbes, R. J.
1955 Studies in Ancient Technology, vol. 3 (Leiden).
Foster, B. O.
1922 Livy, vol. 2 (The Loeb Classical Library, London).
Frazer, J. G.
1914 The Golden Bough, vol. 4/1 (3rd edn., London).
1919 Folk-Lore in the Old Testament, vol. 3 (London).
Galling, K.
1979 Textbuch zur Geschichte Israels (3rd edn., Tübingen).
Gibb, H. A. R./Kramers, J. H. eds.
1974 Shorter Encyclopaedia of Islam (Leiden).
Ginsberg, H. L.
1978 "The Oldest Record of Hysteria with Physical Stigmata, Zech 13.2-6", in: Studies in Bible and the Ancient Near East, Presented to S. E. Loewenstamm (Jerusalem): 23-27.
Gottwald, N. K.
1980 The Tribes of Yahweh. A Sociology of the Religion of

Liberated Israel, 1250-1050 B.C.E. (London) [esp. 611-623: "Mono-Yahwism as the Function of Sociopolitical Equality, Sociopolitical Equality as the Function of Mono-Yahwism"].

Gray, J.
1962   Archaeology and the Old Testament World (London).

Grelot, P.
1972   Documents araméens d'Egypte (Paris).

Gressmann, H.
1913   "Monotheismus und Polytheismus", in: Die Religion in Geschichte und Gegenwart, vol. 4 (1st edn., Tübingen): 475-479.

Grosheide, H. H.
1978   "Een zionistisch-mesiaanse beweging rondom Nehemia?", in: De Knecht. Festschrift J. L. Koole (Kampen): 59-71.

Gunkel, H.
1917   Die Propheten (Göttingen).

Gunneweg, A. H. J.
1967   "Ordinationsformular oder Berufungsbericht?", in: Glaube Geist Geschichte. Festschrift für E. Benz (Leiden): 91-98.

Haag, H., ed.
1968   Bibel-Lexikon (2nd edn., Einsiedeln).

Haeussermann, F.
1932   Wortempfang und Symbol in der alttestamentlichen Prophetie (BZAW 58, Giessen).

Halpern, B.
1981   The Constitution of the Monarchy in Israel (Harvard Semitic Monographs 25, Chico).

Hanson, P. D.
1975   The Dawn of Apocalyptic (Philadelphia).

Harik, I. F.
1972   "The Impact of the Domestic Market on Rural-Urban Relations in the Middle East", in: Rural Politics and Social Change in the Middle East, ed. by R. Antoun, I. Harik (Bloomington): 337-363.

Haussig, H. W., ed.
1965   Wörterbuch der Mythologie, vol. 1 (Stuttgart).

Hengel, M.
1969   Judentum und Hellenismus (WUNT 10).
1976   Die Zeloten (AGJU 1, 2nd edn.).

Henninger, J.
1981   "Über religiöse Strukturen nomadischer Gruppen", in: id., Arabica sacra (OBO 40): 34-47.

Herbert of Cherbury, E.
1967   De religione gentilium (1663), ed. by G. Gawlick (Stuttgart).

Herder, J. G.
1880   Herders sämmtliche Werke, ed. by B. Suphan, vol. 12 (Berlin).

Hermisson, H. -J.
1968   Studien zur israelitischen Spruchweisheit (WMANT 28).

Herner, S.
1926   "Erziehung und Unterricht in Israel", in: Oriental Studies in Commemoration of P. Haupt (Baltimore): 58-66.

Herrmann, S.
1971 "Die konstruktive Restauration. Das Deuteronomium als Mitte biblischer Theologie", in: Probleme biblischer Theologie, ed. by H. W. Wolff (München): 155-170.
1981 A History of Israel in Old Testament Times (2nd edn., London).

Hölscher, G.
1914 Die Profeten (Leipzig).

Hoffmann, H. -D.
1980 Reform and Reformen. Untersuchungen zu einem Grundthema der deuteronomistischen Geschichtsschreibung (Zürich).

Hofmayr, W.
1925 Die Schilluk (Mödling).

Holladay, J. S.
1970 "Assyrian Statecraft and the Prophets of Israel": Harvard Theological Review 63: 29-51.

Holladay, W. L.
1976 "Jeremiah the Prophet", in: The Interpreter's Dictionary of the Bible. Supplementary Volume (Nashville): 470-472.

Holmberg, B.
1978 Paul and Power (Lund).

Honko, L.
1969 "Role-taking of the Shaman": Temenos 4: 25-55.

Hornung, E.
1978 Grundzüge der ägyptischen Geschichte (2nd. edn., Darmstadt).

Hossfeld, F. L.
1982 Der Dekalog (OBO 45).

Hourani, A. H.
1957 "The Fertile Crescent in the Eighteenth Century": Studia Islamica 8: 91-118.

Howie, C. G.
1950 The Date and Composition of Ezekiel (Philadelphia).

Janssen, J. J.
1981 "Die Struktur der pharaonischen Wirtschaft": Göttinger Miszellen 48: 59-77.

Jaspers, K.
1947 "Der Prophet Ezechiel. Eine pathographische Studie", in: Arbeiten zur Psychiatrie, Neurologie und ihren Grenzgebieten. Festschrift für K. Schneider (Heidelberg): 77-85.

Jaynes, J.
1982 The Origin of Consciousness in the Breakdown of the Bicameral Mind (Boston).

Jepsen, A.
1934 Nabi (München).

Jeremias, J.
1970 Kultprophetie und Gerichtsverkündigung in der späten Königszeit (WMANT 35).
1971 "Die Deutung der Gerichtsworte Michas in der Exilszeit": ZAW 83: 330-354.

Johnson, A. R.
1962   The Cultic Prophet in Ancient Israel, (2nd edn., Cardiff).
1979   The Cultic Prophet in Israel's Psalmody (Cardiff).
Keel, O.
1977   "Rechttun oder Annahme des drohenden Gerichts?" Biblische Zeitschrift 21: 200-218.
1980   "Gedanken zur Beschäftigung mit dem Monotheismus", in: id., ed., Monotheismus in Alten Israel und seiner Umwelt (Fribourg): 11-30.
Kegler, J.
1979   "Prophetisches Reden und politische Praxis Jeremias", in: Der Gott der kleinen Leute, vol. 1, ed. by W. Schottroff and W. Stegemann (München): 67-79.
Keil, C. F.
1875   Biblischer Kommentar über die prophetischen Geschichtsbücher des Alten Testaments, vol. 2 (2nd edn., Leipzig).
Kellermann, U.
1967   Nehemia (BZAW 102).
1968   "Erwägungen zum Esragesetz": ZAW 80: 373-385.
Kippenberg, H. G.
1982   Religion und Klassenbildung im antiken Judäa (Studien zur Umwelt des Neuen Testaments 14, 2nd edn., Göttingen).
1983   "Die Entlassung aus Schuldknechtschaft im antiken Judäa", in: G. Kehrer, ed., Vor Gott sind alle gleich (Düsseldorf): 74-104.
Kittel, R.
1898   "Cyrus und Deuterojesaja": ZAW 18: 149-162.
Klein, W. C.
1956   The Psychological Pattern of Old Testament Prophecy (Evanston).
Koch, K.
1976   "Saddaj. Zum Verhältnis zwischen israelitischer Monolatrie und nordwestsemitischem Polytheismus": VT 26: 299-332.
1978/80 Die Profeten (Stuttgart) [Vol. 1, 1978; 2, 1980].
Kraeling, E. G.
1953   The Brooklyn Museum Aramaic Papyri (New Haven).
Krämer, H.
1959   "Prophetes: Die Wortgruppe in der Profangräzität", in: ThWNT 6: 783-795.
Krairiksh, P.
1979   Das heilige Bildnis. Skulpturen aus Thailand (Köln).
Kramer, S. N.
1949   "Schooldays": JAOS 69: 199-215.
Krech, D./Crutchfield, R. S.
1974   Elements of Psychology (3rd edn., New York).
Krech, D. et al.
1976   Psychology: A Basic Course (New York).
Kreglinger, R.
1926   La religion d'Israël (2nd edn., Bruxelles).
Kreissig, H.
1970   Die sozialen Zusammenhänge des jüdischen Krieges

Bibliography

(Schriften zur Geschichte und Kultur der Antike 1, Berlin).

Kuenen, A.
1877   The Prophets and Prophecy in Ancient Israel (London).
1883   Volksreligion und Weltreligion (Berlin).

Kurtz, R.
1904   Zur Psychologie der vorexilischen Prophetie in Israel (Diss. Leipzig).

Kutsch, E.
1980   "Wie David König wurde", in: Textgemäß. Festschrift für E. Würthwein (Göttingen): 75-93.

Lacey, R.
1978   Majesty. Elizabeth II and the House of Windsor (2nd edn., Sphere Books, London).

Lafitau, J. F.
1974   Customs of the American Indians Compared with the Customs of Primitive Times (1724), vol. 1 (Toronto).

Lambert, W. G.
1970   Review of Weisberg 1970: Bibliotheca Orientalis 27: 370-371.

Lambert, W. G./Millard, A. R.
1969   Atra-hasis. The Babylonian Story of the Flood (Oxford).

Lambton, A. K. S.
1953   Landlord and Peasant in Persia (Oxford).

Lang, B.
1975   Frau Weisheit. Deutung einer biblischen Gestait (Düsseldorf).
1978   Kein Aufstand in Jerusalem. Die Politik des Propheten Ezechiel (Stuttgart; 2nd edn. 1981).
1980   Wie wird man Prophet in Israel? (Düsseldorf) [11-30: "Was ist ein Prophet?"; 31-58: "Wie wird man Prophet in Israel?"; 69-79: "Messias und Messiaserwartung im alten Israel"; 137-148: "Ein Kranker sieht seinen Gott"; 149-161: "Vor einer Wende im Verständnis des israelitischen Gottesglaubens?"]
1981a   Ezechiel. Der Prophet und das Buch (Erträge der Forschung 153, Darmstadt).
1981b   (Ed.) Der einzige Gott. Die Geburt des biblischen Monotheismus (München) [47-83: "Die Jahwe-allein- Bewegung"].
1981c   "Prophetie, pophetische Zeichenhandlung und Politik in Israel": Theologische Quartalschrift 161: 275-280.
1981d   "Sklaven und Unfreie im Buch Amos": VT 31: 482-488.
1981e   "Muslimische und jüdische Bibelkritik im Spanien des 11. Jahrhunderts": Biblische Notizen 15: 35-39.

Langdon, S.
1912   Die neubabylonischen Königsinschriften (Vorderasiatische Bibliothek 4, Leipzig).

Langkammer, H.
1965   "Der übernatürliche Charakter des Berufungserlebnisses des Propheten Jeremias": Freiburger Zeitschrift für Philosophie und Theologie 12: 426-438.

Laperrousaz, E. -M.
1982   L'attente du messie en Palestine à la veille et au début de l'ère chrétienne (Paris).

Lautner, J. G.
1936   Altbabylonische Personenmiete und Erntearbeiterverträge (Leiden).
Lawrence, T. E.
1962   Seven Pillars of Wisdom (Penguin edn., Harmondsworth).
Leibniz, G. W.
1961   Philosophische Schriften, ed. by W. von Engelhardt and H. H. Holz, vol. 3/2 (Darmstadt).
Leivestad, R.
1972/73 "Das Dogma von der prophetenlosen Zeit": New Testament Studies 19: 288-299.
Lemaire, A.
1973   "Le sabbat à l'époque royale israélite": RB 80: 161-185.
1976   "A Schoolboy's Exercise on an Ostracon at Lachish": Tel-Aviv 3: 109-110.
1977   "Les inscriptions de Khirbet el-Qôm et l'Ashérah de Yhwh": RB 84: 595-608.
1981a   Les écoles et la formation de la Bible dans l'ancien Israël (OBO 39).
1981b   Histoire du peuple hébreu (Que sais-je? no. 1898; Paris).
1982   "Recherches actuelles sur les origines de l'ancien Israël": Journal Asiatique 270: 5-24.
Lemche, P.
1976   "The Manumission of Slaves": VT 26: 38-59.
Lenski, G. E.
1966   Power and Privilege. A Theory of Social Stratification (New York).
Lévêque, J.
1981   "La datation du livre de Job": VTS 32: 206-219.
Levin, C.
1981   "Noch einmal: Die Anfänge des Propheten Jeremia": VT 31: 428-440.
1982   Der Sturz der Königin Atalja (Stuttgarter Bibelstudien 105, Stuttgart).
Lewis, I. M.
1978   Ecstatic Religion. An Anthropological Study of Spirit Possession and Shamanism (2nd edn., Hardmondsworth).
Lindblom, J.
1962   Prophecy in Ancient Israel (Oxford).
Liver, J.
1971   "David (Dynasty of)", in: EJud 5: 1339-1345.
Lohfink, N.
1969   "Gott und die Götter im Alten Testament", in: Theologische Akademie 6: 50-71.
1981   "Der junge Jeremia als Propagandist und Poet", in: Le livre de Jérémie (Bibliotheca Ephemeridum Theologicarum Lovaniensium 54, Leuven): 351-368.
Long, B. O.
1982   "Social Dimensions of Prophetic Conflict": Semeia 21: 31-53.
Loretz, O.
1975   "Die prophetische Kritik des Rentenkapitalismus": Ugarit-Forschungen 7: 271-278.

Bibliography

1978 "Vom Kanaanäischen Totenkult zur jüdischen Patriarchen -
und Elternehrung": Jahrbuch für Anthropologie und Reli-
gionsgeschichte 3: 149-204.

1982 "Ugaritisch-biblisch mrzḥ 'Kultmahl, Kultverein' in Jer 16.5
und Am 6.7. Bemerkungen zur Geschichte des Totenkultes in
Israel", in: Künder des Wortes. Festschrift J. Schreiner, ed.
by L. Ruppert et al. (Würzburg): 87-93.

Luther, M.
1897 Werke. Kritische Gesamtausgabe, vol. 7 (Weimar).

Maag, V.
1980 Kultur, Kulturkontakt und Religion (Göttingen).

Maloney, R. P.
1974 "Usury and Restrictions on Interest-Taking in the Ancient
Near East": Catholic Biblical Quarterly 36: 1-20.

Mantel, H.
1973 "The Dichotomy of Judaism during the Second Temple
Period": HUCA 44: 55-87.

Marx, K.
1981 Capital. Translated by D. Fernbach, vol. 3 (Harmondsworth).

Mays, J. L.
1969 Amos (Old Testament Library, London).

Mazar, B.
1978 "They Shall Call Peoples to their Mountain": Eretz Israel 14:
39-41 [Hebrew].

Mead, G. H.
1934 Mind, Self, and Society (Chicago).

Mendelsohn, I.
1940a "Gilds in Babylonia and Assyria": JAOS 60: 68-72.
1940b "Guilds in Ancient Palestine": BASOR 80: 17-21.

Merleau-Ponty, M.
1945 Phénoménologie de la percpetion (Paris).

Michel, E.
1947/52 "Ein neuentdeckter Annalentext Salmanassars III.": Welt
des Orients 1: 454-475.

Mettinger, T. N. D.
1976 King and Messiah (Coniectanea Biblica, Old Testament
Series 8, Lund).

Miller, J. W.
1955 Das Verhältnis Jeremias und Ezechiels sprachlich und
theologisch untersucht (Assen).

Miller, P. D.
1980 "El, the Creator of Earth": BASOR 239: 43-46.

Mooren, T.
1981 "Monothéisme coranique et anthropologie": Anthropos 76:
529-561.

Mowinckel, S.
1935 "Ecstatic Experience and Rational Elaboration in Old
Testament Prophecy": Acta Orientalia 13: 264-291.

Müller, E. F./Thomas, A.
1976 Einführung in die Sozialpsychologie (2nd edn., Göttingen).

Müller, K.
1911   Die seit Renan über einen israelitischen Urmonotheismus
       geäußerten Anschauungen (Diss. Breslau).
Neumann, P. A. H., ed.
1979   Das Prophetenverständnis in der deutschsprachigen For-
       schung seit H. Ewald (Wege der Forschung 307, Darmstadt).
Nikiprowetsky, V.
1975   "Ethical Monotheism": Daedalus 104, no. 2: 69-89.
Noort, E.
1977   Untersuchungen zum Gottesbescheid in Mari (Alter Orient
       und Altes Testament 202, Neukirchen).
Obbink, H. T.
1929   "Jahwebilder": ZAW 47: 264-274.
Oldenburg, U.
1969   The Conflict between El and Baal in Canaanite Religion
       (Leiden).
Oudenrijn, M. A. van den
1925   "L'expression 'fils des prophètes' et ses analogies": Biblica 6:
       165-171.
Page, S.
1969   "Joash and Samaria in a New Stela Excavated at Tell al
       Rimah, Iraq": VT 19: 483-484.
Pajak, S.
1978   Urreligion und Uroffenbarung bei P. Wilh. Schmidt (St.
       Augustin).
Patai, R.
1977   The Jewish Mind (New York)[347-351: "The 'Semites'; or, The
       Desert and Monotheism"].
Paul, S. M.
1971   "Prophets and Prophecy (in the Bible)", in: EJud 13:
       1150-1175.
Pavlovsky, V./Vogt, E.
1964   "Die Jahre der Könige von Juda und Israel": Biblica 45:
       321-347.
Peckham, H. H.
1947   Pontiac and the Indian Uprising (Princeton).
Petersen, D. L.
1981   The Roles of Israel's Prophets (JSOT Suppl. Series 17,
       Sheffield).
Pettazoni, R.
1960   Der Allwissende Gott (Frankfurt)[109-118: "Die Entstehung
       des Monotheismus"].
Peuckert, W.-E.
1935   "Deutsche Volkspropheten": ZAW 53: 35-54.
Pfeiffer, R. H.
1926   "Images of Yahweh": JBL 45: 211-222.
1935   State Letters of Assyria (New Haven).
Plöger, O.
1968   Theokratie und Eschatologie (WMANT 2, 2nd edn.)
Porten, B.
1968   Archives from Elephantine (Berkeley).

Bibliography

Porter, J. R.
1981 "BNY HNBY'YM": Journal of Theological Studies 32: 423-429.
Povah, J. W.
1925 The New Psychology and the Hebrew Prophets (London).
Prenzel, G.
1971 Über die Pacht im antiken hebräischen Recht (Stuttgart).
Pritchard, J. B., ed.
1969 Ancient Near Eastern Texts Relating to the Old Testament (3rd edn., Princeton).
Rad, G. von
1939 Fragen der Schriftauslegung im Alten Testament (Leipzig).
1965/66 Theologie des Alten Testaments (München)[vol. 1, 5th edn., 1966; vol. 2, 4th edn. 1965].
Radin, M.
1929 The Life of the People in Biblical Times (Philadelphia).
Ramlot, L.
1972 "Prophétisme", in: Supplément au Dictionnaire de la Bible, vol. 8 (Paris): 811-1222.
Rast, W. E.
1977 "Cakes for the Queen of Heaven", in: Scripture in History and Theology. Essays in Honor of J. C. Rylaarsdam (Pittsburgh Theol. Monograph Series 17, Pittsburgh): 167-80.
Redfield, R.
1956 Peasant Society and Culture (Chicago).
Renan, E.
1953/58 OEuvres complètes, ed. by H. Psichari (Paris) [vol. 6, 1953; vol. 8, 1958].
Reventlow, H.
1963 Liturgie und prophetisches Ich bei Jeremia (Gütersloh).
Ries, G.
1976 Die neubabylonischen Bodenpachtformulare (Berlin).
Robertson, A. F.
1980 "On Sharecropping": Man 15: 411-429.
Robin, C.
1982 "Esquisse d'une histoire de l'organisation tribale en Arabie du sud antique", in: P. Bonnenfant, ed., La péninsule arabique d'aujourd'hui, vol. 2 (Paris).
Rost, L.
1950 "Erwägungen zu Hosea 4, 13f.", in: Festschrift A. Bertholet (Tübingen): 451-460.
Rudolph, W.
1966 Hosea (KAT).
1968 Jeremia (3rd edn., HAT).
1975 Micha Nahum Habakuk Zephanja (KAT).
1976 Haggai Sacharia 1-8 Sacharia 9-14 Maleachi (KAT).
Saggs, H. W. F.
1978 The Encounter with the Divine in Mesopotamia and Israel (London).
Scanlin, H. P.
1978 "The Emergence of the Writing Prophets in Israel in the

Mid-Eighth Century": Journal of the Evangelical Theological Society 21: 305-313.
Schaeder, H. H.
1968 Esra der Schreiber (Tübingen 1930)[= Studien zur orientalischen Religiongeschichte (Darmstadt): 162-241].
Schäfer, P.
1978 Studien zur Geschichte und Theologie des rabbinischen Judentums (AGJU 15).
Scharbert, J.
1982 "Zefanja und die Reform des Joschija", in: Künder des Wortes. Festschrift J. Schreiner, ed. by L. Ruppert et al. (Würzburg): 237-253.
Schleiermacher, F.
1850 Die praktische Theologie, ed. by J. Frerichs (Berlin).
Schmitt, H. C.
1972 Elisa (Gütersloh).
Schölch, A.
1981 "The Economic Development of Palestine, 1856-1882": JPSt 10/no. 39: 35-58.
Schoors, A.
1977 "Isaiah, the Minister of Royal Anointment?" Oudtestamentische Studiën 20: 85-107.
Schürer, E.
1979 The History of the Jewish People in the Age of Jesus Christ. Revised by G. Vermes and F. Millar, vol. 2 (Edinburgh).
Schütz, J. H.
1975 Paul and the Anatomy of Apostolic Authority (Cambridge).
Scott, J.
1977 "Patronage or Exploitation?" in: E. Gellner and J. Waterbury, eds., Patrons and Clients in Mediterranean Societies (London): 21-39.
Seierstad, I. P.
1965 Die Offenbarungserlebnisse der Propheten Amos, Jesaja und Jeremia (2nd edn., Oslo).
Sellin, E.
1912 Der alttestamentliche Prophetismus (Leipzig).
Selms, A. van
1973 "Temporary Henotheism", in: Symbolae Biblicae et Mesopotamicae F. M. T. de Liagre Böhl (Leiden): 341-348.
Shaw, G.
1983 The Cost of Authority: Manipulation and Freedom in the New Testament (Philadelphia).
Sjöberg, A. W.
1976 "The Old Babylonian Eduba", in: Sumerological Studies in Honor of T. Jacobsen (Chicago): 159-179.
Skorupski, J.
1976 Symbol and Theory (Cambridge).
Smith, M.
1963 "II Isaiah and the Persians": JAOS 83: 415-421.
1971 Palestinian Parties and Politics that Shaped the Old Testament (New York).

Bibliography

Smith, S.
1925 "The Babylonian Ritual for the Consecration and Induction of a Divine Statue": Journal of the Royal Asiatic Society, 37-60.

Smitten, W. T. In der
1975 "Erwägungen zu Nehemias Davidzität": Journal for the Study of Judaism 5: 41-48.

Soden, W. von
1955 "Gibt es ein Zeugnis dafür, daß die Babylonier an die Wiederauferstehung Marduks geglaubt haben?": Zeitschrift für Assyriologie 51: 130-166.
1979 "Konflikte und ihre Bewältigung in babylonischen Schöpfungs - und Fluterzählungen": MDOG 111: 1-33.

Sohm, R.
1892 Kirchenrecht, vol. 1 (Berlin).

Spengler, O.
1928 The Decline of the West, vol. 2 (London).

Spieckermann, H.
1982 Juda unter Assur in der Sargonidenzeit (FRLANT 129).

Spiro, M. E.
1953 "Ghosts": Journal of Abnormal and Social Psychology 48: 367-382.

Spiro, M. E./D'Andrade, R. G.
1958 "A Cross-Cultural Study of Some Supernatural Beliefs": American Anthropologist 60: 456-466.

Stadelmann, H.
1980 Ben Sira als Schriftgelehrter (WUNT 2:6).

Steiner, F.
1954 "Enslavement and the Early Hebrew Lineage System": Man 54: 73-75.

Stolz, F.
1980 "Monotheismus in Israel", in: Keel, 1980: 155-183.

Sundén, H.
1966 Die Religion und die Rollen. Eine psychologische Untersuchung der Frömmigkeit (Berlin).
1969 "Die Rollenpsychologie und die Weisen des Religions-Erlebens", in: Wesen und Weisen der Religion. Festgabe für W. Keilbach (München): 132-144.

Swaim, G. G.
1978 "Hosea the Statesman", in: G. A. Tuttle, ed., Biblical and Near Eastern Studies. Essays in Honor of W. S. LaSor (Grand Rapids): 177-183.

Timm, S.
1982 Die Dynastie Omri (FRLANT 124).

Tufnell, O.
1953 Lachish III: The Iron Age (Text) (London).

Urbach, E. E.
1968 "Class-Status and Leadership in the World of the Palestinian Sages": Proceedings of the Israel Academy of Sciences and Humanities 2: 38-74.
1975 The Sages (Jerusalem).

Unger, J.
1976   On Religious Experience (Acta Universitatis Upsaliensis. Psychologia religionum 6, Uppsala).
Vaux, R. de
1961   Ancient Israel. Its Life and Institutions (London).
1971   Review of Oldenburg 1969: RB 78: 124-125.
Veblen, T.
1899   The Theory of the Leisure Class (New York).
Vermes, G.
1968   The Dead Sea Scrolls in English (3rd edn., Harmondsworth).
Volney, C.-F.
1787   Voyage en Syrie et en Egypte, vol. 2 (Paris).
Voltaire
1967   Dictionnaire philosophique (Garnier frères; Paris).
Volz, P.
1938   Prophetengestalten des Alten Testaments (Stuttgart).
Vorländer, H.
1981   "Der Monotheismus Israels als Antwort auf die Krise des Exils", in: Lang 1981b: 84-113, 134-139.
Wallace, A. F. C.
1973   The Death and Rebirth of the Seneca (New York).
Wallis, L.
1935   God and the Social Process (Chicago).
Weber, M.
1920   Das antike Judentum (Gesammelte Aufsätze zur Religionssoziologie, vol. 3, Tübingen).
1947   The Theory of Social and Economic Organization (New York).
Weinberg, J. P.
1972   "Demographische Notizen zur Geschichte der nachexilischen Gemeinde in Juda": Klio 54: 45-59.
Weinfeld, M.
1972   Deuteronomy and the Deuteronomic School (Oxford).
1976   "The Loyalty Oath in the Ancient Near East": Ugarit-Forschungen 8: 379-414.
Weisberg, D. B.
1970   Guild Structure and Political Allegiance in Early Achaemenid Mesopotamia (New Haven).
Weisman, Z.
1976   "Anointing as a Motif in the Making of the Charismatic King": Biblica 57: 378-398.
Wellhausen, J.
1978   Geschichte Israels (Berlin).
1921   Israelitische und jüdische Geschichte (8th edn., Berlin).
Westermann, C.
1978   Theologie des Alten Testaments in Grundzügen (Göttingen).
Weulersse, J.
1946   Paysans de Syrie et du proche-orient (3rd edn., Paris).
Wildberger, H.
1960   Jahwes Eigentumsvolk (Abhandlungen zur Theologie des Alten und Neuen Testaments 37, Zürich).

Bibliography

Williams, S. C., ed.
1930 Adair's History of the American Indians (Johnson City).

Willi-Plein, I.
1971 Vorformen der Schriftexegese innerhalb des Alten Testaments (BZAW 123).

Willis, J. T.
1971 "An Anti-Elide Narrative Tradition from a Prophetic Circle at the Ramah Sanctuary": JBL 90: 288-308.

Wilson, R. R.
1979 "Prophecy and Ecstasy: A Reexamination": JBL 98: 321-337.
1980 Prophecy and Society in Ancient Israel (Philadelphia).

Winnett, F. V.
1938 "Allah before Islam": The Moslem World 28: 239-248.

Wirth, E.
1962 Agrargeographie des Irak (Hamburg).
1969 "Der Heutige Irak als Beispiel orientalischen Wirtschaftsgeistes", in: id., ed., Wirtschaftsgeographie (Darmstadt): 391-421.
1971 Syrien (Wissenschaftliche Länderkunden 4-5, Darmstadt).
1973 "Die Beziehungen der orientalischen Stadt zum umgebenden Land", in: Geographie heute - Einheit und Vielfalt (Erdkundliches Wissen 33, Wiesbaden): 323-332.

Wolf, E. R.
1966 Peasants (Englewood Cliffs).

Wolff, H. W.
1964 "Hoseas geistige Heimat", in: id., Gesammelte Studien zum Alten Testament (ThB 22): 232-250.

Woude, A. van der
1957 Die messianischen Vorstellungen der Gemeinde von Qumran (Assen).

Wright, G. E.
1965 "The Nations in Hebrew Prophecy": Encounter 26: 125-137.

Würthwein, E.
1977 Die Bücher der Könige (ATD, Göttingen).

Yadin, Y.
1978 "The 'House of Baal' of Ahab and Jezebel in Samaria, and that of Athaliah in Judah", in: Archaeology in the Levant (Warminster): 127-135.

Zenger, E.
1982 "'Durch Menschen zog ich sie...' (Hos 11.4). Beobachtungen zum Verständnis des prophetischen Amtes im Hoseabuch", in: Künder des Wortes. Festschrift J. Schreiner, ed. by L. Ruppert et al. (Würzburg): 183-201.

Zimmerli, W.
1963 "Das Wort des göttlichen Selbsterweises (Erweiswort), eine prophetische Gattung" (1957), in: id., Gottes Offenbarung (ThB 19): 120-132.
1974 "Jesaja und Hiskia", in: id., Studien zur alttestamentlichen Theologie und Prophetie (ThB 51): 88-103.
1978 "Die kritische Infragestellung der Tradition durch die Prophetie", in: O. H. Steck, ed., Zu Tradition and Theologie im Alten Testament (Neukirchen): 57-86.
1979 Ezekiel 1 (Hermeneia, Philadelphia).

INDEX OF BIBLICAL REFERENCES

INDEX OF AUTHORS AND SUBJECTS

Index of Authors and Subjects